Poverty and Social Change

Poverty and Social Change

Kirsten Grønbjerg
David Street, and
Gerald D. Suttles

THE UNIVERSITY OF CHICAGO PRESS

Chicago and London

The University of Chicago Press, Chicago 60637
The University of Chicago Press, Ltd., London

Published 1978
Paperback edition 1980
Printed in the United States of America

86 85 84 83 82 81 80   5 4 3 2

Library of Congress Cataloging in Publication Data
Grønbjerg, Kirsten A.
Poverty and social change.

Bibliography: p.
Includes index.
1. Public welfare—United States. 2. Poverty.
3. Social change. 4. United States—Social policy.
I. Street, David, joint author. II. Suttles, Gerald D.,
joint author. III. Title.
HV91.G76   362.5'0973   78-876
ISBN 0-226-30962-2
ISBN 0-226-30963-0 (paper)

KIRSTEN GRØNBJERG is associate professor of sociology at Loyola University and the author of
*Mass Society and the Extension of Welfare,
1960–1970.* DAVID STREET is professor of sociology at the University of Illinois, Chicago Circle
Campus, and the editor of *Innovation in Mass
Education.* GERALD D. SUTTLES is professor of
sociology at the University of Chicago and
author of *The Social Order of the Slum* and
The Social Construction of Communities.

Contents

Acknowledgments

This study began several years back—longer than the authors care to specify. Much of the work involved in creating the volume was initiated in a research project on welfare and poverty directed by David Street and Gerald D. Suttles at the University of Chicago and later at the State University of New York at Stony Brook. This study was a part of a larger effort, the Human Side of Poverty Project, funded by the Rockefeller Foundation and codirected by Street and Suttles along with Donald J. Bogue of the University of Chicago. Important participants in the project included a number of people who went on to complete dissertations and M.A. papers: George Martin, Laura Gordon, Naomi Kroeger, Joseph Helfgot, Richard Forbes, Steve Kalberg, Judith Favia, and Susan Hafner. Others who made important contributions to the research or writing of the volume include Judy Kidd, Malcolm Lambert, and Jane Street.

Some sections of the manuscript have profited from the comments of Morris Janowitz and Blanche Coll, while Meyer Zald and Martin Rein provided helpful advice on the entire volume. We hope that we have returned our debt to their close attention to the manuscript by our own attention to their recommendations.

A genuinely collaborative work is always difficult, especially when it is carried out by three headstrong people. Although separate chapters were written independently by the authors, all went through the pains of many "suggested" revisions and countless discussions. Despite all this, we remain friends and wish here to acknowledge one another's mutual help, encouragement, and attention to detail.

1   The Weakness of Welfare

Progress in the well-being of the majority of Americans in no way guarantees satisfactory improvement for all the nation's residents—witness the present situations of ghettoized blacks, migrant workers, Appalachians, the elderly living on fixed or relatively inflexible incomes, and many others. Indeed, general improvement can make even more apparent and painful the circumstances of those left behind.

Social scientists are aware of the unevenness of social change, particularly of the ways in which alterations in the nonmaterial culture of values and beliefs often lags behind changes in the material culture of technology and economic productivity. It is understandable that Americans put considerable faith in the traditional principles of "invisible hand" capitalism although some of these principles are being made obsolete by the growth of large-scale and oligopolistic industrial enterprise, the rise of mass trade unions, the development of gigantic governmental bureaucracies, and the coming to prominence of interest-group bargaining.

Similarly, the problems of progress in the United States are comprehensible to those who recognize that the nation—in contrast to most other modern industrial states, particularly those of northwestern Europe—still lacks a relevant, agreed-upon theory for dealing with the pains of social change. Such a theory could provide the basis for the rational development of services designed to aid individuals, families, and other groups at various levels of society to achieve satisfactory levels of living and health. Planning of this type implemented on a large and coherent scale would support the formation of a modern welfare state. The United States lacks a comprehensive theory of welfare and shows strong resistance to developing one. Welfare in America is addressed through a mixed bag of programs scattered across various public and private institutions and levels of government.

Important segments of the population view many of these programs as necessary evils at best. With all its welfare programs, the nation has only what the sociologist Harold L. Wilensky (1965) calls a "reluctant welfare state."

ENDS AND MEANS IN IMPROVING WELFARE

The need for welfare may be felt not only by the obviously poor and the unemployed but also by the underemployed, by those threatened with unpredictable layoffs or industrial dislocation, even by many among the apparently affluent who find themselves or their family members facing serious illness or retirement.

To the goal of economic sufficiency must be added those of human dignity and full citizenship for all. Economic adequacy is a matter of relative need, one's expectations for self by comparison with one's peers. Whereas most of America's poor are much better off materially than the hungry millions of Asia and Africa, the experiences of those who are relatively disadvantaged in the affluent society may make them feel a need more strongly than do the starving but resigned masses and they may act on that perceived need. Moreover, it is possible to be in what must objectively be regarded as a satisfactory financial condition without being accepted as a full participant in the community. One can receive needed monies from the state and find them demeaning. Despite the benefits of affluence, one can find oneself effectively excluded from the mass society. The nonwealthy aged in contemporary American society provide a good example: many are considered to be too poor, too insecure, too sick, too "out of it," and too old to be considered full citizens. Private pensions and social security provide a considerable measure of self respect for many of the elderly, at least for a time—but many lose dramatically in self-respect as they become financially dependent and ready for caretaking in home-delivery hot lunch programs, nursing homes, and the like.

A variety of questions beg for answers. For example, what levels of economic security become necessary in modern society for a person to sustain self-respect and function as a citizen? Under what arrangements for economic support can those who live principally on governmental stipends rather than occupational earnings feel respectable—that is, be defined as members of the "deserving poor"? And to what extent could general acceptance of the basic premises of social welfare planning enhance feelings of human worth?

A number of forces resist the movement toward comprehensive planning and programming in the United States. The welfare state is strongly opposed in the name of traditional laissez-faire principles, and this resistance is enhanced by certain social, political, and governmental structures. Important here are the blurring of the American class structure along economic, racial, and ethnic lines; the characteristic fragmentation of American governmental programs and agencies that attend to welfare problems, and of the profession of social work itself; and the turmoil of pluralistic politics that accompany most efforts at welfare reform.

WELFARE AND CAPITALISM

Responsibility for welfare in America lies in both private and public hands, although over the last few decades the public sector has almost eclipsed the former. Public programs are funded and administered through a variety of different agencies and at several levels, typically national, state, and county.

The operation of these programs presents an extraordinarily complex picture, for the location of responsibility, for defining, funding, administering, and providing services varies from program to program. For example, in most urban areas, the same personnel (often known as public aid caseworkers) relate to recipients of both ADC (Aid to Dependent Children) and of what is usually known as GA (General Assistance, a residual program of financial aid for persons with needs not covered by any other welfare arrangements). With respect to the ADC cases, the worker is operating under rules that, although varying considerably from state to state, must be in general accord with federal guidelines as a prerequisite to obtaining federal funds to support the program. In contrast, working with GA cases (not subsidized by federal funds), the caseworker is guided only by state and/or county guidelines, and levels and sources of financial support that have no nationally enforced standards. Handling GA cases usually requires contact with one or more of the following programs or agencies: federal Medicaid, local hospitals and clinics, community school systems, state and federal employment training programs, state unemployment agencies, private social agencies, etc. The chaos that may result from such complexity occurred dramatically during the War on Poverty of the sixties. Federal funds were allocated not only to the public and private agencies which usually administer such programs but also to an array of community groups, church-related organizations, private businesses, and other groupings (gangs, voluntary associations, and professional groups) that joined enthusiastically in the crusade. In the proliferation of what were generally modest efforts at social experimentation, no central thrust was perceptible.

Programs adopted readily in most European countries have been extremely slow to develop in the United States. Federal involvement in welfare was minimal until the Great Depression, and the basic programs and commitments developed in the 1930s have not been substantially altered to this day. The War on Poverty suggested many possible changes, but few of its innovations remain. Developments have come principally through elaborating the basic New Deal programs, for example, broader participation and raised benefits in the social security pension system.

Welfare efforts in America have often been near-sighted, and programs repeatedly have been justified as short-term responses to crises. Many of the welfare accomplishments of the New Deal were originally thought to address merely the temporary economic difficulties of the day. The War on Poverty was defined as a massive effort to "eradicate poverty" within a generation at most. (Such utopian hopes of course boomeranged when the programs were subjected to evaluation in terms of poverty reduction within a period of less than two years.) A break in the pattern of instituting welfare programs as temporary action came when programs could be justified not as handouts from the public treasury but a return of monies invested by citizens toward their own security. Thus social security old age and unemployment benefit programs have had continuity and relatively high public regard as *insurance* even where they have had to be subsidized from the general public treasury.

America's peculiar reluctance to adopt the idea of a welfare state is in large part attributable to the nation's commitment to laissez-faire capitalism. Under this model the system is seen as "self-adjusting." Economic remedies proposed have almost always been minor changes that are supposed to return the economy to its more "natural" state—for example, the passing of antitrust legislation to restore "true" competition, or more recently the matching of a federal deficit of 60 billion dollars with a tax rebate as if both were "extraordinary" measures. Ford's continued "exceptional" deficit followed Nixon's "routine exceptions."

Parallel to these assumptions about the economic and political spheres there developed a view of the natural capitalist man. Motivated by a particularly materialistic version of the Protestant ethic, the natural capitalist was a rugged individualist, a hard worker, and a wholehearted competitor. If he succeeded economically, he was no doubt a hard worker good and true; if he failed, it was his own fault. Support of welfare programs whose assumptions challenged this creed (for example, doubting that the return to economic health would come so normally, or that the poor necessarily deserved their fate) was defined as un-American.

It has come to be recognized, however, that the automatic mechanisms of capitalism do not always work. The adequacy of these mechanisms in providing prosperity and high employment except in times of war or preparation for war, or with the backing of public works measures, has been questioned. Karl Marx, though incorrect in many of his pessimistic predictions about the fate of capitalism, seems to have been accurate about the existence under advanced free enterprise of a "surplus labor pool" that expands and contracts with changes in economic conditions. In the United States this pool now consists largely of minority group members, the young, the elderly, and inner-city residents.

It is also recognized that the New Deal, though designed to save capitalism by getting it back on track, marked a considerable transformation of economics and politics that the ideology did not recognize. The New Deal fostered a high involvement in economic decision-making on the part of the federal government —a far cry from laissez-faire. The government came to play an activist role at mediating conflicts of interest. This change has opened the door to charges that the government compromises its presumed neutral role by intervening in the interests of particular capitalistic or other groupings (Lowi 1969). A corollary to that charge is that the government seldom intervenes on behalf of the beneficiaries of welfare programs because these persons do not ordinarily find it easy to get together to form an interest group.

The theory that all problems of inequality can be handled by extending opportunity has also been revealed to contain mythical elements. Proponents of the capitalist ideology concede that in many instances the competition has been unfair. Such a concession leads to endorsement of educational and other programs designed to open opportunities for minority and other disadvantaged populations. Yet this strategy cannot change the aggregate result that some win and some lose in the capitalist contest for economic success.

Despite its contemporary deficiencies as theory, the traditional ideology still holds great power. Alternative ideologies necessary to justify proposals for the welfare state may still be called "un-American," "socialist," or even "communist." The resistance to anti-capitalist perspectives is so substantial that Americans largely avoid the development of critical counterideologies. Most importantly, the old ideology—even with new terminology—provides a set of ready stereotypes. Those receiving public assistance are still stigmatized. If no longer characterized as willful failures, the poor are now seen, for example, as creatures of a "culture of poverty," under which it is assumed they have been taught to be satisfied with being poor.

AMERICAN PLURALISM

Resistance to the welfare state must also be seen as a function of the pluralism of American politics. Where a proliferation of groupings participates in the political process, ideological clashes over public issues are muted. Pluralist politics can be instructively contrasted with the politics that obtain when two disciplined political parties differ on key issues and organize political conflict over the choice between their points of view. American political pluralism reflects the pluralism of the social structure, which defies analysis along social class lines.

Important aspects of American pluralism that complicate the analysis of class position and politics include the following:

1. *Heterogeneity of economic interests within classes.* The "business interests" range from those of the large industrial corporation to those of the small, family-held store or farm. Within the "working class," interests vary from those of the strongly unionized skilled trades to those of the marginally employed, nonunionized members of the "under class." Within these classes there is a range of interests, for example, in the

priority given to preserving tax loopholes by corporate financiers as compared with that by owners of small businesses, or the concern with boosting social security benefits among assembly line workers as against that shown by migrant workers. Indeed, within classes there is often strong competition, as between small or large businesses or between highly organized crafts and "cheap labor."

2. *Blurring of class lines.* As economic interests fail to produce sharp definitions of social class, so also do characteristics of life style, patterns of association, and patterns of values or beliefs. This is particularly true of the margin between occupants of white collar positions that are not professional, technical, or managerial, and the holders of stable blue collar positions. Members of both categories often have interchangeable incomes, particularly with spouses working, and possess similar kinds of housing, cars, and aspirations for the education of their children. Occupants of white collar positions on the average have greater job security, but in a recession the prospect of unemployment can be as frightening to many white collar workers as it is to assembly line workers, for their affluence is often rooted in mortgages, other kinds of credit, and marginal second jobs particularly precarious in a general economic pinch.

3. *Racial and ethnic heterogeneity.* Particular labor unions or union locals have often been "owned" by specific ethnic groupings, and in the aggregate the unions have generally been much more attuned to the interests and political styles of the white members who have been their traditional membership base than those of blacks more recently moving into crafts and industry. An important example of racial and ethnic schism within the working class is found in the fact that over the past two decades white ethnic working class groupings, prominently Catholic ones in the urban North, have frequently been extremely vocal in their hostility to the demands of blacks. Indeed, the latter have often found their allies mainly in the white upper-middle class. Crucial here are the general lack of trust across racial groups and the fact that minority group members are often viewed as a threat to job security by working-class whites. Also, the racial and ethnic heterogeneity of the working class may be of crucial importance in understanding why American trade unions have so openly rejected the development of ideological politics in favor of "bread and butter unionism." Successive waves of immigration brought

many ethnics who were schooled in European brands of socialism; these perspectives were repeatedly rejected as "foreign
ideology." In its racial and ethnic fragmentation, the United
States stands in marked contrast to those Northern European
societies in which ethnic differences are minimal, where constitutional monarchies have helped tie progress to national identity,
and in which coherent welfare programs have been developed.

4. *Locational differences.* Class distinctions are also complicated in America by variations in areas of residence and origin.
Most obvious in relevance is the sectionalism of the South,
coupled as it has been historically with a racism that splits the
economic classes. Important as well are differences between rural
and urban areas and, within metropolitan areas, the inner city
and the suburbs. Many major American cities are suffering a
sharp exodus of white and affluent populations and of resources
and institutions. The large cities increasingly become the home of
minority groupings facing high unemployment and underemployment—a group that because of high visibility might be on the
way to becoming a well defined "underclass" in cities that are
"administered" by bureaucratic officials.

5. *Political decentralization.* Parallel to the formal governmental decentralization of the federal system is a great dispersion
of political decision-making power. There is considerable truth in
the observation that the nation has a hundred political parties—
two for each state—parties that truly get together nationally only
once every four years to agree about presidential and vice-
presidential nominees. The operations of these hundred parties
enable them to be responsive to local circumstances of economic
interests, racial and ethnic attributes, political traditions, etc.,
and in so doing they reduce further the possibilities of aggregat-
ing political demands into coherent political positions and providing sharp choices between the two national parties on welfare
issues.

Such forces for pluralism make it difficult to obtain consensus
on an elaborated model of social welfare. Instead, governmental
welfare programs as well as other public efforts are largely
hammered out through a process of compromise. Some areas for
potential action remain more or less sacrosanct because of
particular economic interests; for example, until the tide began to
turn recently, national health insurance has been systematically
prevented by the American Medical Association. Other areas are
more open to the bargaining of interest groups.

Because much welfare policy is very close to economic policy, the involvement of business and labor interests in such policy is generally quite high. In contrast, citizens who might benefit from welfare measures are often left out of the political process almost completely. The difficulties of organizing a group such as the aged into a political constituency are huge. This is true as well of the vast majority of the recipients of public welfare, who, despite the fact that their plight has gained considerable prominence through the activities of the National Welfare Rights Organization, generally appear not to have been reached by those activities. Difficulties in the political mobilization of this population include the all-encompassing demands that the daily fight for survival makes on many of the poor, the stigma attaching to welfare recipients that can lead them to avoid publically proclaiming their status through involvement in welfare rights, and the dilemmas of racial identity that have disabled the organization.

It is no wonder, then, that at most times, welfare politics are either quiescent or, if active, show little central tendency or developmental pattern. Political positions swing between that of the conservative Nixon pressing for guaranteed annual incomes for a period, and that of liberals who helped to kill this income measure on grounds it did not go far enough. Many politicians engage in a great amount of posturing to find a popular position, one achieved most often through expressing indignation about the allegedly large numbers of "welfare cheaters." That much of this activity is largely verbal is shown in the short-lived nature of many of the frequent and broadly publicized "crack-downs" on recipients of public aid.

Welfare Agencies and the Social Work Profession

The weakness of the reluctant welfare state in America is displayed well by the character of the organizations that implement welfare in the nation—public and private social agencies and the relevant profession, social work. American welfare institutions are relatively impotent with respect to both goals and means. A number of the critical attributes of these institutions flow from the country's commitments to laissez-faire capitalism and political pluralism. These attributes include the following:

1. *Limited jurisdictions and spheres of influence.* Limitation derives from the decentralization of political structures to state, county, municipal, and even more localized units and from the

fragmentation of programs. A similar pattern obtains among private agencies. Decentralized programs do not provide a coherent approach, and complaints about the lack of coordination and the need for cooperative efforts are continuously being heard. Limitations on autonomy come as well from the residual nature of much social welfare effort: Social welfare institutions are expected to deal with the aspects of human behavior still needing attention after more powerful and explicitly bounded institutions—for example, economic, medical, and educational ones—have had their effects. As a result, social welfare efforts often must operate in counterpoint to the activities of other, nonwelfare organizations and frequently on the "turf" of these other units.

2. *Ambiguous, multiple, and often conflicting goals.* Welfare goals are often stated in excessively general terms—for example, "To promote the economic, social, and emotional well-being of the citizens of . . ." The consequent ambiguity makes it difficult for agencies to make appropriate choices and justify them to outsiders. A dilemma running through many welfare programs involves relative emphasis to be made on such goals as service and rehabilitation on the one hand and surveillance and control on the other. Examples are seen readily in the dilemmas of treatment versus custody in correctional and mental health facilities and of help versus surveillance (to prevent cheating) in agencies serving recipients of public assistance.

3. *Resource shortages.* An expected outcome of the politics of compromise is that resources and tasks will often be mismatched, with severe competition for scarce resources. Expansive words about good deeds are rarely in short supply, so that the mismatch of goals and means often becomes glaring. Further, given the usually illusory but frequent assumption that welfare problems will simply go away with short-term sympathy, resources are perpetually drying up in the face of continued or expanded need. Social casework must usually be practiced with caseloads far larger than originally intended.

4. *Bureaucratic formalism.* Many welfare agencies become hedged about with regulations and paperwork. An extreme example is provided by the research of Richard Forbes on public aid caseworkers in Chicago: On one occasion, he observed that a certain minor service for ADC recipients could not be provided until the neighborhood office received from headquarters new

supplies of a specific request form for the service—despite the fact that the form was blank except for its identification code (Forbes 1973). Although bureaucratic procedures can guarantee the agencies' conformity to law, helping them to defend themselves against charges of error, favoritism, and the like, they can also lead to inertia, rigidity, and dehumanization.

5. *Institutional weakness of the profession of social work.* Slow to develop and still relatively small, American social work suffers from rather low professional prestige and, compared with most other professions, low collegial control over the behavior of other professionals and over the standards of professional practice. These weaknesses derive in part from the fact that social work is concerned mainly with residual social problems and the "losers" who suffer from these problems, and that professional standards must be adapted to the ends and means of the particular agencies where the practitioners are employed. Also important is the fact that American social work developed its professional expertise around the conception of casework—the model of a therapist helping a single person at a time to deal with largely intrapsychic problems. However helpful the caseworker may be to the individual client, this conception provides little substance for comprehensive welfare planning at the community level. Yet it should not be assumed that emphasis upon small-scale change is intrinsic to the social work profession. In other societies, social work has a broader mission, whereas American society has more readily granted legitimacy to efforts to help individual misfortune than to address the social sources of misfortune.

6. *The weakness of the professional ideology of welfare.* Welfare ideology has had difficulties in defending itself against faddish solutions to its problems, such as "scientific management" and its contemporary descendants, "program budgeting" and the like. It has also been weakened by espousing utopian goals (among the aims of some community action programs during the War on Poverty was that of "drastically reducing crime")—a fatal weakness when continuation of programs is made dependent solely upon the achievement of short term results. Indeed, both the welfare and educational institutions recurrently find themselves having to draw back innovations because they have overbought and oversold partial solutions. Public housing, for example, was expected to transform the lives of former slum dwellers. Faith in this single reform, often accompanied by no

other changes, led ultimately to the justification of any kind of public housing, no matter how conceived. Most infamous is the Pruitt-Igoe housing project in Saint Louis, a postwar high-rise development now undergoing demolition whose elevators were designed to stop only at every third floor—because the poor are "used to steps."

Probably the most significant weakness of welfare organizations as well as social workers is the inability to set clear priorities. In the War on Poverty, the character of the federal legislation along with political pluralism led to the bargaining out of multisectored "program packages" that varied from state to state, community to community, and agency to agency. It was nearly impossible to find out which antipoverty efforts "worked," and, perhaps more important, extremely difficult to learn which "didn't work." The lack of priorities and diffuseness of planning is illustrated strikingly in an account by Daniel P. Moynihan, a significant figure in the Johnson and Nixon administrations, on his personal recollections of the development of the antipoverty program. At a critical point in planning inside the Johnson administration, Moynihan recalls, a large-scale employment program for the adult poor was envisaged, but President Johnson vetoed the idea on grounds that he wanted to cut taxes (Moynihan 1969b, xv–xvi). Ultimately there developed diffuse programs like "community action," which, whatever their long-run or peripheral merits, did not attack poverty very directly.

2 Social Reform in America

PUBLIC WELFARE IN THE UNITED STATES

The paradox of American welfare is not niggardliness, but the grudging acceptance of welfare in such a prosperous nation. The richest country in the world has welfare programs which are comparatively modest and remain the object of persistent attacks. Most American welfare programs have been slow to develop, many are mere stopgaps, and the coverage in others is uneven. Wherever possible, the country has explored alternatives to "equalize opportunities," especially educational opportunities, before turning to income redistribution. Programs of income redistribution that have developed since the Great Depression tend to stigmatize some recipients and create further stratification of life chances among the poor.[1] The most respected and generous of our programs—Old Age, Survivors, Disability and Health Insurance (OASDHI), Unemployment, and Medicare—assist mainly those who are not desperately poor, while the more meager and controversial of our welfare programs—Aid to Families with Dependent Children (AFDC), Old Age Assistance (OAA), and General Assistance (GA)—have primary responsibility for the incontestably poor. In either case, welfare draws an additional set of distinctions over and above those of occupation and income.

The general pattern is one where repeated economic crises have forced an adjustment to mass poverty in such a manner that it leaves relatively intact existing ideological convictions about individual responsibility (Turner 1960). Two public philosophies seem to have developed: a progressive one emphasizing reform, and a regressive one stressing deservedness. In short, we have theories of both the carrot and the stick. Though, in general, the former is associated with liberals and the latter with conservatives, the two strategies have been adopted rather opportunistically. Neither has been uniformly successful.

Both of these public philosophies are attempts to keep the

13

nation in one piece either by reducing the most pressing cases of deprivation or by assisting only those having apparent claims to respectability and deservedness. Yet both seem only to shift the lines of inequality rather than to reduce claims of injustice. When benefits are granted to those hopelessly out of the labor market, they become an object of grievance by those who remain in the labor market. When benefits are restricted to those most "deserving," they are characterized as socialism for the rich and capitalism for the poor.

Even our most generous programs usually include some regressive features (for example, the limitation on employment but not on capital income for social security beneficiaries). In consequence, welfare itself tends to become divisive after what is usually a short honeymoon for either the regressive or the progressive approach. Despite their separate limitations, however, these approaches have together provided perennial opportunities to bid for mass support.

CULTURAL FRAGMENTATION AND THE LIMITED STATE

The ethnic, regional, and racial groupings that make up American society have never much trusted one another and for that reason have been loath to put much power in one another's hands. Fiorello La Guardia, probably the most popular man to serve as mayor of New York, was one of those few political leaders with a balanced ticket in his own background: born in Greenwich Village, raised in Arizona, the son of a Jewish mother and an Italian father, he had lived in several places in America and the Balkans. He was raised an Episcopalian and spoke several languages. Practically every constituency in New York could feel that he "belonged to them" (Mann 1959). Such leaders are uncommon, but necessary in a fragmented nation like the United States.

The problem of welding together a nation of distrustful parts found its earliest and one of its most explicit expressions in the formation of the nation itself. The thirteen colonies entered into a confederation only with the gravest misgivings and then only with the assurance of the "limited state": a federal government thought sufficiently weak so as not to threaten their separate powers.

As the state was limited in its powers, the powers of private property were emphasized. The groups involved in this division of power have changed somewhat along with the nature of their mutual distrust. There have been a growing number of regional groupings as the nation has expanded and race and ethnicity have challenged state loyalties. One thing has remained unchanged: no group has trusted the other quite enough to allow for the development of a strong central government that might fall into the hands of another group.

The limited state has, of course, become far more than a mere tax gatherer, confederation for military defense, or printer of money. Yet the federal budget, as Lowi points out (1969), is still divided up among private competitors for federal aid. Washington collects the major part of the funds, but the beneficiaries help cut up the federal pie according to their respective political strength and relative placement in the private sector.

It is also true that the intervening years have not left the separate states, ethnic groups, races, or regions unaltered. The states seem to be gradually coalescing into regions with somewhat greater consensus on their respective interests and a capacity for united action, though the issue of states rights continues to be raised. Ethnic groups have tended to lose first their provincial identification (e.g., Sicilians), then their national identification (Italians), and only then to become an "American ethnic group" (Italian-Americans). Racial groups in America seem to be losing many of their primordial divisions (e.g., tribal and linguistic) in favor of a color scheme (red, black, brown) that has little precedent in their historic background. These amalgamations show diverse groups mobilizing for participation in the division of the federal pie. As they sort themselves out into a smaller number of mutually recognizable groups, they do not necessarily become more trustworthy to one another, but continue to fear a strong government that might fall into the hands of any one group.

The fragmentation of American society consists less in the number of contending groups than in the dramatic and visible inequalities associated with primordial status in a society that holds universalism as sacred. Two groups who have much in common, such as blacks and Southern whites, but who share very differently in the distribution of both private and public goods, can be as divisive as a large number of primordial groups who find themselves the object of discrimination but are hard put to do much about it or to single out those who mistreat them. The situation which may most polarize contenders for power and privilege may be that where only two contenders compete, as in Northern Ireland, Eastern Canada, or Belgium.

The United States may be fortunate in having many relatively small ethnic, religious, and racial groups, each so powerless that it must negotiate to better its life circumstances rather than resort to civil strife. So long as they negotiate rather than fight, however, these groups need a flexible and rather weak central government, so that any temporary alliance among ethnic, religious, racial, and regional groups cannot be made permanent by governmental power.

A nation of such distrustful parts is a fragile thing, and Americans probably owe their continuing unity as a nation to the free enterprise system and to the comparatively low demands that it makes on their social solidarity. It has been a flexible system in which economic power has not automatically been buttressed by strong political power. Wealth might become very concentrated, and indeed the affluent might capture much of the available political power. However, the political power the wealthy could grasp has not amounted to much—or so it was often thought. While the rich might be advantaged in the economic marketplace, others have still had a chance of entering it and making headway without having to contend with those politically advantaged by strong governmental controls as well. The prevailing assumption seems to have been that a strong central government could only further benefit the affluent and well placed.

One cannot help but marvel at how successful the free enterprise system has been in maintaining the unity of the country by not demanding more social solidarity and consensus than the country was able to muster. Aside from Canada, the United States is the only pluralistic nation in the New World that has not resorted to centralized, authoritarian regimes to secure either its unity as a nation or relative peace among its many groups. Undoubtedly it falls short of its own ideals as a democratic nation, but the civil rights it ensures its citizens are broader than those of most other countries similarly fragmented. It is true that some groups, especially the blacks and the Indians, have been placed under exceptional authoritarian control. One can also argue that the absence of a strong central government often has allowed local tyrannies to develop, and it is probably true that many small towns and local governments are run rather arbitrarily by a "power elite." In general, however, the instruments of local or national government in the United States are too weak to be repressive. Americans—hard hats and businessmen alike—may be wise in their persistent loyalty to the free enterprise system. As Boorstein (1953) points out, the United States has not so much a self-governing system as a genius for tolerating high levels of outright disorder.

This rather fundamental achievement of the free enterprise ideology has left in its wake a number of problems, social welfare prominent among them. The limited state gives little room for the development of a public-regarding elite (Banfield and Wilson 1963), whereby the nation's rich and privileged members would sponsor welfare legislation or general public policies in an even-handed way. Without such a reliable elite, the United States has tended to vacillate between witch hunts and reforms, with welfare programs either derided or touted as a solution to disorder.

THE SEARCH FOR TRUSTED LEADERSHIP

If one believes that "that state governs best which governs least," then it is unlikely that government service will attract those who are most talented, ambitious, and public-regarding. The formula for government essentially asks for restraint, and that is not an attractive career for the vigorous and the idealistic. Nonetheless, the country has discovered considerable idealism in its public leaders. In part this leadership has developed because of the dominance and special value commitments of the WASPs (white Anglo Saxon Protestants). The WASPs have remained the largest "minority" group in the nation and they are also the most visible portion of the nation's economic elite. The WASPs were the first subscribers to the Protestant ethic, and one could hope that they would obey some of its precepts of universal otherhood.

For at least the first four decades of nationhood, the WASPs controlled government with little interference or competition. They occupied most political offices, including the presidency. They exercised restraint in government but kept opportunity open—through the Louisiana Purchase, for example, and their continued willingness to accept new immigrants. It was with the Jacksonian presidency that the trustworthiness of the WASPs was first effectively questioned and their role as arbitrators began to be reduced.

The Jacksonian presidency was a revolt against the commercial and landed gentry of the Eastern seabord. Immigrants, small farmers, urban workmen, and people who lived beyond the

Appalachians voted so as to put down the aspirations of a budding aristocracy. With the "spoils system" the Jacksonians immediately turned government into an instrument of economic advancement for a broader class of people (Schlesinger 1945). Political offices were to be divided up among recognizable constituencies—ethnic groups, regions, social classes, and interest groups—roughly in proportion to the votes they could deliver to political parties. The spoils system represented a genuine advance beyond the high-minded indifference of the WASPs for the simple reason that the Jacksonian administration recognized and expanded the role of government in maintaining the fairness of private enterprise.

At this same time the WASPs were themselves divided between the agrarian interests of the South and the commercial interests of the North. With the Civil War, they became even more distrustful of each other's willingness to govern fairly. The growing spoils system and the regional fragmentation of the WASPs jointly reduced their role in government, resulting in a pluralistic process in which ethnic, regional, and racial groups used government to pursue their own specific interests. This way of dividing up the influence of government has continued, and in the main it has benefited several—but not all—lower-status groups. As the Irish, Poles, Italians, Jews, and various other groups gained access to political power, they were better able to compete in the private sector. Thus government began to redistribute income indirectly by rectifying competitive disadvantages in the private economic system. Of course, not all groups were equally benefited by this system of political bargaining, but more and more groups were included. By the end of World War II, it was mainly blacks, Puerto Ricans, Appalachians, and American Indians who remained more or less outside the political and economic market places.

In some sense, then, the spoils or patronage system was a welfare system. It handed out government contracts, gave franchises, provided educational funds, and was the nation's largest employer. But this same system of political bargaining placed politics as a career in low public regard. Americans often express contempt for their elected leaders, and it is not surprising that men of high repute have been reluctant to offer themselves as candidates (Rose 1967). The general pattern is to work for specific favors in the private marketplace—construction contracts, defense industries, subsidies, and the like—which benefit specific constituencies. It is unusual for American political leaders to be concerned with the welfare of the entire population.

One consequence of the functioning of the dominant political system was the extensive development of private self-help ventures among the sectarian and distrustful groups which made up the nation's population. There is scarcely a group in America which has not founded its own colleges, charitable organizations, fraternal associations, or communal institutions. Up to the Great Depression, these were the main "welfare programs." As most U.S. minority groups have succeeded more or less in organizing for self-help, politicians have been more or less eager to offer them the benefits of public welfare. Those groups that have lagged behind are mainly those which have been restricted in their rights to organize for self-help ventures (e.g., blacks and red men) or those which have not had much time to do so (e.g., Puerto Ricans). The U.S. government has proved responsive to organized political pressure but not to those unable to exert political pressure—that is, those usually least able to help themselves.

A second consequence of this dominant and partisan political pattern has been that leaders most concerned with the welfare of the general population have flooded into the private sector. A remarkable number of talented Americans have devoted their lives to the private search for a more affluent and equalitarian society. Dorothea Dix, Jane Addams, and Martin Luther King are only a few whose achievements have overshadowed those of their political contemporaries. All three operated primarily in the private sphere, seeking to bring equality or subsistence to the poor by diverse methods. Even present-day zealots are urged to "work within the system": to contribute to self-help ventures or only to try to extend the number of constituencies taking part in the spoils system. There is no shortage of talented sympathizers with the poor in this country, but most have chosen to work outside the confines of government. Over the long run these idealistic entrepreneurs have been reasonably effective advocates of the poor; they have been in the forefront of movements to establish either governmental or private programs for the poor.

A third consequence of the political pattern is that when some relatively permanent programs for direct aid were established after the Great Depression, these programs were differentiated according to who was most "politically deserving." Thus social security and unemployment insurance went primarily to those who were regular employees, regular voters, and regular union members. Blindness (AB) and total disability (APTD) were apparently recognized as being so uniformly distributed that both received regular legislative support. The programs which were most problematic were General Assistance (GA), Old Age Assistance (OAA) and Aid to Dependent Children (ADC), as it became increasingly evident that each program benefited relatively weak constituencies—the unemployed who were not unionized, the aged who had not had regular employment in the past, and women, frequently black, who were suffering from the wreckage of a domestic union and the continued necessity to support children. The legislated differences are fairly expectable; relatively high payments for the politically deserving and low payments and a heavy burden of bureaucratic surveillance for the remainder. Looking over this entire pattern, one is struck by the partisan role we expect of elected elites and how nearly those expectations are realized in practice.

WITCH HUNTS AND REFORMS

The comparative standing of America's many ethnic, religious, regional and racial groups is a source of grievance and feelings of outraged injustice. The threat of disorder is often great, sometimes manifest in vigilantism, gangsterism, lynchings, racial riots—persistent American forms of violence. The National Commission on the Causes and Prevention of Violence lists thousands of cases of violence throughout the nation's history, the majority of which are somehow connected with preceptions of injustice in the relations among regional, racial, or ethnic groups.

Despite America's rather high tolerance for disorder, national apprehensions have led to two alternating responses: witch hunting and reform. During Reconstruction, the nation made its first timid efforts at federally supported programs for former slaves and people dislocated by the war. This was followed by the Jim Crow period, during which Southern whites reestablished some of their control over blacks. In the subsequent Reform Period, the United States experienced its greatest growth of private charities and self-help ventures. The Red Scare of the 1920s, however, brought these to a halt. It was the New Deal that finally brought the federal government substantially into the business of providing direct aid to the poor, the ill, the unemployed, and the aged.

After the Second World War, however, the country underwent another red scare in the form of McCarthyism. Yet even before the McCarthyites had discredited themselves, the Civil Rights movement was gaining momentum, culminating in the War on Poverty. By the mid-1970s the country seemed to have entered still another period of witch hunting, with the presidency itself heavily involved.

Whenever either witch hunts or reforms fail to contain the potential forces of disorder in the country, the center of gravity shifts from one to the other. The McCarthy supporters, for example, had the ostensible purpose of restraining what they regarded as subversive and disruptive groups in the society. Yet the movement ended by only creating more disorder and acrimony. The Civil Rights movement led to vast reforms, especially in the legislation of equal rights, but it also failed to contain the explosive situation in our inner cities. Each type of period tends to create its own backlash. On balance, neither reforms nor witch hunts can contain the native potential of the country for disorder.

Although World Wars I and II seemed to produce periods of social cohesion that muted many intergroup hostilities, the tendency to sway between extremes has been marked enough to have grave effects on the development of social welfare. Welfare programs have developed in spurts with long intervals between them. Gradually, however, private and localized programs have yielded to public and federally guided programs. As we shall see in chapter 3, all attempts at reform have been heavily conditioned by the close relationship between the nation's identity and the free enterprise system. The alternation between witch hunting and reform has made for a very uneven record in social welfare. Social welfare programs remain among the favorite victims of witch hunts and are frequently accused of being a source of rabble rousing and disorder. In turn, social reformers have often vastly oversold their welfare programs as a final solution to the nation's troubles. The United States does not yet seem able to accept social welfare programs for more limited reasons: to keep people alive and in conventionally accepted comfort.

The Work Ethic as a Test of Citizenship

Despite slackening of immigration in recent decades, Americans remain painfully aware of their torn and fragile loyalties. Being an American, then, is not something to be assumed but something to be actively demonstrated. As Shils (1956) has argued, groups uncertain of their own or other's national loyalties are apt to insist on rather dramatic proofs of citizenship, going beyond native birth or citizenship papers. This insistence probably takes its most overt form in the show of patriotism that accompanies almost any public gathering in the United States: showing of the flag, pledging of allegiance to the flag, singing of the national anthem, and so on. These demonstrations even invade our leisure life and make most team sports—baseball, football, and basketball—occasions to stand up and attest to one's gut, national feeling. In turn, every athletic spectacle is treated as if it were a training ground for the final contest between likely belligerents. Muhammad Ali fights for youth and militants against a "handkerchief head" Joe Frazier; swinging Joe Namath at times shines to dim the glory of a middle American Tarkenton; the *New York Times* likens Woody Hayes to the whole Middle West and turns football defeats into commentaries on Eastern cosmopolitanism.

While sports have always attracted partisan attention, it is work and striving that have been uppermost in the attention of most Americans when it has come to judging one another personally. The most persistent test of citizenship seems to be embodied in what we have come to refer to as the "work ethic." There is a body of analysis on American society which suggests that the work ethic is only a sort of secularized version of the Protestant ethic and that it has endured in this country mainly because the early settlers were successful in establishing it as the central value complex of the society. In short it was seen as providing a value system that could bring some measure of consensus to an otherwise fragmented society. Certainly some of the early immigrants to the country did adhere to the Protestant ethic. However, it is difficult to establish a direct line from their early dominance in *some* areas of the nation to the present very widespread acceptance of the work ethic among such diverse groups as Poles, Italians, Southerners, or Irishmen. In most instances the work ethic seems to have been self-imposed as if to dispel doubts about the worthiness of those very people who did *not* share in the Protestant tradition.

Thus there seems to have been a rather sudden conversion to the work ethic by groups historically distant from the Protestant tradition. Well-off WASPs have always been able to live lives of relative leisure without much social criticism. It is mainly those who are just making it into the labor market or into the business world who are the most outspoken adherents of the work ethic. This pattern occurs irrespective of their cultural traditions. A novel but interesting example of this seems to be the recent rejection of feminine dependency ("They just gave me dolls...") among American women in favor of a militant work ethic as they enter the labor market in growing numbers. One can argue, then, that the work ethic is not just the historical legacy of a few early and pushy settlers, but a test of citizenship most favored because it was the most universal one available. If the Protestants invented the ethic, their creation did not keep others from practicing it. If public service provided little or no warrant for determining a citizen's loyalty—and the usual reaction was simply to distrust self-proclaimed public servants as charlatans or politicians—then private economic conduct was the plausible alternative. And if free enterprise was seen as uniquely American, then success at economic enterprise became especially suited as the American way to citizenship.

The work ethic may have been a fairly good test of citizenship in the United States because it gave immigrants hope, though many had a long wait before being able to demonstrate their industry. However, widespread acceptance of the work ethic has also resulted in gross distortions in our definition of the poor and our manner of distributing aid. Some observers have seen the work ethic as a personal choice and have been tempted to view poverty as self-inflicted. Others have regarded the work ethic as only an external imposition and have taken poverty to be an incorrigible characteristic of the present economic system. Theories of racial or cultural inferiority have had about the same appeal as have those which have assigned all the fault to "the system." These theories, however, have had considerable effect in shaping public opinion, so that hope for the full citizenship of some groups, such as the blacks, has been regarded as too futuristic by many liberals and too optimistic by some conservatives. All such views have tended only to complicate life for those too far from the mainstream of society to be able to prove themselves by the work ethic.

A metaphor useful for thinking about this problem is to view the entire American society as a huge sports complex where about 80 percent of the population is inside the stadium playing a game called "work ethic" while the other 20 percent stand in a queue outside the stadium awaiting their chance to join the game. The people inside rejoice at their good fortune and, out of guilt, self-righteousness, or fear, explain the presence of the outsiders as either a malevolent conspiracy by the monopolistic owners of the stadium or as the result of a persistent inability of those outside to get up early enough in the morning to gain entrance to the game. Each interpretation leaks outside to those in line, adding to their chagrin and their perplexity as to why they are not inside playing the game.

Not only does word of these views leak outside to those in line, but well-meaning liberals inside see to it that those outside get "welfare tickets" or vouchers which will encourage them to stay in line rather than tear down the stadium, which is what the liberals say they would do if they were in the same position themselves. The conservatives in the stadium are frightened by the apprehensions of the liberals, and while they agree to the plan they insist that different-colored tickets (OAA, ADC, AB, APTD, GA, OASDHI, UI, etc.) be given according to how likely a person is to stay in line in the first place. They also insist that if a person gets out of line he must be given a ticket of lower denomination. Incorrigible latecomers are not to be given tickets at all.

A large bureaucracy is formed to hand out the tickets, but, much to everyone's surprise, many of those in line will not take them; these persons resent the leaked allegation that they do not have the personal fiber to keep their own place in line or are threatening to tear down the stadium. Others accept the tickets and then find they are not all the same color or denomination. Some are mortified by the low denomination given them and withdraw into mute isolation. Others gloat at their large-denomination tickets. Occasionally a knot of people who have already met one another while in line will compare their different-colored tickets and "break up" over the inexplicable differences among them. Some groups who have been in line a long time will be outraged that they got low-denomination tickets while others who are behind them got high-denomination tickets. Some people take the whole affair as a joke; they exchange tickets, buy them, sell them, or lie about how long they have been in line or are willing to stay there.

The line outside the stadium gets noisy. Some people take the tickets so lightly or so seriously that they actually break a few windows in the stadium. Both the liberals and conservatives inside the stadium get worried and take time out to increase the denomination of all the tickets—but under conservative pressure the procedures for surveillance are increased, and those guilty of laughter, acrimony, wailing, or outrage find deductions made from their tickets. When news of this leaks to those outside in line there is a large outcry; encouraged by their first success in window breaking, some try it again, and this time they dislodge a couple of bricks in the stadium. This escalation of disorder discredits the liberals within the stadium and they relent to the use of a police force to keep those outside in line. The police arrive, and those outside get back in line, though resentfully.

Time out is over in the stadium, and the game of work ethic goes hot and heavy. There are even a few new players from the outside, a concession to the liberals that the conservatives have had to grant in order to call in the police force. But then, the police cannot stand the taunts of the rabble outside the stadium and beat up a few, some in possession of high-denomination tickets and others who turned out to be stray liberals from inside the stadium. There are more windows broken and more falling bricks. The police panic, crush a lot of heads, and then threaten to strike unless they are given hazardous duty pay—an expense far greater than the cost of all the tickets given to the outsiders in line. The arguments of the conservatives are discredited, and a bipartisan committee proposes that most of the old welfare tickets be replaced by one that has a single denomination. At first this proposal has wide conservative and liberal support, but then the conservatives insist that those who get the new welfare tickets do janitorial duties inside in order to get their tickets. The liberals balk, saying that this is only another attempt of the monopolistic owners to curtail individual freedom. They counter-propose that all the tickets be printed in new colors and the denomination of each be increased. Word of this leaks outside the stadium and . . .

The point of the metaphor is that those who can play the game of the work ethic tend to shape the lives of those who are waiting to do so. Those unable even to subscribe to the work ethic are seen as a subversive force not fully deserving of being called citizens. According to the liberals, this unruly lot is likely to revolt unless it is bought off. According to the conservatives, this rabble

s to be closely watched and policed. Both groups, then, tend
e social welfare as an instrument of social control, the one as
arrot and the other as a stick. Thus most social welfare
programs in the United States consist in varying proportions of
both carrot and stick. Those usually employed and unionized
receive fairly generous subsidies with a minimum of surveillance.
Those whose citizenship or subscription to the work ethic is more
questionable, such as blacks or American Indians, receive smaller
payments and a great deal more surveillance. Neither prescription leads to an even-handed distribution of social welfare
benefits which might mitigate—or at least not exacerbate—existing feelings of injustice among the nation's poor.

Nowhere is the liberal conception of social welfare as an
instrument of social control more explicitly developed than in a
study by Piven and Cloward (1971). It is their contention that
most of the 1960 riots and demonstrations were a successful effort
of the poor to expand welfare payments. It is our view, however,
that almost the reverse took place: that a liberal presidential
administration, by expanding welfare payments, promoted agita-
tion for further expansion of benefits. The riots and demonstrations did not taper off as welfare payments rose but, if anything,
grew more clamorous. They slackened only when the White
House was occupied by a far more conservative and unresponsive
administration and a score of large cities began to spend increasing amounts on their police budgets. Then, with some grumbl-
ing, the poor did get back in line—and the nation soon recoiled
at several gross excesses of police authority and official subversion. It is too soon to judge the effects of these developments on
welfare policies. What does seem clear is that the initiative does
not belong to the poor and that their responses are often
orchestrated by those who take the difference between being at
work or being on welfare as a critical judgment of one's state of
citizenship and corresponding need for discipline or appease-
ment. Neither reaction may quiet the threat of disorder among
the poor; in fact, it may worsen it.

THE FUTURE OF SOCIAL REFORM

We have emphasized the country's difficulty in finding non-
partisan leaders who would sponsor a more even-handed distribution of public welfare. We have argued that periodic witch
hunts have castigated welfare programs while reformers have

oversold them as a panacea to all the nation's disorders. We have also tried to highlight the way in which either conservative or liberal doctrine has tended to turn welfare into an instrument of social control over those still unable to subscribe to its requirements of first-class citizenship. Despite all these obstacles, the outstanding characteristic of American welfare programs has been their growth, especially since the Great Depression. American welfare has progressed from private or locally supported efforts to the point where almost everyone takes the term "welfare" to mean the federally mandated programs. These programs are no longer the temporary expedients of the past but are acknowledged—whether grudgingly or willingly—as inevitable in a highly industrialized and urbanized society where most people are dependent upon wage labor in a single labor market.

It would be easy to argue that the obstacles to the welfare state—partisan leadership, cycles of cultural fragmentation, and the use of welfare as an instrument of social control—have weakened over time in response to persistent economic crises that have produced mass poverty. Such an argument does not fully capture the forces now taking the initiative in new welfare programs and likely to play a large role in their future. The debate over public welfare is now occurring on a national level. However localized, conservative, primordial, liberal, or bigoted the constituencies who oppose or support welfare legislation, they look to Washington to settle their disagreements. Whatever their reluctance, Washington legislators are being asked to devise programs which will satisfy all their constituencies. Social welfare is no longer buried in local politics, no longer something that can be farmed out to high-born private entrepreneurs. It is a national issue in which the various parties—some of them still extremely provincial and partisan—must work with the whole nation as an audience.

Local disorders and expressions have been redefined so as to require federal intervention. This is due in part to legal changes which began with the New Deal but were most marked in the 1960s. The 1964 Civil Rights Act and a number of Supreme Court decisions have increasingly made the federal government responsible for seeking out and redressing local claims of injustice. As the federal government enlarges its own welfare programs, it seems increasingly to entangle itself as referee in the counterclaims of diverse, often local groups. The national media can only increase the likelihood that these diverse sources of discontent get compiled in a single report available both to the discontented themselves and to newspaper readers and TV viewers in Washington, Des Moines, and New York. The reluctance of states and municipalities to shoulder the burden of reform has left the nation's foundlings at the federal doorstep.

It is for reasons of this kind that an obscure sit-in in Greensboro, N.C., could become escalated into a national issue that required the attention of U.S. marshals, the Supreme Court, Congress, and the presidency itself. The same can be said of what has happened or what will occur in Little Rock, Arkansas, Selma, Alabama, the Hough district of Cleveland, and numerous other places. The federal government has become a principal participant in even the most primitive and localized debates occurring in the country. Paradoxically, even the States' Rights movement looks to the federal government to finance its efforts through "revenue sharing." And the local control movement is financed largely through federal subsidies.

This sort of national aggregation does not necessarily presage an era of tranquillity or consensus. As we can see from the recent past, federal welfare programs may only make diverse groups more acutely aware of their favored or unfavored position in the total society. Welfare programs can divide people as easily as they can unite them, especially where there is a multiplicity of programs responsive to select constituencies. The mere expansion of current programs is unlikely to do much more than increase disputes among diverse beneficiaries. What seems to be needed is a more general notion of welfare programs, one that benefits all elements of the society in a more uniform fashion. Here, the Medicare program probably comes closest to establishing a model, since it extends to all the same potential coverage.

In the future, the national aggregation of welfare issues and solutions should make it easier for politicians to respond in this general way to the very unequal availability of resources and rights to our citizens. The sheer plurality of parties involved in such debates makes such an inclusive response more likely. There are two major obstacles which continue to lie in the way of such a political program, however. One is the American fear of a strong government, and the other is the stubborn tendency of both conservative and liberal leaders to see welfare programs as only an instrument of social control. Both of these obstacles were prominently displayed in the controversy over the Family Assistance Plan proposed by the Nixon administration. While the administration's support may have been half-hearted at times, the FAP was still a far more universal and less "constituency-specific" plan than the ones currently in force. It was the liberals who defeated it in Congress, and while some of the work rules included in the plan could have been considered punitive, it was mainly the apprehensions of liberal congressmen about how the federal bureaucracy *might* use the work regulations which gave them pause. In their view, like that of most Americans, the government could not really be trusted with strong powers for fear that it would differentially enforce them.

Equally an obstacle is the tendency of conservatives and liberals alike to consider welfare programs necessary only when there is "trouble on the streets." Both sides develop responses that are narrowly conceived. The liberals are apt to respond quickly to each separate disturbance with a separate program. The conservatives tend to entail each program with so many conditions that it begins to look like a probationary program for a recently released criminal. Neither response is apt to diminish the recipient group's sense of relative deprivation or of alienation in American society. Because of this widespread sense of relative deprivation or alienation, Americans seldom trust their government to legislate with skill and fairness and to manage its bureaucracies without respect to race, creed, or religion. Thus the two obstacles to a unified welfare system feed into and perpetuate one another.

By comparison to the experience of a few well developed welfare states, the record of the United States is nothing to brag about. Considering the obstacles, however, the nation's reformers have achieved much, and there is little reason for them to decrease their efforts.

3 The American Way of Welfare I: Fusion of Economic and Patriotic Doctrines

Before the beginning of the twentieth century, most industrialized nations had initiated extensive social welfare programs at a time when the United States had barely begun social welfare legislation on a state level. Whereas Germany had established comprehensive social insurance programs in the 1880s under Bismarck, it was not until the 1930s that the United States did so. The few preexisting state programs to aid the blind, mothers, and older persons were of limited coverage.

In terms of formal program experience in five areas of social security categorized by HEW as old age and invalidity, sickness and maternity, unemployment, work injury, and family allowances, the United States in the mid-1960s ranked twenty-first out of twenty-two rich industrialized nations (outranking only Israel).[1] In the proportion of its gross national product channeled toward social security, it was also twenty-first (outranking only Japan). By the beginning of the 1970s the United States had raised its social security standing a little, ranking seventeenth out of twenty-one nations (surpassing Japan, Australia, New Zealand, and Switzerland) (Wilensky 1976, p. 11). These and other measures (Heilbroner 1970) reveal the extent to which the United States lags behind other industrialized nations in terms of formal welfare policies, welfare expenditures, and indexes of general well-being (f. ex. infant mortality rates).

Most western nations have been more willing than the United States to deal with poverty as a matter of social responsibility and to follow policies which involve the total population as beneficiaries. These countries have generally relied on a strong sense of nationalism and national welfare, subsequently combined with modern economic theory, in recognizing the inevitability of economic fluctuations in industrialized nations, and have placed the responsibility for dealing with these economic conditions fully on the central government (see Heclo 1974, pp. 285–88). The

United States has only recently recognized that unemployment and poverty are recurring conditions which must be dealt with as structural rather than as individual phenomena. To explain this lag, we focus on the development of *federal* welfare legislation in the United States, for only a central government can effectively make economic policy (see Appendix for a chronology of welfare-related events).

The character of social welfare in the United States has been conditioned, as we saw in chapter 1, by the laissez-faire economy. The year 1776 saw the publication of Adam Smith's *The Wealth of Nations* as well as the Declaration of Independence. The intellectual movement started by Adam Smith played an important role in the conceptualization of the American nation. As Lowi (1969, p. 5) puts it, "If the principles of nineteenth century economics had not existed, the Americans would most certainly have invented them." This identification of the nation and its particular economy is evidenced by the vocabulary that laissez-faire economics shares with the wording of the Declaration of Independence and Constitution itself. Individual property rights were guaranteed by the Fourth and Fifth Amendments (1791), and individuals were granted broad protection against governmental interference.

Within a relatively short time after the American Revolution, the combination of laissez-faire and the American Constitution with its guarantees and principles of government came to spell "the American way." A number of American social characteristics deriving from this combination have retarded the development of social welfare in the country. Perhaps most important in this respect is the establishment of free public education, which on an ideological level was essential for the successful operation of the laissez-faire system. However, the absence of major collectivist movements and the cultural fragmentation of the United States prevented major challenges to that system. The constitutionally mandated political fragmentation of the country strengthened the connection between the laissez-faire ideology and the national identity.

Nevertheless, the concentration of economic power that has occurred especially since the late nineteenth century has increasingly challenged the laissez-faire system as an adequate description of the American economy. The highly complex and economic structure characteristic of a mature industrial society, as well as wars and other national disasters, have pointed to failures of the system in providing for those in need.

It is our argument, therefore, that the changes which have occurred in federal welfare legislation have taken place in a field of opposing forces, including, on the one hand, a defense of the laissez-faire system in the name of patriotism and, on the other hand, a series of social and economic crises which have compelled government intervention. As a result, the expansion of social welfare in the United States has followed a distinctive pattern: welfare programs have been slow to develop except during wars or depressions; coverage has always been incomplete; welfare programs have often been disguised as insurance or work incentive programs; much of the legislation has been temporary; and federal welfare legislation has been accompanied by an emotion-laden controversy over patriotism as well as over the particular crises of the period. This gradual, ad hoc growth of social welfare and other governmental functions has resulted in a vast accumulation of departures from the laissez-faire model to the point that, by the late 1960s, a crisis in the national identity itself was partially responsible for the first major proposal of universal welfare aid put forth by a president of the United States (Nixon's Family Assistance Plan).

HISTORICAL TRENDS IN THE DEVELOPMENT OF SOCIAL WELFARE IN THE UNITED STATES[2]

Before the Civil War

Until the Civil War the laissez-faire ideology fairly accurately described the economic conditions of the United States and provided reasonably adequate models for the behavior of its citizens. The United States was essentially a rural society with a preponderance of small, independent farmers and entrepreneurs. Industry as such was of small importance and the existence of the frontier made it possible to export those poor who did gather in the larger cities. This, on the whole, warranted the absence of state or federal legislation for welfare purposes in place of local almshouses and indentureship or "putting-out" systems, and the short-term private charitable efforts undertaken at the time (Axinn and Levin 1975, chaps. 2 and 3; Coll 1969). It was under these circumstances that the distinction between the "deserving" and the "undeserving" poor became especially important. Underlying this distinction was the notion that poverty was a just payment for one's failure in life, barring physical disability or accidents.

The "deserving" poor constituted those who were unable to work or care for themselves because of age, illness, infirmity, or widowhood, while the "undeserving" poor consisted of those able to work, yet unemployed. Ideally, the undeserving poor should not receive aid and should be forced to work or punished if they did not, since it was assumed that everyone who really wanted to could find work or go West. Over time, the undeserving poor has also come to include those who have disqualified themselves by immorality aside from violation of the work ethic—namely, unwed mothers, alcoholics, drug addicts, etc. (For documentation of these observations, see Bremner 1956, chaps. 1 and 2; Axinn and Levin 1975, chaps. 2 and 3; Trattner 1974.)

Before the Civil War, problems of poverty remained largely a local and private charge, as is evident from the general absence of state and federal legislation. There were clear symptoms of public concern, however, mainly in the Eastern seaboard cities where both private and public charities had been founded, and where some social surveys were undertaken.[3] In New York City, as in most of the Eastern cities, the consequences of poverty, rather than poverty as such, were the main issue of social concern. The depressions of 1819 and 1837, when, for example, more than one-third of the workers in New York City were unemployed, did not prompt outspoken criticism of the economy. This general lack of interest can probably be attributed to three widespread beliefs: first, that industrialization would abolish all kinds of human want; second, that unemployment was due to the inefficiency and indolence of the unemployed; third, that poverty was at worst temporary. Indeed, poverty was still publicly acclaimed as a positive value by inspiring the rich to charity and the poor to gratitude, ambition, and patience. Without poverty men would not work and able men could not assert their innate abilities. The latter notion, that any able man could rise to the top, became an integral part of the ideological orientation of laissez-faire economy and, as well, of the "American dream."

The heavy influx of German and especially Irish immigrants in the 1840s and 1850s and the consequent problems of unemployment and overpopulation in the coastal cities resulted in gross poverty which was difficult to explain within the laissez-faire state (Pickett 1969, chap. 1; Bremner 1956, chap. 1). The tendency was to categorize these immigrants as the "dangerous classes," and the children of the poor were often identified as a serious threat.[4] This is best exemplified by Stephen Allen's statement that the "rising generation of the poor" constituted a menace to the republic (Pickett 1969, p. 15).

This interpretation represented an important and enduring outlook often adopted by the older Anglo-Saxon, Protestant elites and later by other groups as they rose to respectability. Up to the 1920s, such beliefs gave rise to the temperance movement and other coercive attempts to reform the ethnic poor (Gusfield 1963). The same beliefs aroused serious misgivings about the entrance of the Irish and the Southern Europeans into political life. Assumptions about the unreliability of immigrant groups spurred great efforts at political reform and some state regulation of consumer behavior.

The preservation of the laissez-faire vocabulary of motives seems to have produced circumstances in which the poorest and most disadvantaged citizens became supporters rather than critics of a weak government. Naturally the older Anglo-Saxon elites were apprehensive of the new immigrant groups' entrance into what had become a relatively strong government. But under the governing belief that all men follow narrowly defined or individual interests, the new ethnic groups seem to have been equally reluctant to assign great power to a government which might fall into the hands of the "wrong people." Thus, both the new and the old immigrants often conspired to keep a limited government limited. The irregular and illegitimate pattern of "patronage politics," in turn, became a major way in which government itself aided the poor (Hofstadter 1955; Dahl 1961, book 1).

Aside from the distribution of patronage, limited outdoor relief and the maintenance of almshouses and hospitals, all of which were local undertakings, the first efforts at publicly financed state aid were developed shortly before the Civil War. This development was restricted almost exclusively to those who were believed unable to compete in the struggle for survival: the aged, the sick, the infirm, and the orphaned.[5] Similarly, the problem of the insane was taken up by a number of states before the Civil War. The immediate response to proposals for having the federal government participate in similar programs was expressed by

President Pierce, who, in 1854, declared that the federal government cannot become "the great almoner of public charity throughout the United States" (Bremner 1960, p. 70). However, this did not mean that there was any greater enthusiasm for the involvement of state governments in social welfare. Ideally, there was no need for state public assistance, since private and local charity would take adequate care of the needy. As early as 1781, Thomas Jefferson had written, "[This estimate of the public expenses of Virginia is exclusive] of the maintenance of the poor, which being merely a matter of charity cannot be deemed expended in the administration of government" (Jefferson 1964, p. 164).

The Civil War

The Civil War was a very important turning point. For the first time federal government agencies became involved in meeting the physical and spiritual needs of people in need—specifically soldiers, sailors, and former slaves. Through the Bureau of Refugees, Freedmen, and Abandoned Lands, established in January of 1865 (extended in 1866 and 1868) under the War Department and over two presidential vetoes, the federal government spent fifteen million dollars between 1865 and 1869 in relieving physical suffering, overseeing the beginnings of free labor, buying and selling land, establishing schools, paying bounties, and administering justice in the South. Even more important, the bureau set a precedent for future crisis situations, particularly the depression of the 1930s.[6] The intervening depressions of the latter part of the nineteenth century, however, were dealt with primarily on the local and state level.

The Bureau of Refugees, Freedmen, and Abandoned Lands was created to serve what was seen as the temporary predicament of former slaves and a devastated land. Though an extensive program in the South, it did not spread to other parts of the country and continued to attract strong opposition. The bureau ceased to exist in 1869, well before the freedmen had achieved economic security. It was among the first of a series of federal programs and controls which were retrenched or eliminated as the South regained local control. It was also the first major federal program to relieve inequality and poverty but, like others which would succeed it, was legislated with termination dates. Once dissolved, the program left no residual organization, its leaders returned to their previous anonymity, and it was largely forgotten except in the writings of W. E. B. DuBois (1965) and a few others. There were, however, a number of private organizations which supplemented the work of local, state, and federal agencies in relieving distress during and after the Civil War (Bremner 1956, chap. 3).

At about the same time, some states began to appoint permanent boards to inspect, report on, and suggest improvements in public charities, such as reformatories, asylums, and almshouses which previously had been entirely under local control (Brackett 1903, pp. 18–53; Bremner 1956, pp. 48–50). This expansion of government responsibilities was associated with an enormous growth of industry and population. The government assumed the role of arbitrator and standard maker—a departure from the view that competition alone was sufficient to ensure minimum standards of health care, housing, etc. The establishment of inspection boards may be regarded as the first in a number of *indirect* efforts to intervene in the competitive economic process, and it remains a favored method in adjusting the economy to compensate for imperfections in the laissez-faire model. Such indirect methods of regulation offered an alternative to direct governmental aid to individuals.

The growth of federally supported welfare in the 1860s was short-lived. It accommodated to the laissez-faire ideology by repairing some of the worst consequences of slavery, while defining them as an exception. The congruence between the nation and its particular claims for a special economic organization remained secure. Indeed, the latter part of this period saw the beginning of a further consolidation of the American identity with capitalism. As the West opened and as wartime prosperity continued, city boosters were joined by industrial magnates in defining the American way as that of the laissez-faire state (see also Glaab and Brown 1967; Wade 1958).

A Period of Social Concern, 1870–1915

The period 1870–1915 brought forth both a multitude of welfare problems and a number of solutions which fit more or less satisfactorily into the conception of a limited state. The country experienced some of its most severe depressions. The increase in slums, crime, and urban misery was difficult to dismiss for even the most enthusiastic proponents of the American way. Yet the period also saw the growth of reform, the private welfare movement and public education. Strains on national pride were high, and for the first time collectivist and populist movements attempted to revise both the national identity and its attendant economy (Bremner 1956; Wiebe 1967; Hofstadter 1955).

A number of private charities, especially in the cities along the Eastern seaboard, had by the 1870s become well-known and sizable organizations: the Association for Improving the Condition of the Poor, founded in 1843; the Children's Aid Society, in 1853; and the Young Men's Christian Association, in 1851 (Bremner 1956; Zald and Denton 1963). All of these organizations attempted to induce some form of moral change in the poor, but some went further, aiming to improve general conditions of housing, health, and child welfare. They formed the general approach which was to be adopted or advocated with some important modifications by the Settlement House and the Progressive movements.

These efforts may be seen as an expression of middle-class concern over social dislocation in the industrial cities, located mostly in the North, after the Civil War (Wiebe 1967). Slum dwellers were often recent immigrants, and the early welfare agencies approached their difficulties as an educational problem. Their poverty and distressing living conditions were thought correctable by moral instruction, public education, and "Americanization" classes. Because it was believed that opportunity existed for the willing and able, it was logical to try to alleviate poverty through improving the individual. This was indeed the direction taken by most private welfare agencies and became a major emphasis of the Settlement House movement.

The recurring economic depressions in 1854–55, 1857–58, 1873–77, 1893–97, 1907–8, and 1914–15, unparalleled in the previous history of the country, gave rise to a new era of social concern and in turn to the Charity Organization movement, "Scientific Charity," the Settlement movement, the Populist movement, and the Progressive movement.

During the earlier depressions aid was granted on an ad hoc basis as emergency relief, provided mostly in almshouses and by private agencies. From the 1870s until World War I, the increasing need for coordination was met in part by the Charity Organization movement, originating in England and appearing in the United States in Buffalo, New York, in 1877. "Scientific

Charity" involved systematic implementation of investigations, coordination, and personal service. A sharp differentiation was made between the paid professional administrative agent of a private welfare organization and the "friendly visitor," who by her "treatment" and her relations with the poor was to inspire the desired moral changes (Trattner 1974; Axinn and Levin 1975).

With the onset of the depression of 1893–97, the increasing professionalization of social workers, eager to establish a separate position for themselves, produced new emphasis on "differential casework."[7] Social workers argued that they, and not volunteers, possessed the required skills to deal with all problems of poverty. They emphasized the importance of a wholesome physical and social environment, defining this as the proper area of concern for the social worker. Their success at this time was generally limited to the establishment of an occupational role for themselves in hospitals, schools, and psychiatric work. Much of their effort was directed toward the protection of a precarious professional image, which led them to oppose both amateurs and standard governmental stipends without "treatment."

During this period, welfare workers took the view that public aid was inefficient and would produce economic dependency on the part of the recipients—"pauperizing the poor." Their supporting arguments and evidence in some cases led to city charters (New York 1897, Baltimore 1898) that outlawed outdoor relief, i.e., relief given to individuals in their homes and not in poorhouses and the like. Public aid was also attacked because of increasing expenditures which seemed to have no corresponding increase in effect; and both the social workers and defenders of the laissez-faire ideology came to agree that most any form of public aid was detrimental.

While social workers became defenders of the doctrine of individualism and individual treatment, the Populists were criticizing the doctrine. In part, the Populist movement was a reaction to dramatic changes in the American economy. Small private entrepreneurs were being overshadowed both economically and politically by the large industrial corporations, and free competition was in some instances being replaced by oligopoly. The number of people who were not self-employed increased enormously. The Populists drew their support from farmers, small businessmen, and a large class of people who felt that they were being excluded from an important role in the economy and that the laissez-faire system itself was eroding. Support for the Populists grew during the depression of 1893–97. The Populists, however, were not so much aggressive anti-capitalists as eager restorationists. They offered a criticism of the system in operation rather than of the ideology itself. Essentially they sought a return to the small-scale economy of pre–Civil War enterprises. Their accomplishment, then, was not to provide an alternative to the laissez-faire ideology but the exposure of how little the American economy conformed to this ideology. The Populists also revealed the degree to which Americans were willing and able to accept simplistic solutions to the evils of the current system, such as a substitution of a silver standard for a gold standard.

The "exposure" of economic disparities became a prevalent orientation reflected in the "Ash Can" school of art which became prominent around 1900 (Bremner 1956, chap. 7). Also journalistic reports (e.g., Jacob Riis), articles, and books reflected this expansion of interest in the poor. Riis's *How the Other Half Lives* (1890) and William T. Stead's *If Christ Came to Chicago* (1964), published in the beginning of the 1890s, presented vivid descriptions of actual situations of poverty in New York and Chicago. This new interest in factual information was also reflected in several social surveys undertaken around this time, for example, the New York Tenement House Investigation (1900), John A. Ryan's estimate of poverty (1905), and the Pittsburgh Social Survey (1907–8). A number of reports were published in the *American Journal of Sociology* (founded in 1895) which documented actual conditions of poverty.[8] Slowly a more complete understanding of the situation was obtained, one which led to questioning and some changes of attitude toward poverty.

Of greater importance, however, in this new era was the Settlement movement, which started in London in 1884 and spread to the United States around 1890, primarily to New York, Chicago, Baltimore, Boston, and Philadelphia. The settlement workers were instrumental in raising some of the main issues which came under attack from 1890 to 1915, namely, slum conditions, child labor, and women's hours and wages. In the process they helped shift emphasis from idleness, improvidence, and intemperance to unemployment, high living costs, and low wages. This new view of poverty, defined in terms of insufficiency and insecurity, was felt to be more "scientific" than the older view. It should be noted, however, that neither the settlement workers nor, later, the Progressives advocated any radical changes, and that both movements stressed working within the system in order to gain as much as possible without challenging the "American creed."[9]

The influence of the settlement house workers was concentrated on shaping public opinion and the further development of national standards. They helped women organize into labor unions, gathered important statistics, made speeches, wrote articles, lobbied for legislation, and organized committees on various subject matters. Legislation concerning women's hours was challenged in 1908 in the United States Supreme Court (Muller vs. Oregon) on the basis that it violated the freedom of women. Brandeis wrote a famous brief for the hearing about "the world's experience regarding women's hours of labor" and the statute was declared constitutional. Yet, a minimum wage law was declared unconstitutional in 1917, and legislation regulating children's wages and hours was declared unconstitutional in 1918.

The settlement workers were first involved in political battles on the municipal level, fighting the ward boss or promoting municipal reform (1895–1909). They failed to be effective in both areas, and consequently turned their attention to state and national policies, at which time they became involved with the Progressive party. Theodore Roosevelt adopted almost unchanged a platform developed by leading settlement workers for his presidential campaign of 1912. The cure for poverty suggested by these Progressive reformers was the correction of unjust and degrading conditions of work and living. Nearly all reforms proposed during this period involved some limitations on private property rights and the extension of public authority into areas previously regarded as the exclusive preserve of individual initiative. Yet no broad demand was made for changes in the economic structure, nor was public aid defended as a right. The government's role was restricted to setting standards and providing short-term and limited state aid, while long-term individual needs were the responsibility of private welfare. Industry remained its own authority in other matters, and the basic beliefs in a laissez-faire model were unchanged. The high point of the reform movement was reached in 1915 with the legislation of mother's pension, aid to the blind, and workmen's compensation, the first social insurance program in the United States.

By comparison with earlier times, much was accomplished between 1870 and World War I. Federal government responsibility for welfare standards and working conditions were strengthened toward the end of the period, following severe criticism of governmental corruption at the turn of the century. It was also clear that the number of poor was beyond the capacity of private agencies during economic crises and that local governments would have to provide some aid to the unemployed in addition to their traditional responsibility for those unable to work. Further aid was provided the "deserving" poor, and aid in the home (outdoor relief) became the predominant form despite public controversy.

The United States still lagged far behind the northern European industrial nations, where all or most of the reforms passed in the United States in the period 1900–1915 had been adopted in the previous century. Moreover, the aid provided by the states and private organizations was short-term and pitifully small. Most importantly, the level of governmental standards and regulations was to prove completely inadequate in allaying the effects of cyclic fluctuations of the American economy. But in 1915 these shortcomings were not apparent, and the First World War produced a period of prosperity that seemed to warrant the high hopes of social workers and businessmen that prosperity was here to stay. For the next fourteen years, until 1929, very few Americans found it necessary to raise the soul-searching questions that had been asked between 1870 and 1915.

World War I

While the First World War brought prosperity, it also brought a degree of government regulation unparalleled in previous periods. Much of what the Progressives had earlier advocated in vain became law out of necessity. This was especially true of the regulation of labor, of working conditions for women and children, and of female suffrage. The legislation passed in this period aroused neither violent protests nor presented any recognized challenge to the laissez-faire ideology. Most of the legislation was seen as a response to the duress of war and much of it was abandoned in the 1920s. Such programs as employment services, established because of the labor shortage during the war, were left without funds in the twenties.

In the First World War, as in the Civil War, some important precedents were set. The Civil War anticipated state and especially federal involvement in social welfare, while World War I saw the beginning of labor regulation, employment services, and other regulatory practices that restrained private enterprise. Private enterprise, however, was favored in several ways by the war. On the one hand, wartime prosperity was attributed to the operation of a free market, while on the other hand the extensive governmental control and investments were dismissed as wartime emergencies.

The First World War gave Americans some experience in organizing mass programs. It also introduced a permanent federal income tax, which had been tried only for a short time during the Civil War. This was later to place the government in the position of being able to support universal welfare programs. However, the net effect of this added financial burden seems to have been to exacerbate the "antiforeign" sentiments implicit in the arguments developed earlier to explain away the poverty of European immigrants. The belief that drink and improvidence were at the root of most unemployment and distress received formal endorsement in the Eighteenth Amendment of 1917, and a foreign war did little to discourage the sentiments behind the Prohibition movement (Gusfield 1963).

The Interlude of the 1920s

The 1920s began with a mild business slump and an agricultural depression following the war, but nothing so severe that available aid and charity could not handle it. Prosperity returned, and the decline of interest in poverty which had been noticeable before the war became more evident in the 1920s. One important reason for this decline was the view that nothing more need be done. Foreign immigration had slowed to a trickle due to the restrictive immigration laws of 1921 and 1924, and the broad expansion of public education was thought sufficient to Americanize the foreign and equalize opportunity for the disadvantaged. The stage seemed to be set for a quiet period of prosperity and unity. Instead, the United States experienced an increasing ethnic and racial fragmentation which made it difficult to obtain broad support for any new social programs.

At the same time many of the forces which had pushed for reform before the war lost their strength. Having lost its raison d'être and most of its older leaders, the Settlement movement declined, accompanied by the collapse of the Progressive movement. Southern Negroes started migrating to northern cities in the 1920s, replacing many foreign-born immigrants in the worst residential districts.

The professionalization of social workers had continued, so that by the 1920s a professional subculture was emerging. A large number of professional organizations were established in the 1920s, which helped to channel interest away from external causes of poverty to the defensible skills of casework (Lubove 1965). A professional self-image could more easily be created in the area of casework deriving from established psychiatry than in the area of amateur social reform. Social workers, then, became technicians rather than social agents. In the process, the volunteer had been almost totally excluded from any important place in social work.

Even more important for the decline in interest in social problems was the high degree of cultural fragmentation which was evident in the 1920s. A number of groups in that decade developed an elaborate and defensive system of unquestioned beliefs, designed to combat the insecurity of a modern, pluralist world while also hanging on to a narrowing set of patriotic images. The 1920s were characterized by deep and divisive conflicts between intellectuals and businessmen; violent antiradicalism, often directed at recent immigrants (the Palmer raids in 1919; see Murray 1955; and the Sacco-Vanzetti case in 1920–27); a Protestant counterreformation directed against "modernists" (e.g., the Scopes trial in 1925); and a cult of Anglo-Saxon supremacy as evident in the spread of the Ku Klux Klan movement (founded in 1915 but not gaining momentum until after the war) and in the new immigration restrictions of 1921 and 1924.

The result was greatly intensified group consciousness. Intellectuals often felt alienated from the American society and in many instances became expatriates. Immigrants such as the Italians, some of whom started a movement in support of Mussolini, often dissolved former identifications with the United States and started nativistic movements; the Jews supported the establishment of an independent Palestine; the Irish started a movement for a Free Ireland; and the Negroes in large numbers followed Marcus Garvey and his Universal Negro Improvement Association.

The fear and distrust of other groups was evident at many

levels, and the result was an unwillingness to support legislation that might benefit one or several groups in particular. No major group, however, challenged the laissez-faire economy as a proper and integral element of national identity. Instead, the field of what was considered "American" narrowed, and groups spread out across a spectrum ranging from those who endorsed a rigid version of the American creed to those who simply detached themselves from the country either symbolically or as actual expatriates. The Ku Klux Klan, the prohibitionists, city boosters, and Attorney General Palmer so narrowly interpreted the concept of patriotism that any criticism of free enterprise was considered subversive.

The Great War had also produced much disillusionment, especially among the intellectuals (see Dos Passos 1921). The alienation from American society, moreover, was greatest in those groups that would have been most likely to provide leadership in social reform movements. Many intellectuals with a strong genealogical claim to national membership (Hemingway, Fitzgerald, Dos Passos) reacted to the Anglophobia by becoming expatriates. Throughout this period, then, there was no significant national legislation in the area of public welfare. The settlement houses mainly marked time. No new charitable organizations were established on a national scale, and few individuals or great figures made themselves known for their efforts to meet social needs.[10]

Although prosperous, the twenties brought to the United States a crisis of identity and a severe test of its attachment to the free enterprise system. Much of the activity of the decade can be seen as an attempt to come to grips with a twentieth-century America in which the departures from the original laissez-faire model were so glaring that they provoked an extremely defensive posture among advocates and alienation among those whose loyalties were at all suspect. Certainly, the owners and managers of business continued to operate with a relatively free hand, and President Coolidge prided himself upon the reduction of government expenditures. However, even though the government did not then intervene into the public operation of business, it made a strong attempt to regulate private morality (e.g., prohibition) and played a role of partisan on behalf of private businesses in other ways (e.g., use of the army to quell labor strikes). Big business came fully to overshadow the small farmers and businessmen. The formation of trusts, the growth of government contracts, and frequent scandals involving collusion between government and business (e.g., the Teapot Dome) all made the laissez-faire model a questionable description of American society. The "old" ethnic groups, the conservatives, and the wealthy rose to the occasion with a righteous and defensive claim for the reality of the free enterprise system and distrust of those suspected of any disloyalty. In the meantime, large pockets of poverty remained, frequently invisible because those who might have pointed them out had become "detached" from the society as expatriates, bohemians (Ware 1965), or members of a growing "international set."

Up to the Great Depression, then, the laissez-faire ideology had remained largely intact and continued as a prescription, if not a description, of economic behavior. Even into the Great Depression, public leaders such as President Hoover clung tenaciously to the notion that the free enterprise system was the only acceptable economic system for the United States and, indeed, that it was still the distinctive ingredient of the American way.

4 The American Way of Welfare II: The Reluctant Compromise

The period between 1932, when the Great Depression reached its low point, and the start of World War II, when many of the effects of the Depression had been ameliorated and the unemployed energies were beginning to be absorbed by the war effort, was a turning point in the history of social welfare in the United States: responsibility for leadership and relief was placed unequivocally on the federal government.

As a result of the Depression, many people came to realize that the fortunes of individual Americans were interdependent, and many adopted the belief that it was the duty of the federal government to prevent new depressions, a duty which entailed a mandate to engage in fiscal and monetary policies. A thorough revision of public welfare was recognized as both possible and necessary (for documentation see Heilbroner 1968; Elder Jr. 1974; Piven and Cloward 1971). The 1930s saw the greatest volume of direct and indirect welfare legislation in the history of the United States, of which the most permanent pieces were the Wagner-Peyser Act (establishing a United States Employment Service, similar to what had existed during World War I), 1933; the Tennessee Valley Authority, 1933; the Fair Labor Relations Act (The Wagner Act, acknowledging the rights of workers to bargain collectively with employers thus legitimizing labor unions), 1935; and the Social Security Act, August 1935. All were adopted without termination dates.

The Social Security Act, the most important of these, established or reaffirmed a number of precedents. For the first time since the Bureau of Refuges, Freedmen, and Abandoned Lands right after the Civil War, federal responsibility was assumed on the grounds that national crises could occur irrespective of individual enterprise; welfare became a matter of right for certain groups of the population who were unemployed for reasons acknowledged to be other than personal. The Social

Security Act embodied the realization that at least some of the causes of poverty were old age, unemployment, injury, and disability. In emphasizing social rather than personal conditions, the act made its greatest departure from the past. It distinguished two primary kinds of support: social insurance, where the individual receiving support had contributed directly to this support; and public assistance, under which the individual had made no direct contribution because he was considered physically incapable of doing so or because of circumstances beyond his control. Although the act was constructed to aid the victims of an industrial society's systemic poverty, the schedule of payments was painfully low. This was due largely to the widespread fear that aid would compete with available wages.

Among other accommodations to the laissez-faire system in the Social Security Act, the most apparent was the social insurance part of the program. Having contributed to his own support, the individual was later to receive support in proportion to his contributions. This is essentially an elaboration of the old self-help theme, the major difference being that the individual was guaranteed a minimum amount of support, his contributions were deducted from his pay, his employer was also required to contribute, and the program was under government administration.[1] The noncontributory parts of the act can be seen essentially as aids to the deserving poor and, it was argued, would eventually "wither away" as the social insurance program covered more and more persons. Thus, the part of the program most in conflict with the laissez-faire model was adopted with the expectation that it would become obsolete in the future and thus would be eliminated. Afterward, President Roosevelt could vow that "the Federal Government must and shall quit this business of relief" in support of the Social Security Act (Steiner 1966). The "withering away" of the public assistance part of the act was therefore of crucial importance in making it acceptable to a large proportion of the politicians and the general population.

The massive public assistance which was initiated during the Depression shifted the center of private welfare from the economic to the emotional side of dependency. Voluntary private agencies seemed to take exclusive responsibility for problems of family structure and personal emotional balance when financial need was not involved. In the process, these agencies built up a new clientele consisting mostly of a lower-middle-class population, able to pay at least in part for received services (Cloward 1964; Cloward and Epstein 1965). The great increase in public welfare further alienated many professional social workers from public relief, which was still denounced by some as producing economic dependency without providing necessary treatment. Not only did professional social workers view public welfare as aggravating the situation of recipients, since these received no treatment which could "improve" them, but the great influx of untrained and inexperienced workers who were employed in the public agencies endangered the professional self-image of social workers. This factor was probably also important in extending private welfare further in a direction where "treatment" was possible and away from direct concern with social and economic causes of poverty.

Perhaps even more significant than federal relief and social insurance was the adoption of fiscal and monetary policies through, for example, the deliberate use of the federal budget to stimulate the economy and attempts by the Securities and Exchange Commission to regulate the supply of money, thus continuing the tradition of indirect regulation started after the Civil War. Following the faltering attempts of the Roosevelt administration (Schumpeter 1942, p. 64), these monetary and fiscal policies were to remain the most extensive means of economic stabilization over the next forty years. The Social Security Act, the next most durable legislation of the 1930s, was to remain basically the same until the 1950s, when it was expanded. Finally, the Depression saw the first legislative attempts to establish and enforce minimum wage and hours standards. Thus, the Federal Contracts Act of 1936 (the Welsh-Healy Act) required that companies with government contracts exceeding $10,000 conform to such standards; and the Federal Wage and Labor Hour Law (the Fair Labor Standards Act), October 1938, established standards for minimum wages, overtime pay, and child labor for some portion of the work force involved in interstate commerce.

It is difficult to assess the success of these welfare measures in ameliorating the economic impact of the depression, since World War II intervened to restore prosperity.[2] It is somewhat clearer, however, that the challenge to the nation's identity was incompletely met. The nation seemed unable to bring itself to accept the point of view that the economic system alone could be considered responsible for unemployment. In other nations less closely identified with a particular economic system (Germany, Great Britain, the Scandinavian countries, etc.), the recognition that industrialism produces unemployment and dependency, irrespective of the system of ownership, did not strike at the roots of national identity. Attempts at extensive income redistribution could be undertaken without shame or self-criticism.[3] In the United States, however, it seemed difficult for people to distinguish between the inevitability of unemployment and dependency produced by any industrial economy and criticism of the American way.[4]

Nevertheless, the new monetary and fiscal policies openly admitted the necessity for "tinkering" with the "free" market. In addition, the 1930s was the period during which American labor unions finally became an effective political power and achieved recognition in federal legislation (the Fair Labor Relations Act of 1935). For the first time a mass organization directly representing some of those most likely to become dependent was given rights to bargain collectively for the welfare of its members (Greenstone 1969, chap. 2). The legitimation of the industrial labor unions (CIO)[5] not only created a potential partisan for further welfare benefits but also introduced a new principle of collectivism into American life.

World War II

As with World War I, a number of social and legislative changes took place in World War II, such as the regulation of labor, and increasing employment of Negroes and women. The war also facilitated the continued development of standards, especially with regard to hours of work and wages, thus setting important precedents.

The need for effective use of manpower and raw materials justified extensive government involvement in both the economy itself and the labor market. The war effort also required that standards for performance and the distribution of resources be established by the central government through some method other than the free market. The Office of Price Administration and the War Food Administration established in 1943, were both concerned with establishing minimum family budgets which could be used in the actual distribution of food and the development of rationing programs.

Once established, however, the concept of a national standard was an important step in the field of social welfare. Discrepancies between such standards and reality document the failure of the economy to provide adequately for the country's citizens. Thus, by 1953, under the Social Security program, every state had calculated minimum budgets for ADC families living in the state; however, no state provided a needy family with aid that amounted to more than a fraction of such budgets. The incongruities of the system became progressively difficult to overlook. Likewise, when an individual was being paid less than what had publicly been established as fair or ideal, the result must ultimately be either a rejection of that particular standard or a realization that at least some change in the economy is necessary.

While the implications of such standards may be slow in coming to the attention of the general public, there is reason to believe that they do have a long-term effect. The early 1960s saw a major resurgence of interest in national standards and the many "invisible poor" were discovered by the use of such standards, especially the "low-income" or "poverty" budget (developed in 1963). Some of the more immediate consequences of the development of these national standards were observable during World War II and the period immediately following it. Rent controls were implemented during the war and lingered on in some cities, notably New York. Standards for the equal treatment of blacks and whites were enforced through the Fair Employment Practice Commission (1943) but were most fully developed in the United States armed services, which have continued to set the pace of racial integration. The passage of an Open Housing Act in Massachusetts (1945) followed similar standards and, although incompletely enforced, set the stage for open housing acts in the 1960s. Federal standards for minimum wage rates and the rates for overtime work were not only expanded during the Second World War but were more thoroughly enforced.

Without minimizing the impact of these national standards, we must acknowledge that the demands of the war itself had much to do with them. Because of the demand for manpower, America was forced to make some concessions to blacks, the largest underprivileged group in the nation.[6] In the process of forcing an expansion of the labor market to include more blacks, World War II encouraged the continued migration of rural blacks to southern cities and of southern blacks to the big industrial cities in the North. In time (the 1950s and 1960s) this increased concentration of blacks in the slum and ghetto areas of central cities outside the South was an important reason for the tremendous increase in the number of ADC recipients during the late 1950s and the 1960s.

The Second World War also brought to the United States extensive controls on interest rates, prices, wages, and the use of taxation as an anti-inflationary policy. While price and wage controls were quickly abandoned after the war, policies which were attempted during the period have found an unquestioned place in the practice of both conservative and liberal administrations since the war and were formally implemented in the Employment Act of 1946. Terms such as "wage policy," "presidential price guidelines," and "federal subsidies" were introduced into political platforms and public life.

Within the living memory of most Americans, World War II was also their longest period of full employment. The prolonged return of "good times" not only demonstrated the possibility of full employment but also showed that most people were willing to work. This put into question the argument that unemployment was the result of individual laziness and that the existence of unemployment was a necessary incentive for the industrious. In addition, World War II again demonstrated the link between heavy armament production in the United States and prosperity. For at least some people this raised the question of whether or not the laissez-faire economy in the United States could experience prolonged peacetime prosperity. In some circles there was the growing suspicion that the cost of prosperity in the laissez-faire economy was a tremendous armament production and that the system had survived repeated crises only because of war-time production and governmental controls. These questions, first arising in the postwar period, were to be more explicitly formulated in the 1950s and 1960s as the Korean War and the Vietnam War both rescued the country from economic recession and threatened its domestic programs and expenditures.

Above all, the Second World War brought a change in scale to both private and public organizations in the United States as well as to the rest of the world. Some business enterprises (e.g., General Motors, General Electric) became enormous organizations having vast international holdings and considerable political influence. Armies, research institutes, labor unions, and government bureaucracies all underwent a transformation in size that further removed them from intimate contact with ordinary citizens and brought them together into a complex of loose cooperation that belied the classical model which sharply separated private and public sectors. The immediate reconciliation between such large-scale public and private undertakings and the laissez-faire model was Schumpeter's concept of interindustrial competition for technological advances (Schumpeter 1942, chaps. 6 and 7). While Schumpeter's arguments were satisfactory to many scholars in the early 1950s, individuals as different as C. Wright Mills (1956) on the one hand and Dwight D. Eisenhower ("the military-industrial complex") on the other were to raise serious doubts. Their observations anticipated what was to become a massive reaction against "the Establishment" during the late 1960s. The situation was complicated by the fact that the well-to-do have benefited from government expenditures as much or more than the poor and that arguments for the reduction of one type of expenditure could easily imply reduction of the other.

The Interlude of the Late 1940s and the 1950s

The United States entered the Second World War with a federal budget of $8.995 billion in 1940 and emerged with one of $63.714 billion in 1946. Such a massive change in the extent of governmental operations could not help but bring a reaction from those who believed in a severely limited role for the government. This reaction was not long in coming, and a good deal of its force was spent on the growing budget of welfare expenditures. At the same time a wide range of public and private organizations—research institutions, oil producers, defense industries, colleges, and universities—sought and obtained extensive federal economic support.

The mid and late 1940s brought considerable legislation which touched on social welfare though not directly related to it. Among these were the G.I. bill (1944); the Servicemen's Readjustment Allowances Program (1944); the Employment Act of 1946, establishing a national goal of full employment and the President's Council of Economic Advisors; the George Barden Act of 1944, which dealt with the problem of facilitating vocational training; and the Labor Management Relation Act, which restricted the discretion of unions to strike. There were also a number of amendments to the Social Security Act. The amendments of 1950 included for the first time adult benefits in the ADC category; previous benefits had only covered children and not heads of the families. The same year, Aid to the Permanently and Totally Disabled (APTD) was added to the Social Security Act (Title XIV).

The 1951 Jenner Amendment to the Social Security Act, requiring that welfare data should be available to the public but could not be used for political or commercial purposes, represented a general shift of focus from unreliable state and local politicians to unreliable recipients. This shift was to some degree caused by increasing rolls in a time of prosperity, but equally important was the fact that confidentiality could be attacked and eliminated without endangering the basic principle of providing minimum benefits for the unemployed and unemployable. Although very little resulted from the amendment in concrete terms, the political impact was great. The act represented a turning point in authority relations of federal and state policy-makers; it brought strength to those opposing federal liberalization of eligibility requirements; and it revealed the distance between social workers and politicians, each of whom viewed the other with distrust and saw the other as being narrow-minded (see Steiner 1966). The long-term mistrust of governmental involvement was reawakened after the scare of the depression had waned.

The NOLEO Amendment,[7] passed in 1950, further illustrated a change in attitude toward welfare recipients, especially those in the ADC category. Originally ADC had been designed for widowed mothers having dependent children, but during the 1950s the image changed to that of illiterate, unwed black women with many children. This change produced a great deal of controversy because of assumed cultural differences between the black and white populations, racial prejudices, varying sex mores, and "hefty" moral judgments. As had usually been the case in American public welfare, more stringent behavioral codes were prescribed for welfare recipients than for others (hence the welfare search to find "a man in the house.") The conception of the ADC category shifted from "involuntary dependency" due to death of the provider (i.e., the "deserving poor") to "voluntary dependency" due to desertion and illegitimacy (i.e., the "undeserving poor").

The concept of honest dependency was a cornerstone in establishing the Social Security Act and was essential in accommodating the act to the laissez-faire model. It is not surprising, then, that a shift toward seemingly voluntary dependency would appear threatening and that to support such a group of people would appear misguided or un-American. Once again, of course, the cultural fragmentation of the United States was important. As had been the case with newly arrived immigrant groups, blacks were viewed with distrust and fear. In particular, their relatively high rate of illegitimacy seemed to disqualify them in the eyes of whites from any claim to being able to manage their own affairs. In turn, efforts to revise welfare legislation in the 1950s seemed to return to the view that unemployment and poverty were due to individual shortcomings. Though not unopposed, this outlook held sway in legislative circles during the fifties.

The controversial nature of the ADC program was made clear in the Newburgh crisis in 1961 (see May 1964, pp. 17–37). The crisis occurred when the city of Newburgh, New York, attempted to introduce thirteen new requirements which individuals had to fulfill in order to receive ADC. Many of these requirements seemed specifically designed to embarrass recipients (for example, public registration at the police department) and to prevent blacks from obtaining aid (long residency requirements and refusing aid if the individual supposedly had entered the city with the intent of obtaining it). The goal was to cut down on welfare rolls, to discourage people from applying for aid, and to provide minimum benefits only. On the surface, the struggle concerning which conditions should be present before relief could be given was about municipal rule versus federal or state control, but it had racial undertones in addition to outright discrimination against all persons receiving ADC.

During the 1950s it became quite clear that most of the welfare programs created during the 1930s would not wither away. On the contrary, the programs expanded with regard both to the levels of benefits provided and the absolute and relative numbers of people covered. The latter change can be explained partly by the increase in the size of those groups of the population most exposed to risks provided for in the Social Security Act. Thus, between 1947 and 1965 the proportion of the population over sixty-five increased from 20 to 31 percent and the proportion of broken families from 16 to 23 percent. In terms of the number of recipients, the most striking increase occurred in the ADC category: from 2.2 million in 1950 to three million in 1960.

This increase in the number of dependent people took place despite a wartime economy between 1950 and 1955 and was accompanied by inflationary pressures. Once again, war seems to have been essential to high employment, although few commentators pointed this out at the time. Instead, the Korean War seemed to fit into the widespread anticommunism sweeping the United States in the fifties and to provide some substance to the claims that the enemy of the country was collectivism in general.

The late 1940s and the 1950s represented a period of uncertainty about the direction of welfare. The legislation that occurred benefited primarily the moderately well-off (e.g., the G.I. bill) or the "deserving poor." Congressional and public discussion was highly critical of aid to the poor. The movement surrounding Joseph McCarthy was one of a number of voices aroused by the increasing role of the federal government. The McCarthy movement itself attacked welfare measures as communist-inspired and un-American.

The McCarthy movement and others like it were in large part attempts to reaffirm the nation's identity as a simple, orthodox laissez-faire society with a firm root in Christianity and rural virtue. In all fairness it must be emphasized that the movement was correct in claiming that welfare measures were antithetical to the nation's past identity, if quite wrong in claiming that they were "communist-inspired." McCarthyites detected a wide disparity between the laissez-faire model and United States society. Some of the same discrepancies between the ideal model and social reality were to give impetus to another kind of social movement more favorable to social welfare.

Discrimination against blacks in the United States is one of the nation's greatest violations of the laissez-faire model. The disenfranchisement of the black population from the right to compete at all levels of society is also a long-standing practice. By the late 1950s the predicament of blacks was worsened by their location in urban ghettos and their inability to obtain proportionate political representation. The Civil Rights movement, which got started in the late 1950s, then, could make a strong case for itself without being considered "unpatriotic." In part, it avoided this accusation by appealing strongly to Christian ideology. The timing of the movement, however, seems to have been most directly due to the decline of McCarthyism and to the 1954 Supreme Court decision which ruled that segregated schools were unconstitutional (Brown versus Board of Education of Topeka). With these two favorable circumstances and the end of a war opposed to communism, it was again possible to favor a broader extension of rights and benefits to all citizens.

The Civil Rights movement and reports of it helped to bring federal financing into state and private organizations as a way of claiming federal guarantees against discrimination in employment, the allocation of services, and individual treatment. In turn, the widespread federal involvement in the financing of private industry, the public schools, hospitals, and transportation gradually urged the federal government into stricter enforcement of fair employment and fair treatment practices.

Inevitably the Civil Rights movement encountered the question of welfare benefits, because so many blacks were poor and dependent upon public support. As a result, there was a renewed interest in the social and structural causes of poverty, in contrast to the individualistic interpretations of the early 1950s. The Civil Rights movement also drew some attention to the broad extent of governmental support of private industry as compared to the relatively small sums spent on poor people. Finally, the movement dramatized the existence of poverty, misery, and primitiveness in America to a large middle class accustomed to think of their country as the most prosperous and modern in the world. Guilt-stricken or aroused by the idealism of the well-protected, thousands of middle-class American youths joined the ranks of the Civil Rights movement and an intellectual debate which by the 1960s came to touch on the national identity itself.

An Era of Unrest: The 1960s

If the 1950s were characterized by an attempt to restore the congruence between the national identity and the laissez-faire model, the 1960s were marked by an insistence that the nation live up to its claims for prosperity and equality. To some extent both social movements had their roots in the great postwar expansion of government. While the McCarthy movement used the symbols of the traditional laissez-faire framework, the movements of the 1960s were to demand that the vast government and business organizations which had developed during and after the Second World War should be more equitable and effective.

The crises of the sixties were in some ways qualitatively different from those which had provoked welfare legislation in the past. The decade was comparatively prosperous and the gross national product increased without a major recession. Yet the country faced the nearest thing to an authentic "crisis of identity" which it had encountered since the Civil War. The growth of huge government subsidies to farmers and large industries completely overshadowed the honorable image of the small independent entrepreneurs struggling alone. The exclusion of blacks from the labor market and electoral politics raised grave doubts about the pervasiveness of democracy and other basic freedoms. The inability of popular opinion to control the country's entrance into a new war and the government's faltering attempts to enforce national standards of nondiscrimination aroused a credibility gap which not only plagued three presidents but raised questions about the national identity itself. On the one side, critics launched a full-scale attack on the nation's identity, which in some cases was explicitly expressed by desecrating the nation's flag. On the other side, defenders of the American creed launched unrestrained counterattacks which were most fully expressed in some of Vice-President Spiro Agnew's speeches.

The problem of welfare legislation was often lost in disputes about even broader issues. First, at the beginning of the decade the United States voted into office a president who not only accepted the existence of "big government" but supported the idea of government playing a very positive role. Second, the Civil Rights movement, along with several other movements supporting the poor (e.g., Mexicans, Indians, Puerto Ricans), began to take extensive action. Third, for the first time since the 1930s, scholars and social commentators turned their attention to income distribution and thereby "rediscovered" poverty. Fourth, riots and social unrest called attention to slums and residential aggregations of the poor. Fifth, the federal government itself sponsored a variety of new agencies, groups, and policies that culminated in an official "War on Poverty." Finally, by the late 1960s a widespread student movement with leftist tendencies had come into existence, however incoherent and fragile its organization. By the end of the sixties all of these changes of direction had been interrupted by the Vietnam War and the election of a new president far less favorable to either social welfare or significant changes in the national identity. Nonetheless, the development which took place in the 1960s may ultimately prove to be irreversible, since the United States had committed itself, at least theoretically, to the elimination of poverty.

When President Kennedy assumed office in 1961, there was already widespread dissatisfaction among legislators and the public with existing welfare programs, and a major overhaul of the system was considered necessary. Conservative groups had long been unfavorable to public welfare in general and the ADC category in particular on the grounds that such measures were contrary to the American tradition of self-support. This particular orientation, strengthened in the late 1950s, had resulted in the Newburgh crisis in 1961 and the Byrd investigations in 1962. That year Senator Robert Byrd of West Virginia undertook a study of eligibility of ADC cases in the District of Columbia. His claim that 60 percent of the cases examined were ineligible for aid was received by his co-legislators, the news media, and the population at large in a way which furthered the impression that ADC recipients were undeserving. Further, of all public assistance programs, ADC seemed to have the worst fate, being either left out when benefits were increased or receiving minimum increases. This was in contrast to programs for the blind and to a certain degree the aged, the only recipients who had organized or attempted collective action by the early 1960s and who were, incidentally, the main beneficiaries of an exclusive Medicare program established in 1965. Of course, it continued to be more respectable to be poor because one was old or blind than because one had been deserted or had illegitimate children.

The failure of the withering-away programs and the shift in composition of ADC clients to a less influential and less respected group had produced an orientation toward change which was shared by those who had "rediscovered" poverty and were seriously disturbed by the fact that poverty was both severe and widespread in "the richest nation in the world." It was increasingly clear that a major overhaul of the welfare program was needed, and the 1960s produced the largest volume of anti-poverty legislation since the 1930s, including the Social Security Amendments of 1961 and 1962 emphasizing services to the poor, Medicaid, and Medicare, the War on Poverty, and work incentives for public assistance recipients (1967).

Much of the legislation was accompanied by broader public recognition of the plight of the poor in the United States. Starting with the publication of Michael Harrington's *The Other America* (1962), a large body of literature on the poor accumulated through the decade. Unlike the literature of the fifties, that of the sixties focused more closely on the social or systemic causes of poverty, and criticism ranged from the welfare system itself to the public school system and the labor market. Additional criticism of welfare coverage, especially in the ADC category, was voiced by some members of the Civil Rights movement as well as by black nationalists. By this time there were ample statistics to document the condition of the poor, thanks to the development of standards and record keeping during the Second World War.[8] An actual decrease in the average life expectancy may not have been too significant, but, taken together with the relatively high infant mortality in the United States, it caused embarrassment in some circles.[9] Unemployment and underemployment due to automation and industrialization could now be documented. Within a few years, this literature expanded to include a wide range of social problems associated with poverty: violence, delinquency, discrimination, broken homes, the deterioration of housing, health, and so on. The extraordinary riots which occurred in the late 1960s gave further impetus to this concern with the consequences of poverty and were the reason for several government reports which focused on the entire social context of poverty (President's National Advisory Commission on Civil Disorder 1968).

There were indications that the lesson of the 1930s was beginning to be accepted—namely, that a thorough revision of economic policies was necessary and that adequate provisions should be made for those who for some reason or another were unable to provide for themselves (Grønbjerg 1977). This attitude was reflected especially in the professional literature (economists, sociologists, social workers, etc.) which since 1962 had taken a serious interest in a guaranteed annual income, negative income tax, and similar schemes.

Because the Cold War had opened the United States to international comparisons, it became increasingly difficult to defend a system showing so many apparent injustices. A rapidly rising standard of living in Europe and the claims of the United States to be a model of prosperity made many public officials aware that the nation could lose ground in the world competition for prestige if it failed to live up to its own image. This was in fact a major issue in the 1960 presidential debates between Kennedy and Nixon. The poverty of American blacks and the inequity of their treatment became especially embarrassing with the rise of African nations and the United States' attempts to gain their support in international policies.

The War on Poverty program, introduced in 1964 as a new approach to fighting poverty, was different in several respects from the basic concepts of the Social Security Act of 1935 (see Lowi 1969, pp. 214–50). An important segment was the Community Action Program (CAP), which sought to promote community-based groups that were then to take action to improve the local community and the situation of its residents. Similarly, VISTA, the Model Cities program, and the compensatory education programs were either demonstration programs or attempts to incorporate the poor as a new interest group comparable to labor unions.

Whether or not the War on Poverty was a success, it soon aroused considerable criticism. On the one hand, some of the community groups formed were seen as political threats and made many mayors uneasy. On the other hand, specialists examining the War on Poverty drew up a number of criticisms including the difficulty of identifying community units (Suttles 1972, chap. 3), the promotion of a culture of poverty (Lowi 1969; Huber 1974b), and the inability of community groups to effect wide-scale changes or materially to change their own circumstances (Greenstone and Peterson 1968; Vanecko 1970; Blau 1969; Piven and Cloward 1971). By the late 1960s it was clear that neither welfare expenditures nor the number of people receiving support had decreased as a result of the new programs; on the contrary, welfare rolls were growing rapidly.

In the long run, of course, the War on Poverty may have extensive consequences, for example, by making the controversy over decentralization and local control a major issue. Yet the War on Poverty reverted in many ways to the 1920s. Once again the personal shortcomings of the poor were often identified as the central problem, and many of the measures undertaken were at heart efforts at individual rehabilitation. Many of the demonstration projects were meant to inspire comparable grass-roots and private efforts rather than be significant in their own right. The heavy emphasis on "community organization" indicated a focus on "remotivation" and voluntarism rather than on direct aid or realistic sources of employment. Finally, the absence of adequate administrative structures and the very name "War on Poverty" indicated the characteristic temporary nature of such adventures in the United States. Essentially a "crash program," the War on Poverty seems to have incorporated the belief that unemployment and dependency would disappear once people had been remotivated, organized into interest groups, and instilled with civic responsibility.

The War on Poverty failed to recognize some of the more obvious sources of dependency in the United States economy—for example, deflationary monetary policies, automation, the obsolescence of skills, and the migration of industry. It received heavy criticism after two years of operation and might have declined in any case had not the Vietnam War intruded to absorb most of the funds available. The riots which occurred in 1965–67 did much to undermine the support of moderate whites for the Civil Rights movement and, in the eyes of some, directly implicated the federal government in the charge that it had sponsored "irresponsible troublemakers" or "outside agitators." Once it became clear that the Vietnam War was to be expensive in both lives and resources, President Johnson lost the support of liberals as well as conservatives. Considering the extent of public unrest and controversy occurring up to 1968, the slow rate at which changes took place is more impressive than the few changes which were made.

When President Nixon took office in 1969, public discussion of the guaranteed annual income had progressed so far that it could scarcely be neglected, and the Nixon administration itself had promised legislation in this area as a way of assuring critics that it was not exclusively tied to capitalist interests. In the fall of 1969, Nixon announced his Workfare Program or Family Assistance Plan (FAP), and in 1970 the bill was finally introduced into the Congress.

The progress of the Family Assistance Plan was marked by its slow passage through legislative channels, the constant necessity to accommodate the bill to the laissez-faire ideology to the point where it became unacceptable to its original liberal supporters, and finally its death in early 1973. In the original presentation of the bill, Nixon emphasized the work incentive aspects of the bill rather than its provisions for universal aid in case of unemployment, and argued that it would be self-reducing. Similarly, the term "Workfare" was meant to draw attention to the incentive system and away from the support measures.

Such window dressing was probably essential for congressional and popular acceptance of the FAP and typical of the evasive vocabulary which had been used historically to describe welfare programs in the United States. Even so, the FAP remained in the Congress for more than two sessions before being shelved, while some came to doubt President Nixon's intentions in initially presenting the bill. Public reaction to the proposal seemed confused by an administration which publicly espoused the most progressive welfare legislation in the history of the United States while doing little to get it enacted.

Nonetheless, it is the opinion of many journalists and academicians that something like the FAP will eventually be enacted in the United States. Preliminary reports of President Carter's welfare reform proposals suggest strong lines of continuity to the FAP. If some type of universal program does become implemented, it will represent another public institution which has become essential because the laissez-faire system does not function as hoped. Designed as permanent programs, the FAP and Carter's Better Jobs and Income Program (BJIP) assume that low wages, dependency, and unemployment are problems endemic to industrial society. Also, while the vocabulary and provisions of both proposals include a great deal of emphasis on work incentives and job training, they also include the expansion of previous welfare measures to insure universal coverage for all those who are dependent or have low incomes. Such provisions amount to an admission of failure for the classic laissez-faire system.

Certain elements of the Nixon as well as the Carter proposals could make it easier for Americans to accept universal welfare coverage while these same characteristics could make such a program less effective than anticipated. As critics have pointed out, the FAP proposal continued the distinction between the "deserving" and "undeserving" poor by continuing to provide for those who cannot work at all for reasons of health or child-bearing through older programs (ADC, APTD, OAA). Thus, the work incentive program, which was supposed to match grants to earned income below certain levels, placed an extreme emphasis on employment and implicitly condemned those unable to work or to find work to an inferior status bordering on penury. Most important, however, the level of support proposed by the federal government was well below any publicly defined "minimum living standards." While the program would relieve people of the threat of starvation, it might not rescue many from poverty. The Carter proposal maintains the distinction between those expected to work and those not expected to work, but would provide a higher level of support to both than FAP. However, the passage of a program such as the FAP or BJIP is likely to elicit a new round of controversies focusing on the familiar themes of stigmatization, regional inequality, and the level of support offered. It may be expected that all of these controversies would be taken up in the heated emotional climate of patriotism.

Certainly the United States in the 1970s is drastically different from that of 1800 or even that of the McCarthy period of the 1950s. Yet conservatives are still able to appropriate to themselves many of the national insignia of patriotism in their struggle to give business and industry a free hand without responsibility for the maintenance of the broad masses. This point was eloquently demonstrated by Ronald Reagan's 1976 presidential campaign.

Conclusion

The close identification of the United States with its particular form of economy has been pivotal in maintaining conditions unfavorable to direct welfare programs. This identification may account not only for the absence of a major socialist movement in the United States but also for the absence of any other collectivist movements or reforms of any magnitude.[10]

Despite the idealization of the laissez-faire economy, the United States has seen a tremendous expansion of government functions and public intervention into the area of private business. Protection of business interests, antitrust laws, extensive subsidy programs, and direct participation in the economy constitute a vast part of the government's operation and expenditures. While some businessmen speak derisively of the "welfare state," governmental protection for large corporate enterprises has advanced to the point where they have "cradle to grave" paternalism ensuring corporate immortality. There is, indeed, some justice in Bayard Rustin's comment that the United States is a society with "socialism for the rich and capitalism for the poor." This advance of governmental functions on behalf of industry has increased the number of departures from the laissez-faire model and heightened the defensive patriotism of adherents. In turn, proposals for further welfare measures have been surrounded by an emotion-laden controversy that cannot be justified by either the immediate crises or the anticipated expenditures.

In the long term, governmental aid and assistance extended to private business and the well-to-do can be expected to enlarge the discrepancy between the laissez-faire model and social reality in the United States.[11] Such a development is already well underway and it provides the fulcrum by which the poor and dependent can lay claim to equal aid. Their claims gain justice not only in their appeal to fairness but in the declining plausibility of an ideology which many Americans, including businessmen, have abandoned in practice.

5   Who Is What Among the Poor

Once outside academic or policy-making circles, but sometimes inside them as well, poverty is usually discussed as if it were a clearly recognized state of being, seen as such by the poor as well as by others. Yet much of the controversy over what to do about poverty in the United States has arisen because of differing assumptions about who the poor are and, implicitly, why they are poor. This is not because the United States has been reluctant to adopt official public definitions of the poor, for it was one of the first nations to struggle with this problem. The federal government and the various states continue to come forth with numerous definitions (for greater detail see United States Department of Health, Education, and Welfare 1976a). However, no definition has received uncontested or enduring majority support.

Each definition has an implicit theory of poverty underlying it and tends in varying degrees to shift the responsibility for poverty onto the collectivity or the individual. If poverty is defined as having an income of under $3,000, then the elderly, the handicapped, and blacks tend to be singled out as "the poor" and their individual backgrounds are emphasized as the cause of poverty. If a relative definition of poverty is preferred, say 50 percent of the median income, then poverty is seen as concentrated among the working poor and among the residents of certain regions. More important, the relative definition indicates that the country as a whole has maintained a stable distribution of income despite the changing backgrounds and capabilities of its members. To define poverty, then, has been continuous with making a political statement. The inability to settle on a satisfactory consensual definition of poverty of course reflects the debate over free enterprise. However, to the American self-image of inevitable progress and wealth, the very discussion of poverty is distasteful. Yet it is exactly this inability to come to grips with the basis of poverty in the United States which has made most attempts to combat poverty through governmental programs ineffective, self-defeating, or partial. Each "war on poverty" has had to cater to both structural and individualistic theories about the causes of poverty (see Grønbjerg 1977, pp. 3–8).

CHANGING CONCEPTS OF POVERTY

From a sociological point of view, certain definitions of poverty are more appropriate than others. Particular ideological or political connotations do not necessarily make a definition less scientific but mainly emphasize the intricate relationships between reality, science, and politics. The "reality" of poverty has continuously been identified, observed, and analyzed. To that extent, poverty is a social, perhaps even a sociological creation. However, it is crucial to examine in which ways society creates, maintains, and selects the victims of poverty.

Certainly we should avoid the circular definition of the poor as those who have a culture of poverty—a definition taken to its logical absurdity by Banfield (1970). There are of course many people who are poor, yet hardworking and possessed of standards of self-improvement and achievement. Our definition of poverty must be objective and standardized, so that the causes of poverty can be critically assessed rather than just relabeled.

A number of writers have suggested that poverty should be considered in its broadest sense to include all social aspects of low income. One study has defined it as the relative absence of income, assets, basic services, self-respect, opportunities for education and social mobility, and participation in many forms of decision making (Miller and Roby 1970). Since such a blanket definition makes it next to impossible to assess who is poor or how many poor there are, it can only obscure our capacity to identify the various economic and social conditions it envelops.

Poverty is most commonly defined in terms of low income. But economic definitions are only partially agreed upon and tend to change over time. Robert Hunter, for example, proposed that an annual income of less than $460 for a family of "average size"[1] in the industrial states of the North in 1904 would make that family poor (Hunter 1965). Adjusted for price changes that figure would equal about $3,001 in (January) 1977 dollars. In 1950, an annual income of $2,000 for a family of four was used as the poverty level by the Joint Economic Committee of Congress. In 1977, that $2,000 corresponded to $4,867.[2] But in 1977 the Social Security Administration's low income level for a family of four was set at $5,981,[3] 99 percent higher than Hunter's 1904 poverty level and 23 percent higher than the Joint Economic Committee's 1950 poverty level. Clearly, the notion of what constitutes poverty reflects partly the change in the overall level of income (see also Huber 1974a).

In fact, these changing standards constitute one of the major dissatisfactions with using a particular income level as a cut-off point to separate the poor from the nonpoor. As economic conditions change, so do notions of what constitutes need. Poverty in this sense is relative deprivation: it measures how much worse off a person is compared to the rest of the population. Using such a comparative approach, poverty may be defined as, for example, income which is less than one-half of the median income. This is the definition advocated by Fuchs (1965, p. 75), and it emphasizes the notion that the poor are those who have fallen behind the standards of the society as a whole, recognizing, however, that those same standards are constantly changing.

Since 1947 the proportion of families with incomes less than one-half the median family income has hovered around 20 percent, ranging between 18.9 percent and 20.9 percent (Miller and Roby 1970, p. 36). In 1975, the percentage was 19.4 percent.[4] This indicates that there has been no great change in the relative deprivation of the poorest members of the American population, although the notions of what constitutes adequate income may well have changed considerably. There is, for example, strong evidence that what the general public sees as the minimal income necessary for an average family to get along on is closely related to the general level of family income, not the cost of living (see Schiltz 1970, pp. 21–22).

An attempt to include the total income distribution more directly in the definition of poverty is, a priori, to view those in the "bottom" part of the income distribution as poor, regardless of the actual incomes. The issue here is even more directly one of relative deprivation. An important question is, for example, how much of the total income goes to the poorest fifth? Since 1947, the lowest fifth of families in the United States have received between 4.5 and 5.6 percent of the total money income. In 1975, they received 5.4 percent (United States Bureau of the Census 1976c, p. 17, table 5).

Neither the definition of poverty in terms of comparative income nor the definition in terms of income share has received any wide endorsement in the United States. This may be for ideological reasons, since such definitions clearly tie the condition of the poor directly to the economic conditions of the rest of society and not just to the individual poor. Numerous other monetary definitions of poverty based on certain budgetary considerations have been proposed. Among the most important of these are the various state standards used to determine eligibility for public assistance and the Social Security Administration's low-income level. There are, of course, many other proposed poverty levels. Most definitions are based on budgetary assumptions about what consumption items are needed by a poor family and how much these items cost.

Each state, then, has established its own definition of poverty. In July of 1976, the annual threshold levels for an AFDC family of four ranged from $2,244 in Texas to $6,228 (almost double) in Vermont.[5] The Social Security Administration's low-income level for a nonfarm family of four headed by a woman was $5,492 in July 1976 (United States Bureau of the Census 1976c)—lower than Vermont's standard, but higher than that of Texas.

The definition of poverty developed by the Social Security Administration in 1964 is the most commonly used and seems to be winning wider support. This index provides a range of income cutoff points adjusted by such factors as family size, sex of family head, number of children under eighteen years of age, and farm-nonfarm residence (Orshansky 1965a, b, 1969). At the core of this definition is a nutritionally adequate food plan (the "economy plan") designed by the Department of Agriculture for "emergency and temporary use when funds are low" (United States Bureau of the Census 1976b, p. 143). The annual income level is then constructed by multiplying the cost of food by three on the assumption, based on research among low-income families, that food constitutes about 33 percent of the total family budget. The definition was revised in 1969 to allow for annual adjustments in the poverty levels based on changes in the Consumer Price Index, rather than on changes in the cost of food included in the economy food plan. These revisions also allowed the poverty levels for farm households to be increased from 70 to 85 percent of the corresponding nonfarm levels (United States Bureau of the Census 1971, p. 5).

TABLE 1   Weighted Average Thresholds at the Low-Income Level in 1974 by Size of Family and Sex of Head, by Farm–Nonfarm Residence, 1974

Size of Family	Total	Nonfarm			Farm		
		Total	Male head[a]	Female head[a]	Total	Male head[a]	Female head[a]
Unrelated							
Individuals	$2,487	$2,495	$2,610	$2,413	$2,092	$2,158	$2,029
14 to 65 yrs.	2,557	2,562	2,658	2,458	2,197	2,258	2,089
65 yrs. & over	2,352	2,364	2,387	2,357	2,013	2,030	2,002
All families							
2 persons	3,191	3,211	3,220	3,167	2,707	2,711	2,632
head 14 to 65	2,294	3,312	3,329	3,230	2,819	2,824	2,706
head 65 & over	2,958	2,982	2,984	2,966	2,535	2,535	2,533
3 persons	3,910	3,936	3,957	3,822	3,331	3,345	3,133
4 persons	5,008	5,038	5,040	5,014	4,302	4,303	4,262
5 persons	5,912	5,950	5,957	5,882	5,057	5,057	5,072
6 persons	6,651	6,699	6,706	6,642	5,700	5,700	5,702
7 or more persons	8,165	8,253	8,278	8,079	7,018	7,017	7,066

[a]For Unrelated Individuals, sex of the individual
Source: United States Bureau of the Census 1976b, p. 146.

The SSA poverty level is inadequate in several respects. By most standards, it is too low. For a family of four not living on a farm, the poverty level was $5,501 in 1975 for a family headed by a male and $5,472 for one headed by a female (United States Bureau of the Census 1976c, p. 33). Compare this to a $9,588 income level for an urban family of four, deemed as modest but adequate by the U.S. Department of Labor in 1975 (Weir 1976). Excluding other expenses, such as gifts, contributions, personal life insurance, and taxes, this latter income level is lowered to about $7,795, still more than $2,290 higher than the SSA's poverty level.[6]

In spite of its low level, the SSA-defined poverty threshold is useful for looking more closely at the poor. First, by using the most conservative definition of poverty, the conditions of the very poorest can more clearly be demonstrated. Second, it is the only definition which at least attempts to adjust for variations in economic needs due to such important factors as family size and rural-urban residence. Third, aside from small-scale surveys, we know very little about the characteristics of the poor if they are defined in any other way. Because the federal government and a number of other important bodies use it, it is the poor by that definition that we must know about. It is largely, then, for practical, but also for theoretical reasons, that this chapter will be based on the SSA low income levels.

It must be recognized that any definition will tend to focus attention on a particular segment of the population and thus emphasize certain policies for reducing or eliminating poverty. An absolute definition of poverty, like the budgetary definitions, will tend to identify as poor those who are not employed for various reasons. Therefore, policies to combat poverty have generally focused on employment opportunities and emphasizing to the poor the value of hard work. A relative definition of poverty, on the other hand, would tend to include among the poor a large segment of the working population who are already deeply enmeshed in the cultural celebration of hard work and for whom increasing employment opportunities will be of little importance. The policy implication of such a definition, therefore, is to change the income distribution itself.

What is not often acknowledged, however, is that policies utilizing either type of definition are not likely to have much effect on the poor except for selective groups. As our findings will indicate, those groups whose poverty may be most reduced by increasing employment opportunities are small segments of the black population, some female heads of households, and some of the aged.

POVERTY IN THE INDUSTRIAL SOCIETY

The industrial society is based on a money economy. Very few, if any, members of such a society can supply themselves directly with all the necessities of life, including food, housing, clothing, tools, etc. Consequently, money income is of paramount importance for maintaining life at any but the most desperate level. There are several ways of obtaining such money income.[7] In an industrial society, earnings from work are the most important source. In capitalist societies, income may also be obtained from investments. Finally, income may be transferred directly or indirectly from one person to another. Although such income originally may have derived from employment, the person who uses it may not be required to work for it. In this latter category fall all private and public transfer payments, including alimony, retirement benefits, and public assistance. Most of these transfer payments are granted because the recipient is thought to be in some financial need, perhaps even is poor, although much of the transfer income also goes to the nonpoor (for example, veteran's benefits). There have been increasing governmental expenditures for transfer payments in recent years which have aided some segments of the needy population, but the distribution has been very uneven and may have neglected the very poorest and those least able to benefit from expanding employment opportunities.

In 1974, 62 percent of all poor families received some income from earnings, although relatively few (6.4 percent) of all families who had income from earnings were poor (see table 2).

TABLE 2   Incidence and Distribution of Poverty by Type of Income, 1974

Source of Income	All families			
	Total pop. (thousands)	% Poor	% of Poor families	% of Nonpoor families
Total	55,712	9.2	100.0	100.0
Earnings, total	49,529	6.4	62.0	91.6
Wage or salary income	47,048	5.8	53.9	87.5
Nonfarm self-employed	6,539	7.2	9.2	12.1
Farm self-employed	2,576	14.6	7.4	4.3
Income other than earnings				
Social security	12,162	10.0	23.9	21.6
Dividends, interest, rent	27,243	2.5	13.3	52.5
Public assistance	4,359	46.9	40.0	4.6
Other transfer payments[a]	10,296	5.0	10.0	19.6
Private pensions, alimony	6,581	8.3	10.7	11.9

Percentages do not add up to 100 percent because a family may have income from more than one source.
[a]Includes Unemployment and Workmen's Compensation, Government Employee Pensions, and Veteran's Payments.
Source: Calculated from United States Bureau of the Census 1976b, tables 38, 39.

This indicates that although employment is a very important source of income, (91.6 percent of the nonpoor had income from earnings, compared to 62.0 percent of the poor), it is no guarantee against poverty.

As is obvious from table 2, the general pattern of income sources is quite similar for the poor and the nonpoor. For both categories, the majority have income from earnings, mostly in the form of wage or salary income. There is very little difference between the poor and the nonpoor in terms of income from self-employment. There are only two types of income where there are major distinctions between the two population categories. As one should perhaps expect, the poor are much more likely to receive income from public assistance: 40.0 percent of the poor have income of this type, compared to only 4.6 percent of the nonpoor; public assistance is after all designed to aid the poor. It is also not surprising that only 13.3 percent of the poor have income from dividends, interest, and rent, compared to 52.5 percent of the nonpoor.

The Societal Creation of Poverty

Nonworkers and Their Support

Children. The argument that many people are poor because of the particular workings of the social structure may be easier to demonstrate if we look at different categories of the poor. First of all, children can scarcely be held responsible for their poverty. In 1974, 38.4 percent of all poor persons were under the age of sixteen[8] and thus by law restricted from most types of employment. Children, of course, are the responsibility of their parents, and from time to time the argument has been made that the poor were irresponsible either in having children or in not supporting them adequately.[9] Most poor, however, have only a few children: 53.3 percent of poor families with children under eighteen have two children or less and 32.2 percent have three or four children, whereas only 14.6 percent have five children or more. Large families are overrepresented among the poor, since family size is built into the definition of poverty: 38.3 percent of families with six or more children were poor in 1974, compared to 9.5 percent of families with one or two children.

Families headed by females were also much more likely to be poor than those headed by males (32.5 percent and 5.7 percent respectively), but most poor people live in families headed by males (54.0 percent). The accident of being born into families which are large or headed by females (or blacks) thus are primary factors in the poverty of children. The high proportion of children among the poor only places greater emphasis on understanding the poverty of those who are responsible for such children—poor adults.

Many of the poor over the age of sixteen are unable to work because they are ill, disabled, aged, unable to find work, or have other responsibilities, such as keeping house or attending school. When taken together, they and their children constitute a large proportion of the poor.

The disabled. A sizable segment of the poor American population is too ill or disabled to work (13.1 percent of males and 15.4 percent of females aged fourteen to sixty-four). To be ill or disabled greatly increases the likelihood of being poor: 29.1 percent of all those aged fourteen and over who were too ill or disabled to work were poor in 1974.

Relatively few data are available about those who are poor because of disability. In 1966, almost one of every two disabled adults did not work at all.[10] Of those who did work, 36 percent were employed full-time, 12 percent part-time, and 39 percent were unemployed (President's Commission on Income Maintenance Programs 1970, p. 139). As one would expect, the proportion who worked declined with increasing severity of disability. Of all families headed by an ill or disabled person in 1966, 41 percent were poor, with the incidences of poverty being greater for those families headed by a disabled person under fifty-five (48 percent) compared to those aged sixty-five and over (39 percent). This probably reflects the longer working life of the older disabled person, who may only recently have become disabled and thus may be entitled to relatively high social security payments.

The same age pattern holds for both male and female disabled heads of households, although more of the families headed by a disabled female were poor than of those headed by a disabled male (62 percent versus 44 percent, under age fifty-five). Women, of course, are less frequently covered by social security or public income maintenance programs among the disabled. Thus only 38 percent of severely disabled women, but 60 percent of severely disabled men were entitled to public program benefits in 1966. In 1966, 34 percent of several disabled men received OASDHI (social security) benefits and 26 percent public assistance and other public income, while 40 percent received no public income. The corresponding figures for severely disabled females were substantially lower, indicating that 22 percent received OASDHI benefits and 16 percent received other public income; fully 62 percent received no public income at all. Presumably some of these women may have working husbands who can support them. It is clear, however, that neither public income maintenance programs nor private funds are sufficient to maintain a minimum standard of living for disabled citizens, especially female, who are unable to support themselves through their own work.

Ablebodied nonworkers. In 1974, 18.7 percent of poor males between the ages of fourteen and sixty-four did not work because they were attending school, while 7.3 percent did not work for other reasons, including unemployment and the belief that no work was available. Lack of work, for whatever reason, is an important factor in the creation of poverty: 36.4 percent of all male heads of households who could not find work in 1974 were poor, while 21.2 percent of those who did not work for "other reasons" were poor. It may be assumed that these families received some income in the form of unemployment benefits, public assistance, or employment income from other members of the family who work, but evidently not enough to keep them out of poverty.

Many able-bodied adults, especially females, do not work because of other obligations. Thus 26.8 percent of all female family heads indicated in 1974 that they did not work because of housekeeping responsibilities. Of these 1,941,000 female family heads, 50.1 percent were poor. The incidence of poverty among black women not working for this reason was almost twice that of white women (74.3 percent and 41.8 percent respectively).

To eliminate poverty among these women it would be necessary not just to make well-paying jobs available but, more important, to provide adequate child-care facilities to allow them to work. It is generally estimated that the cost of such child-care facilities would be somewhat less than supporting the women and their children through public assistance.

Ironically, it is those proponents of the laissez-faire ideology most eager to chastise the poor for their apparent unwillingness to work who most strenuously oppose a policy which would make it possible for the poor to work and be responsible parents at the same time. That many poor parents are willing to forego income from work to care for their children indicates a far greater commitment to responsible citizenship than that with which they are usually credited.

The aged. Old age in America has long been closely associated with poverty. In 1974, close to one-sixth of all persons aged sixty-five and over were poor (see table 3). The proportion was somewhat less for heads of families: 9 percent of male heads of families aged sixty-five and over and 13 percent of female heads of families in the same age group. For unrelated individuals, the proportion of aged who were poor rose to 27 percent for males

TABLE 3   Incidence of Poverty Among the Aged
by Race and Household Status, 1974

Population aged 65 and over	Total population (thousands)	% of Total population poor
Persons	21,127	13.7
White	19,206	13.8
Black	1,722	36.4
Male heads of family	6,925	8.9
White	6,410	7.7
Black	454	23.9
Female heads of family	1,108	13.0
White	909	8.1
Black	187	36.8
Male unrelated individuals	1,455	26.8
White	1,233	23.7
Black	195	44.3
Female unrelated individual	5,047	33.2
White	4,641	30.3
Black	381	68.8

Source: United States Bureau of the Census 1976b, tables 6 and 23.

(44 percent for black males) and 33 percent for females (69 percent for black females). Thus a substantial proportion of America's old, and particularly of America's elderly females and elderly blacks, are poor despite income from public and private pensions and insurance programs. It should be pointed out, however, that these figures do represent a decline in absolute poverty among the aged. Thus 13.7 percent of all aged were poor in 1974 compared to 28.5 percent in 1966.

Those aged seventy-three and older are more likely to be poor than those slightly younger (see table 4). This is due to several factors. Social security has been covering an increasing proportion of the work force, and several of the very old are not eligible for social security payments because they were working in jobs uncovered under social security at the time they were employed. Also, most of those in the oldest age groups have been forced to

TABLE 4   Mean and.Median Income of the Aged Population by Age, Sex, and Marital Status, 1974.

Sex and marital status of aged population	Age category		
	Aged 62–64	Aged 65–72	Aged 73 and over
	Mean income		
Married couples	$13,586	$9,711	$7,579
Unmarried, living in families			
Males	7,127	5,098	3,639
Females	5,046	3,642	2,642
Unmarried, not living in families			
Males	5,926	5,717	4,963
Females	5,578	4,402	3,541
	Median income		
Married couples	$10,000+	$7,396	$5,891
Unmarried, living in families			
Males	5,304	3,477	2,660
Females	3,355	2,560	2,162
Unmarried, not living in families			
Males	4,748	3,819	3,216
Females	4,339	3,102	2,765

Source: United States Bureau of the Census 1976a, table 54.

give up employment because of disability or health problems, even though persons aged seventy-two and over are not subject to the earnings test before receiving social security as are those aged sixty-two to seventy-two.[11] More than one-fifth of male beneficiaries aged sixty-five to seventy-two worked in 1963 (compared to 53 percent of nonbeneficiaries), while only 18 percent of beneficiaries and 5 percent of nonbeneficiaries worked at the age of seventy-three.[12] However, by the time the old person has reached the rather high age of seventy-three, he or she is not only more likely to be unable to work but has often exhausted private funds and savings. In 1974, the median income of married and unmarried individuals in different age categories over the age of sixty-five was as indicated in table 4.

Females seem to be consistently worse off than single males, both with regard to incidence and degree of poverty. It is the relatively poor economic condition of women that partly accounts for the difference existing between aged married couples and aged unrelated individuals with regard to poverty. While most aged poor family heads were male, most aged poor unrelated persons were females. This is in part a reflection of the fact that women live longer than males and thus outlive their husbands, but it also reflects the fact that women have less income than males throughout their lives, particularly in their old age (see table 4).

The better financial situation of married couples is due in part to the traditionally better employment status of married men (in 1970, families headed by a male aged thirty-five to forty-four whose wife was not in the labor force had a mean income of $12,649) compared to unrelated males of the same age group (mean income of $7,895 in 1970; United States Bureau of the Census 1973, table 250). In 1963, 90 percent of old couples, but only 80 percent of old unmarried persons, had some form of income from a public income maintenance program (Bixby, Murray, and Belmore 1967). By 1974, however, there was no difference between the two categories in the proportion receiving social security benefits. Nevertheless, the result is not only that higher social security payments go to married men because of their higher earnings, but also that married couples are supplied with the additional income from social security payments to the spouse.

As in all other age categories, blacks are more likely to be poor than are whites. In 1974, 36.4 percent of aged blacks were poor compared to 13.8 percent of aged whites. The figures were again somewhat higher for females than for males: 16.3 percent of aged white females and 41.9 percent of aged black females were poor, compared to 10.1 percent of aged white males and 28.7 percent of aged black males (United States Bureau of the Census 1976b).

Nonwhites—especially males—traditionally have lower earnings than whites and, therefore, receive less income from social security payments once they retire. They are also likely to have fewer assets. Thompson (1975, p. 35) reports that the average monthly social security benefits for blacks in 1973 ($134.70) was only about four-fifths of the average monthly benefits for whites ($169.20). Most of this difference can be explained by the lower earnings of blacks in jobs covered by social security and by the shorter period of time blacks generally work in covered employment. Not only do aged blacks receive lower benefits from social security, but fewer of them receive any social security benefits at all (80 percent) than is the case for whites (92 percent; Thompson 1975, p. 31). This is not because older blacks continue to work after the age of sixty-five and thus postpone obtaining social security benefits to which they otherwise would be entitled. On the contrary, such a pattern is more typical of whites (Rubin 1974). Instead, higher disability and illness rates among nonwhites are likely to be important and seem to be reflected in the tendency for nonwhites to become social security beneficiaries before the age of sixty-five and thus receive a lower rate of benefits than they would have received had they waited until they reached the age of sixty-five (Bixby, Murray, and Belmore 1967). Blacks are also more likely to have worked in jobs which are not, or have only recently been, covered by social security (Bixby, Murray, and Belmore 1967; Thompson 1975).

Although there has been a substantial increase in the extent to which blacks are covered by social security (from 49 percent of aged blacks in 1960 to 80 percent in 1973), there has not been much change in the average monthly benefits of blacks relative to whites between 1960 and 1973. And as Thompson (1975, p. 40) indicates, there are substantial differences among young black and white males, "which means that the present discrepancies in social security benefit levels are likely to persist for some time to come."

Contrary to what seems to be a popular assumption, a

considerable proportion of the aged work. In 1974, 69 percent of males aged sixty to sixty-four, 32 percent of those aged sixty-five to sixty-nine, and 14 percent of those aged seventy and over were in the labor force. Over time the labor force participation rate has decreased from 57 percent of those aged sixty-five to sixty-nine, and 28 percent for those aged seventy and over in 1954 to the present levels. The decline in labor force participation rates has been greater for nonwhites than for whites. Nonwhite males aged sixty-five and over experienced a decline of 56 percent from a participation rate of 50 percent in 1948 to 22 percent in 1974. For white aged males the decline was 52 percent from 46 percent to 22 percent. The labor force participation rate was lower for aged females than for males in 1974: about 8.2 percent of aged females worked compared to 22.1 percent of aged males. The participation rate was about the same for both white and nonwhite women (8.1 percent and 9.4 percent respectively) and white and nonwhite men (22.1 percent and 21.7 percent respectively; United States Department of Labor 1974, tables B, B-1).

The white-nonwhite difference is considerably larger for aged poor males who work. Only 6.3 percent of aged white males who worked in 1974 were poor, compared to 22.3 percent of aged nonwhite males. Of those who worked, a fairly large proportion worked full-time year-round, but still remained poor: 16.9 percent for nonwhites, 6.4 percent for whites. The incidence of poverty was also lower for aged white women than for aged nonwhite women. However, the difference between the two racial groups was larger than for males: 25.7 percent of nonwhite working females aged sixty-five and over were poor in 1974, compared to only 7.6 percent of aged white females.

Aged blacks were somewhat more likely than whites not to work because of illness or disability (34.7 percent for blacks, 15.2 percent for whites), and of those who did not work for this reason, a much greater proportion of blacks than of whites were poor (46.7 percent of aged black males, 17.0 percent of aged white males). Thus aged blacks tend to work more than aged whites, but earn less, and they are affected by illness and disability to a greater extent. This relationship holds for both males and females.

A considerable number of the aged are not working for "other reasons." In some cases, they have presumably not been able to obtain work. Few employers are willing to hire aged persons, and some are unwilling to keep aged employees on the payrolls. When old workers are allowed to continue to work, it is often at lower wages and in less demanding positions. However, the structure of many private pension systems is such that older workers are undesirable employees because they impose a comparably higher economic burden on the employer than do younger workers (Davis 1973). Also, the structure of the social security system discourages older workers from continuing to work, especially at any but the lowest wages (Alberts 1974).

It is therefore not surprising that a considerable proportion of the income of aged persons comes from some form of public income (social security, public employees' retirement, veterans' benefits, and public assistance). In 1962, OASDHI (social security) provided about 30 percent of the income of persons aged sixty-five and over, and programs for railroad and government workers about 6 percent (Bixby, Murray, and Belmore 1967). Since then, the level of social security payments has increased considerably, coverage has been extended, and employment of the aged has perhaps correspondingly declined. Therefore, we would expect social security and other government programs to be of increasing relative importance for the income of the aged. More than 94.7 percent of persons aged sixty-five and over received some social security cash benefits in 1974, providing the largest coverage of any single program (only 10.8 percent of persons aged sixty-five and over received income from Supplemental Security Income [SSI] for the aged, i.e., public assistance; calculated from *Social Security Bulletin Statistical Supplement* 1974, pp. 108, 161, and United States Bureau of the Census 1976b).

The social security program is important because of its acceptability and its capacity to remove the old person from poverty: 67 percent of all aged heads of households were poor before receiving social security payments in 1965, and 35 percent remained poor after receiving their checks (President's Commission on Income Maintenance Programs 1970, pp. 118–19). Considering public programs other than OASDHI and public assistance, 50 percent were poor before receiving these benefits, while only 16 percent were poor after receiving them. Public assistance programs were the least effective in this respect: 87 percent were poor before, 69 percent after receiving Old Age

Assistance. In general, all public programs had the combined effect of cutting the incidence of poverty in half, leaving 37 percent of the old still poor after receiving these benefits. Since 1965, social security payments have increased substantially, but the proportion remaining poor after receiving benefits probably may not have been reduced (Garfinkel 1977).

It is frequently argued that private pensions should be the main way to support the aged. If so, such programs would have to be radically expanded. Private pension plans provided only 3 percent of the total income of the aged in 1962 (Bixby, Murray, and Belmore 1967). This proportion may have increased somewhat since that time as more and more workers have become eligible for pensions under union-negotiated programs. In 1974, however, private pensions were still a relatively small proportion of all income received: for only 5.8 percent of all families did unearned income from nonpublic sources (including dividends, interest, rent, annuities, alimony, and private pensions) constitute more than 50 percent of all income, and for 85.7 percent of all families, these sources of income amounted to less than 25 percent of all income.

It has been estimated that only a fraction of those contributing to private pension plans ever receive such benefits. A federal study of selected private pension plans covering 7.6 million of the 23 million workers with such pension programs indicated that over a period of twenty years only 4 percent of the participating workers received any benefits (Bernstein 1974). Over the years, private pension plans have been the subject of similar criticisms (Henle and Schmitt 1974). Many workers have not received private pension benefits to which they were legally entitled because the pension plan was terminated or because of inadequate management of the plan. Two additional problems which have beset private pension plans concern the determination of who is entitled to benefits. First, in most cases workers have not been able to transfer their benefit rights from industry to industry, or even from company to company within the same industry. Where benefit rights were portable, only a fraction of the amount usually could be transferred. Second, almost all pension plans require the worker to work for a minimum length of time for the same employer (often as long as eighteen years, but occasionally as much as thirty years) before he or she would be entitled to any pension. The requirement of many years of employment before a nonforfeitable right to benefits, known as vesting, may be obtained has been particularly troublesome in combination with restrictions on portability of benefits. People who work in volatile industries or who change jobs for other reasons have often been unable to accumulate sufficient vesting to obtain any sizable benefits upon retirement.

A not unimportant side effect of such pension provisions has been to encourage some employers to dismiss their older workers, sometimes before these have worked for the minimum length of time to obtain vested retirement benefits. There are also indications that some retirement plan provisions discourage employers from hiring older workers because of the relatively high retirement costs to the employer of such workers (Davis 1973).

A law designed to overcome some of these problems, the Employment Retirement Income Security Act (ERISA), was enacted in 1974, to become fully effective by 1978 (Henle and Schmitt 1974). Clearly, it is too early to assess the degree to which ERISA will accomplish all of these goals. However, there are likely to continue to be significant problems of vesting and portability. There is hope, however, that provisions about termination insurance, funding, and fiduciary responsibility will make it possible for more workers to obtain the benefits to which they are legally entitled than is currently the case.

For some workers, but not most, combined public and private benefits will approximate preretirement living levels (Henle 1972; Kolodrubetz 1973). Low-wage earners are likely to be relatively worse off in their retirement because they are least likely to have supplementary private pensions. Only 30 percent of those with wages and salary below $5,000 in 1972 were covered by private pension plans, compared to 76 percent of those with earnings of $15,000 to $20,000, and 71 percent of those with earnings of $25,000 or more (United States Bureau of the Census 1975, p. 295). Furthermore, low-wage earners are more likely to retire early because of unemployment or disability (Henle 1972). Low-paid workers in small nonunionized plants are also least likely to have contributed to (and thus benefit from) employer-supported private pension plans, although their participation is growing (Bell 1973). Already in 1962, Bixby, Murray, and Belmore (1967) concluded that "relatively few of those at the very low income levels received any income from private pensions, and this source was less important at the levels above $5,000 than in the $2,000–$5,000 range" (p. 12).

Unless things have changed dramatically since 1962, the old do not get much income from their families. "Cash contributions by relatives not living in the same household, or by friends, amounted to barely 1 percent of the aggregate income [of the old]. Only 3 percent of the couples and 5 percent of the nonmarried reported cash contributions. These included occasional contributions as well as contributions received regularly. Not included were lump sum inheritances and larger cash gifts" (Bixby, Murray, and Belmore 1967, p. 12). It is probable that the old do receive some income from relatives or friends in the form of income-in-kind. However, there exists little information on this subject.

Other possible sources of income for the aged include income from assets, such as rent or dividends. By 1962, the median holdings of couples over 65 were $11,180, with nonfarm homes accounting for about one-third of all assets. When assets in the home were excluded, median assets were $2,950. Unmarried men and women had assets about one-third that of married couples (Bixby, Murray, and Belmore 1967, p. 4).

A study reporting on various types of financial assets and debts of married males and nonmarried males and females aged fifty-eight to sixty-three in 1969 confirmed the continuing bleak financial situation of the aged (Sherman 1973). It should be emphasized that this is the age group in which one might expect assets to be greatest: homes have more or less been paid for, the children have left home and are presumably taking care of themselves, and most people have not yet retired to live off their pensions and other assets. Although some of the persons surveyed were financially comfortable, in general people in this age group were found not to be very well off, especially when the amount of homeownership was excluded. Thus 14 percent of married men, 47 percent of unmarried men, and 37 percent of unmarried females had a net worth of less than $1,000. Married men are more likely to own assets and the values of these assets are likely to be higher. Homeownership is especially important both because of the value of the home and because homeowners are more likely than nonhomeowners to have other assets as.well (Sherman 1973).

There is, then, no reason to believe that the old are living high on their savings, especially as inflation reduces the buying power of savings and fixed retirement incomes. As health care improves and life expectancy increases, it is even possible that the median level of assets will actually decline as the old consume their assets over time and as various economic emergencies arise.

The cost of poverty to the old does not come just in terms of physical want or health. The psychological costs are very high, although unmeasured. Loneliness, fear, distrust, and feelings of inadequacy and self-disgust among the aged have been documented by many observers. The old can contribute to society only to a limited extent because of illness or disability, but even those who can and do work are often unable to find employment because they are considered too old. To be useless and unwanted is a misfortune in any society: to be that in the United States with its emphasis on self-reliance and achievement is worse.

The Working Poor

Although relatively few male family heads who worked full-time (forty hours per week) for fifty to fifty-two weeks during 1974 were poor (2.5 percent), full-time working males headed more than one-quarter (28.5 percent) of all poor families. Full-time work throughout the year is thus no guarantee against poverty. Part of the reason for this, of course, is the type of work available to a large segment of the population in the United States. Looking at male family heads who worked during 1974 but who were still poor, most of these were farmers and farm laborers (24.7 percent) and operatives (17.0 percent, see table 5, column 3). Farming was clearly the occupational category most risky with regard to poverty: 24.1 percent of all farm laborers and managers and 20.9 percent of all self-employed farmers were poor, compared to only 4.3 percent of operatives (see table 5, column 2). A large proportion of the poor farm laborers are migrant workers, who generally work only part of the year and often at far below the minimum wage level. It is clearly those occupations which require no skills or only very little formal training which have the highest incidences of poverty.

Low-paying occupations are among the few open to people with low educational levels (29.1 percent of all poor family heads had less than eight years of education in 1974). The lower the educational level obtained, the more likely is the individual to be

TABLE 5   Incidence and Distribution of Poverty for Male Family Heads, by Occupation, 1974.

	Families with male head		
	All Families		
Occupation of male family heads	Number of families (thousands)	% of Families poor	% of Poor families with working heads
Wage and salary workers	35,894	3.1	64.7
Professional, technical, managers and administrators, except farm	10,643	0.7	4.4
Clerical and sales	4,342	1.5	3.8
Craftsmen and kindred	8,666	2.6	12.7
Operatives	6,929	4.3	17.0
Service, incl. private household	2,585	5.2	7.7
Laborers, except farm	2,196	9.3	11.7
Farm laborers and managers	532	24.1	7.3
Self-employed, farm	1,456	20.9	17.4
Self-employed, other	3,445	8.8	17.3

Source: United States Bureau of the Census 1976b, table 14.

poor: 21.3 percent of all family heads with less than eight years of education were poor, compared to 3.1 percent of those with some college education. Lack of adequate education makes it very difficult for an individual to improve his job situation through promotion, job changes, or job training.

In all occupational categories, for males and females and blacks and whites alike, labor union membership is crucial. Not only are the poor much more likely to be restricted to certain lower occupational categories, but even within these categories they are less likely to have the benefits of labor union membership than do their nonpoor fellow workers. In 1970 only about 12 percent of poor males were labor union members, compared to 28 percent of all male workers.[13] However, the discrepancy between the two groups is largest in most of the occupations where the poor are found. For operatives, exclusive of transport equipment operators, 48 percent of all males were union members, while only 28 percent of all poor males working in this capacity were members. Forty-four percent of transport equipment operatives carried union cards, while only 15 percent of poor males in this occupation were union members, constituting 6 percent of all such workers.

Similar patterns are found among service workers and nonfarm laborers. Farmers and farm laborers tended not to be members of any unions (less than 2 percent of all farmers and farm laborers were union members). However, even in this group, union membership seems to guarantee higher wages: 29 percent of farmers and farm laborers not members of any union were poor, while only about 14 percent of union members were poor. Less than 4 percent of union members in all other occupational categories were poor, while the corresponding percentages for nonunion members varied from 1 percent among managers, officials, and proprietors, except farm, to 14 percent among nonfarm laborers.

The picture for females is very similar to that of males except that females are less often members of any union (only 10 percent of all female workers were union members in 1970), in large part reflecting the unwillingness of labor unions to recruit female workers to become union members or apprentices, and the tendency for unions to survive mainly in the so-called male occupational categories. Poverty rates for both union and non-union members are higher for females than for males for all occupational categories. This is in part due to the lower pay women receive for the same work that men perform, and the fact that women (and blacks) tend to occupy the lesser-paying, lower-status jobs within each occupational category.

For blacks, the general pattern is the same as for whites, but blacks are less likely to be members of labor unions than are whites (Hammerman 1972), except for the categories of professionals and managerial workers and clerical and sales workers. In all occupational categories, black union members are about twice as likely to be poor as are their white counterparts. Black males who are not members of any labor union are considerably more likely to be poor than are white males in the same occupations. In general, the poverty rates for blacks who are not members of unions are approximately three times that of white nonunion members for all types of occupations.

These statistics not only testify to the known discrimination against blacks and females which exists in labor unions but also indicate that union membership is more important for blacks and females than for white males in insuring a sufficient income. Both blacks and females have relatively insecure job positions located on the lower end of the scale within each occupational category. Union members are less likely to be fired or laid off, and they are in a much better bargaining position for obtaining increased wages, fringe benefits, and improved working conditions. While union membership does not insure self-sufficiency, it certainly seems to reduce the likelihood of becoming and staying poor. Some occupations, such as farm and service occupations, have little or no union organization, leaving most, if not all, the workers in this category with little bargaining power and in insecure and low-paying job positions (Bluestone 1974).

If the head is working full-time rather than part-time, the incidence of poverty is reduced from 20.1 percent to 4.9 percent. Also, as expected, the more members of the family who work, the lower the incidence of poverty. However, even having two or more wage earners in a family cannot definitely remove the family from poverty, especially if the family is black. Almost 11 percent of black families with two or more wage earners in 1974 were poor. The fact that one-fifth of all poor families have two or more wage earners and almost two-thirds of all poor families have at least one wage earner does not lend much credence to the culture-of-poverty notion that the poor cannot and do not want to work.

DEGREE OF POVERTY

Assuming that we know more or less accurately who the poor are and perhaps why they are poor, the question of just *how* poor they are remains to be examined. Almost two-fifths (37.3 percent) of all families in 1974 had incomes which were $2,000 or more below the level defined by the federal government as being a minimum income for providing a nutritionally adequate diet.

Although the defined level was only $2,610 for unrelated males not residing on a farm and about $2,160 for unrelated males residing on a farm and for females, almost 23 percent of all unrelated poor males had incomes at least $2,000 below this level in 1974. In other words, of those unrelated males who were poor, 22.8 percent had less than $600 in total income. About two-fifths of all poor unrelated males (40.3 percent) had an income deficit[14] of more than $1,250, that is, their income was less than half the minimum budget. The average deficit was about $1,001 for unrelated individuals, and the deficit was slightly higher for males ($1,189) than females ($907) and for blacks ($1,068) than for whites ($979). (See Table 6.)

TABLE 6   Mean Income Deficits for Selected Categories of the Poor Population, 1970 and 1974.

| | Mean income deficits | | | Change in mean deficit between 1970 and 1974 | |
| | 1974 | 1970 | | | |
Categories of the poor	in 1974 dollars	in 1970 dollars	in 1974 dollars	in actual dollars	in constant dollars
Families	$1,845	$1,419	$1,802	$426	$ 43
Male head	1,781	1,309	1,662	472	119
Female head	1,921	1,604	2,037	323	-116
Black families	2,005	1,621	2,059	384	- 54
Male head	1,853	1,427	1,812	426	41
Female head	2,080	1,769	2,247	311	-167
Unrelated individuals	1,001	806	1,024	195	- 23
Males	1,189	917	1,165	272	24
Females	907	762	968	145	- 61
Black unrelated indiv.	1,068	894	1,135	174	- 67
Males	1,286	983	1,248	303	38
Females	945	844	1,072	101	-127

Source: United States Bureau of the Census 1971, table 30; and United States Bureau of the Census 1976b, tables 40 and 41.

Among families we find that almost 64 percent of poor families have a deficit of $1,000 or more. The mean income deficit for families was $1,845 in 1974, but the deficit is larger for families headed by females than by males ($1,921 and $1,781 respectively). The deficit per family member was $485 for all families, $451 for male-headed families, but $527 for female-headed families. The same pattern holds for black families: $404 deficit per family member for male-headed families compared to $509 for female-headed families. Compared to white families, black families have a lower deficit per family member, but this seems to be mainly the function of the larger family size among blacks (4.25 for poor black families, 3.59 among poor white families), because the mean deficit is about $200 larger for black families than for white families. Black families headed by females show the largest average deficit: $2,080. Clearly, most poor people are very poor. This conclusion is also confirmed by the observation that the mean income deficit is always higher than the median income deficit for all poor groups. The difference between the two measures of central tendency ranges from $396 for male-headed white families to $215 for male-headed black families. These data indicate that the distribution of income deficits is skewed toward the end with high deficits.

CHANGES OVER TIME

Using the low-income level, there seems to be no doubt that there has been an overall decline in the number of poor people between 1959 and 1974, from about 39.5 million to about 24.3 million.[15] In 1974 there were approximately 5.1 million poor families and 4.8 million poor unrelated individuals. There has been some change in the relative distribution of poor people; poor families headed by females constituted a larger proportion of poor families in 1974 (46 percent) than in 1959 (23 percent). In general, conditions thus seem to have improved, but this improvement has benefited mainly male heads of households and particularly white male heads of households. There has been no significant change in the number of unrelated individuals who are poor (4.9 million in 1959, 4.8 million in 1974) indicating that single adults have not been able to participate fully in the economic development between 1959 and 1974.

In recent years, there has also been a significant decline in the proportion of poor people who are over the age of 65, from 18.9 percent in 1970 to 13.6 percent in 1974. This, as we have already indicated, is largely the result of increased social security benefits during the last few years. With continuing high levels of inflation, however, it is likely that more of the aged will become poor in the future because of their reliance on fixed retirement benefits. For those below the age of sixty-five the changes that have taken place would seem to be mainly a reflection of an improved employment situation between 1959 and 1974. Such changes have traditionally affected male heads of households the most and this seems to be borne out more recently by our data.

Thus, in 1959, 75 percent of poor male heads of households were working compared to 52.7 percent in 1974, and 17.3 percent were unemployed in 1959 compared to 12.6 percent in 1974. Whether this trend toward a nonworking poor population will continue in the future is not entirely clear. It is important to keep in mind, however, that we have used a definition of poverty throughout this chapter which is not adjusted for changes in the standard of living. It should come as no surprise, therefore, that the extent of poverty as defined by the Social Security Administration has been reduced, or that we are now faced with a poor population increasingly deprived of those most able to participate in the economic life of the nation. Most of those who are poor now are likely to be less able to benefit from whatever improvement is obtained in the general standard of living without considerable support from public and/or private income maintenance programs. Furthermore, since many workers may have a difficult time keeping up with inflation, the proportion of working poor may well increase in the future.

CONCLUSION

People are poor then because they are unable to work, or find work, or because they work in semi- or unskilled jobs which pay low wages. Some people are poor because they do not work full-time, whether because the cannot find full-time work, or because the work they do is only available at certain times of the year. Union membership is also an important factor. But even a person working for a minimum wage of $2.50, 40 hours a week, for 52 weeks would not earn enough, before taxes, to support a spouse and three children. Furthermore, the poor must rely to a large extent on nonearned income, in part at least because of factors beyond their control. There is no question that family dissolution may be caused by poverty and itself can cause an intensification of poverty. This has been debated considerably in the literature. For blacks, at least, it would seem that Liebow (1967) has presented a well-documented and convincing argument that the failure to obtain a decent job (both with regard to wages and job status) is a major cause, if not the most important one, of family dissolution (see also Schiller 1973; Scanzone 1970; Goode 1962; Monahan 1955; Udry 1966, 1967; Ross and Sawhill 1975).

We place here the major burden for the production and

maintenance of poverty on the fluctuating economy, the inability
of the labor market to provide enough jobs which pay a decent
wage, and the inability of the American society to provide
adequately for its aged, sick, and disabled population and their
dependents.

The poor of 1974 seemed to share characteristics which make
for permanent and long-term poverty (see Myrdal 1962): they
have low education in a time where a college degree is becoming
increasingly necessary for obtaining a reasonably good job; they
are unskilled or semi-skilled when many jobs of this type are
disappearing; they are old, disabled and ill at a time when
medical costs are increasing rapidly; they are underemployed and
unemployed and have given up finding work at a time when the
"acceptable" level of 4 percent unemployment seems an impossible dream; and they are black and female, both disadvanta-
geous characteristics on the job market.

There are strong indications that the poor have become poorer:
in almost all categories of the poor, the average income deficit
was greater in 1974 than it had been in 1970 (see table 6), not
adjusted for price changes.[16] In fact, the total income deficit, that
is, the total amount of money necessary to bring everyone above
the low income level, was greater in 1974 ($14,250,925) than it
was in 1970 ($11,447,204, $14,537,850 adjusted for inflation).
This is particularly important since there were about 1.2 million
fewer poor people in 1974 than in 1970.

Our conclusion then, must be that there may be fewer poor
people in America today than before, but their poverty is in some
ways more desperate. This conclusion is also supported by a
recent study of changes in the distribution of income before and
after government transfer payments. Danziger and Plotnick
(1977) found that the distribution of pretransfer income in the
United States has become more unequal between 1965 and 1974
and can only in part be explained by changes in the demographic
composition of the population, that is, an increase in female-
headed households and in the aged population—both groups
which traditionally have low incomes. An examination of the
posttransfer distribution of income suggests that, at best, government transfer income programs have not quite been able to keep
up with those demographic and economic forces which push
toward greater inequality. A 1976 study found that 58.1 percent
of all pretransfer poor families were still poor after receiving

social insurance benefits. Welfare benefits removed an additional 8.1 percent from poverty, and certain in-kind benefits, such as food stamps, removed 3.5 percent more. However, after all of these public transfer benefits, 46.5 percent were still poor as defined by the SSA low-income level (Garfinkel 1977, p. 5).

6   Culture and Life Style Among the Minority Poor

The weaknesses of the culture-of-poverty theory have discredited almost any attempt to identify the cultural accompaniments of poverty in the United States. The central weakness of that theory was that it ignored structural conditions and made poverty self-inflicted and self-perpetuating. It was also presumed to be a "universal" culture, shared by all poverty-stricken groups, although, in practice, its adherents (Lewis 1965; Moynihan 1965; Banfield 1970) narrowed its usage to where it seemed to apply only to blacks and Hispanics or to the recent poor in the United States. In addition, those who supported this interpretation of poverty (Miller 1958) provided very little in the way of cultural materials to document its existence, but concentrated instead on family and peer group structure. At the same time, each apparently assumed that the culture of poverty was created and shared exclusively by the poor rather than being the collective product of groups whose members— some of them not poor—had felt or shared in the disgrace of poverty.

Despite the weaknesses of this approach, it is our view that there is a cultural component in the way that diverse groups in the United States have shaped and reshaped the meaning of poverty among themselves. It is not a monolithic or universal culture of poverty as Oscar Lewis (1965) would have it, but a series of cultural traditions: those that divide the native WASPs, the immigrants, and the racial poor. These cultural traditions have not been created or admired by the poor alone, but are interpretive and expressive accounts of group poverty which are created and carried by expressive elites as well as those submerged in poverty—by novelists, by disc jockeys, by preachers, by politicians, by prize fighters, and by the poor themselves. The cultural traditions we have in mind are especially present in what has been called "popular culture," those songs, dances, ritual forms, slang terms, or styles of dress which have mass appeal although they are somewhat restricted according to their origin and primary audience. These traditions also have their "high cultural" forms as in the novels of Mark Twain, the plays of Eugene O'Neill, or the poems of Langston Hughes.

Since we are concerned with the cultural elements which have emerged from group poverty, our focus is on those forms of behavior which are primarily an evaluative commentary on other forms of behavior or social structure among the poor. This evaluative aspect is especially prominent in the case of collective representations, the celebration of folk heroes, in poems, dances, novels, or linguistic forms. Such commentaries bear no mechanical relationship to other forms of behavior, and while they often provide a blueprint for behavior, it is not always one that is followed. More often, they provide an account of group poverty so that they transform the isolated, day-to-day miseries of individual poverty into the drama of group life. It is not just that these day-to-day events are made important and meaningful, but that they are recast as archetypical group experiences. Largely through such cultural forms, the poor have become conscious of their distinctive place in American life. Among the remaining WASP poor, for example, country and western music provides the public drama for defining their relation to the wider society. The blues have played a similar role among blacks, just as the ethnic radio has for numerous immigrant groups. As Morris Janowitz puts it, ethnicity or minority group status is the "poor man's genealogy," a collective source of historic identity so that one can lay some claim to having mattered in the past and thereby, possibly, to matter in the future.

This is not to say that these cultural traditions are consequential only in promoting minority group consciousness among the poor, for each tradition is accompanied by a distinctive style of life. This style of life embodies a sort of compromise between each separate tradition and that of the cultural mainstream: minority group identity is celebrated yet combined with the patterns of conduct of the dominant culture. There are, of course, individuals who retreat almost entirely to their own cultural tradition, just as there are others who are ashamed of it and reject it. Most commonly, however, individuals move in and out of their own tradition and the mainstream as financial and situational conditions permit.

In the United States we can identify three broad cultural traditions which are responsive to visible group poverty and which dramatize its collective character: the native ethnic, the racial, and the immigrant (for a fuller explanation of these terms, see the section "Public Conceptions of the Minority Poor," below). They are not simply the remnants of an imported cultural heritage (e.g., Scotch-Irish, African, or European), although they may selectively retain some of these cultural elements. Rather, they emerge from the same fragmentation— regional, racial, and immigrant—that we have already emphasized in describing the nature of American welfare. The different traditions depend upon how their members have been separated from the mainstream of American culture—whether they have been "left behind," "kept in their place," or experienced partial acceptance as "hyphenated Americans." Each tradition, then, must be viewed in terms of the transactions across the barriers which divide American life and restrict participation in its cultural mainstream.

THE VISIBLE POOR

How the other half lives has been a continual source of conjecture in the United States, and one can fill entire libraries with accounts of what life is like "on the other side of the tracks." This preoccupation has yielded both extreme liberal and extreme conservative conceptions of the poor—conceptions that typically attribute poverty either to the stubborn discrimination of the wider society or to the stubborn profligacy of the poor. Both liberal and conservative interpretations, however, fail to recognize how fateful they are for the poor themselves. The most important adaptive problem facing the poor beyond immediate privation is the conception of them held in the wider society. The key element in this conception is a profound uncertainty about the attachment of the poor to the total society and to conventional lines of conduct. In a society where utilitarianism is a common mode of thought, it is almost inevitable that the poor be expected to have little stake in conformity or in the persistence of collective institutions. Conservatives are likely to distrust those whose material investments are thought insufficient to command loyalty or endear them to respectability. Liberals and radicals are likely to believe that the social detachment of the poor will make them easy recruits for the causes of reform or even revolution. To the extent that the poor themselves share these beliefs, their own interpersonal relations will be shot through with distrust and fear.

If most of us work at trying to fulfill the wider society's expectations, then the poor must work at altering, selecting among, transforming, or evading those expectations. What we expect of the poor is unruliness, profligacy, radicalism, false humility, a short temper, sexual license, and opportunism. The special burden of the poor is to get past these stereotypes and to discover among themselves a social order which allows them to keep life and limb together in a day-to-day routine—one that usually confines aggregates of poor people together in single residential areas. Their efforts are only more or less successful, but they all gravitate toward a more provincial world which provides its own social order while insulating them from the destructive stereotypes of the wider society.

Stereotypic expectations do not fall evenly on the poor, and the poor themselves have responded to them in various ways. Public suspicion of the poor appears greatest where poverty is compounded with other widely held reasons for doubting a person's national allegiance and commitment to respectability. If a person's residence, race or ethnicity, regional origins, religion, or property coincide to raise doubts about his attachment to national institutions and conventional forms of conduct subcultural development seems especially likely. One is inevitably led into discussions of ethnic, racial, and minority groups.

We use the term "visible poor" to indicate those who are not just poverty-stricken but are also brought to public attention by their race, ethnicity, religion, regional origins, or some other public claim that they have a distinctive background. In the United States, such bounded groups tend to be confined to residential enclaves that both separate them from the wider society and heighten their visibility: reservations, ghettos, slums, mountain hollows—some place, fairly notorious, on the wrong side of the tracks. It is also an American habit to explain affluence or poverty in terms of character, which is more easily done by paying selective attention to bounded groups where one can assume uniformity in background.

Though by no means the only poor in the United States, it is the visible poor who have been the main objects of the debates on poverty, whether conducted on television by Archie Bunker or in

Washington by Harvard social scientists (Moynihan, Miller, and Banfield). Among the many nonvisible poor are those whose poverty is not connected with their primordial status—the aged, the disabled, the slow-witted, and those who have been so damaged by institutional care that they cannot care for themselves. But the primordial groupings seem to be the only ones who have the necessary social propinquity to develop a shared style of life. Pressed together in their residential enclaves, blacks, Indians, Puerto Ricans, and groups like themselves can develop some unity in outlook and behavior.

PUBLIC CONCEPTIONS OF THE MINORITY POOR: NATIVES, RACES, AND IMMIGRANTS

By "native ethnic" we mean those groups like the hillbillies, Okies, Arkies, Cajuns, or Creoles who are seen as having an unquestioned claim to being "Americans" but who are also seen as having a distinct and in some ways anachronistic way of life. This stereotype seems to betray a profound ambivalence toward such groups, for it often combines heroic and patriotic images with a common belief that these people are unsuited for life in an urban and industrial economy. Both Daniel Boone and Sergeant York are American heroes, but it is difficult to imagine either of them working eight hours a day in a local factory.

The minority poor who are objects of this public image have often claimed to be the only "real Americans" and have held the sober ways of blue-collar America in contempt. Such an attitude seems to produce a provincial and not very steady community which extolls the independent craftsman but which also promotes a great deal of hard drinking, a prompt and physical defense of one's autonomy, and an extraordinary readiness to leave job and residence when there is any challenge to one's independence; it honors, in short, what Howell (1973) has called "hard living."

Racial stereotypes, such as those which apply to blacks, Puerto Ricans, Mexicans, Filipinos, Japanese, and Chinese, dwell less on the group's distinctive way of life as on their organic unity and the way in which indissoluble bonds among them preclude attachment to other races. Americans seem to take racial groups as descent groups within which natural and thus unalterable qualities inhere (Tannenbaum, 1946). The differences between racial groups, then, are thought to be almost insurmountable, while the features which join them are taken to be involuntary, primordial, collective, and mysterious. Since the features which identify these racial groups are those presumed to inhere in physical resemblances, the tendency is for both the racial group and the host society to emphasize what are considered to be physiological "traits" and an inborn commonality which is nearly like that of the "herd instinct."

American minority groups who have this public image may choose to emphasize their physical attributes—their sexual prowess, their strength, or their volatility—or promote equally their animal-like image as a docile but conniving herd of "natives." These various aspects of the total image are not so contradictory as they first appear. The animalistic image of American blacks leads easily to the conclusion that they can act like a troop of baboons in the collective fright of a riot or panic. The conspiratorial and insidious ways ascribed to Orientals are easily extended to an image of languorous sensuality. Like all social images, these may have little basis in fact, but they encourage the construction of racial subcultures—a pattern which emphasizes both an animalistic magnetism and a collective hesitation to join the host society. For each racial group, then, the inclination has been to model itself after the "society within the society": a people who were in, but not "of" the surrounding society. In this sense the world of Suzi Wong and that of Shaft are similar.

It is with the immigrant groups that we find the least problematic and certainly the most widely applied images. Public stereotypes of immigrant minorities stress their labor on the one hand and their alien loyalties on the other. The emphasis on labor suggests a willingness to do hard work but an incapacity to do much else. The act of immigration is taken to indicate a heartfelt expression of one's preferences, but as with the conception of all free choices in America, this preference has been regarded as potentially fickle and uncertain should it run up against material losses. The streets of America are not really paved with gold, and usually we have depended on far less to attach immigrants to the country. Immigrant status is seen as remediable, however. The outstanding attribute of our image of the immigrant has been the potential for achieving full citizenship. If the first-generation immigrant could not be trusted fully to perform skilled tasks, more could be expected of the second generation.

The immigrant, then, worked hard and lay low. This did not

mean giving up opportunities for political and economic advancement, but it did mean waiting for the opportune time. For the immigrant poor there was a long-term incentive which said, in effect, that if you work hard and look after one another, you can "raise yourself by your own bootstraps." Not all the immigrant poor bought this image of themselves, but it has remained true enough to make understandable to Americans a cautious Mollie Kaminsky or an outraged Archie Bunker.

Of course, all these images are only stereotypes, and to recognize them is only a start in understanding how the career of the minority poor has been shaped in this country. A host of additional circumstances have altered and reshaped that career. Yet it would be wrong to underestimate the power of the stereotypes and the accompanying style of life associated with each. They are not just self-fulfilling prophecies but a set of images which have "conditional appeal" in a society that does not have a well-developed national culture (Shils 1956). Under conditions of intense group competition, uneven mobility, and widely publicized inequities, these images become compelling sources of self-identification particularly for those who are especially sensitive or pessimistic about their status in the wider society. The 1960s was a period of intense minority group awareness because the growing affluence was unevenly distributed among minority groups despite the government's widely publicized claims that it was rectifying past inequities. The result was an explicit effort to foster black culture as well as many other group cultures.

The Natives: Hard Living

As Howell (1973) describes it, "hard living" is a life style especially prominent among the descendants of early settlers in the remote regions of the South. His observations probably apply equally well to a number of other groups in the Southwest, the West, and the lower Mississippi valley who have lived in remote areas long enough to have submerged their origins and to have assumed a regional, "American" identity. The difficulty in the self-definition of these people lies in the reasonable claim that they are "just Americans" (or, as they are apt to put it, "just plain folks") while finding themselves in a position subordinate to many whom they consider "foreigners." This problem is especially acute when they are faced with the unheroic discipline of factory work under alien supervision. Situations of this kind put into jeopardy both their self-conception and their faith in the "American way." What is involved here is not simply the retention of a "frontier tradition" but the selective reshaping of radical conceptions of individualism. Whether or not such virtues were always prominent in the remote agrarian regions of the United States—and often they were not—they have become the key means of turning aside destructive stereotypes and of adopting a strategy for creating a more provincial world in which some measure of self-regard is possible.

A feature of this strategy is to avoid employment in large factories and bureaucracies and to engage in work that requires little supervision or provides great flexibility: that of tinkerer, independent painter, solo mechanic, or itinerant miner, lumberjack, or construction worker. The armed services, of course, are attractive not only for their heroic roles but because they reduce the mundane responsibilities of family and home. Such occupations may work to the detriment of family stability and community life. Within the general scheme of things, however, these misfortunes can be viewed as romantic adventures.

Within this loosely articulated style of life, demonstrations of personal independence make the construction of social ties treacherous. Equalitarianism—being just another "good old boy" —is demanded, and any sign of "putting on airs" may provoke violence. Commensualism must be complete, and the "drinking bout" is probably the archetypical and most acceptable form for reducing everyone to the same status. Hard living means hard drinking. Consequently the perceived need for self-discipline is often very great, and hard living is frequently accompanied by a respect for or engagement in "hard religion." Fundamentalists, like the "hard shelled Baptist," provide the only conceivable bridle to rein in such recalcitrant individualism. In its more extreme forms, hard religion provides for unusually stiff demonstrations that one will subject himself to discipline, to a collective moral code, or to the demands of social living. "Snake handling" may be too extreme for even most hard livers, but public confessionals, speaking in tongues, and ecstatic experiences are widespread means by which hard livers convince themselves and others that they have abandoned their natural and sinful ways.

Since the demand for total affiliation is so great, the likelihood of betrayal is equally great. Associations, then, tend to be fragile, and their breakage is often accompanied by violence and re-crimination. The automobile and the ability to "just pick up and go" are especially valued. In general, individual pride is protected by only a thin skin.

Such a style of life is hard put in our central cities where there are numerous regulations, many policemen, and a labor market that does not leave much room for the nonunionized worker making a living by his wits. Hard livers have generally congregated in the unregulated shanty towns of the nation, in the old buildings left in small towns at the margin of the central cities, in trailer camps, in mining and lumbering company towns, or in shanty towns of their own construction. When forced to live in the central city, hard livers have concentrated around the most deteriorated "skid rows" which allow maximum freedom from surveillance and a minimum of community and bureaucratic responsibilities.

Because it is difficult for hard livers to participate in most forms of collective life, social observers have usually discounted them as an effective voice in the nation's political life (e.g. Greeley 1974). This judgment probably underestimates the strength of their episodic ventures into public life. As devout equalitarians, hard livers are attracted into political life when they can ride the crest of a strong populist movement or become private agents of a vigilant and "patriotic force." The candidacies of William Jennings Bryan and the Ku Klux Klan may represent the high points of their political participation. They are not insensitive to their own collective interests, but they generally recognize the hopelessness of these interests—having a desire to dismantle large-scale institutions and put "just plain folks" back in charge.

Yet, for most hard livers, Franklin Delano Roosevelt and the New Deal represented the nearest thing to a bridge between themselves and other Americans. The New Deal aimed to give Americans a new grub stake and to right the imbalances which had been produced by big government, big business, and "city slickers." Roosevelt was a Yankee and a rich man; yet somehow he inspired more trust among hard livers than either Henry Wallace or George Wallace have done. Undoubtedly the New Deal did not quite live up to their expectations. Still, the symbolism of this political venture was in the correct direction to attract hard livers—a restoration of the "American way" and some sympathy for the "little guy."

Such a style of life has been the subject of an enormous volume of fiction, ranging from Mark Twain's unrepentent Huck Finn to the more troubled and divided heroes of Wolfe and Faulkner. In Tennessee Williams's plays, even rich folks act like hard livers. These high cultural expressions have been accompanied by an incredible number of folk heroes who probably subscribe to these cultural images a good deal more closely than do their admirers. Evel Knievel, Woody Guthrie, and an entire pantheon in Nashville provide the objects of adulation if not emulation.

In an earlier period of American history, hard living was a frequent style of life and its practitioners so numerous as to be considered a major "social problem." During the early 1920s Nels Anderson (1923) estimated that 300,000 to 500,000 of these rootless rebels annually passed through Chicago alone. During the same period, Harlan County, Kentucky, achieved a reputation for rootlessness and violence that is unparalleled. Hordes of "hard livers" became visible during the time of the "dust bowl" and the Great Depression. Over the intervening years, however, their numbers have declined or, at least, they have become less visible. Vast numbers of them have found an economic niche as self-employed artisans; factory discipline relaxed to admit others during periods of high employment (e.g., the Second World War); and federal welfare programs have advanced to care for most of the aged and disabled.

However, the prosperity of the nation and especially that of the sunbelt seems to have progressively altered this tradition into mimetic gestures. The nation is receiving a mild dose of this from President Carter's beer-drinking brother (the nation's first official black sheep) and the president's own stand up confession in *Playboy* magazine. The widespread use of regional dialect on CB radio and the spread of country and western music turn the tradition into something that is more a form of entertainment than to be taken in earnest.

Still there is no reason to assume that this country has seen the last of its hard livers. There remains quite a population reservoir in the backwoods of America, and numerous other hard livers may become visible if factory discipline grows tight or there is another dust bowl (Morrill and Wahlenberg 1971). Numerous groups can on occasion emphasize their "native American" status to the exclusion of racial or immigrant statuses. The American

Indians and long term Mexican settlers in the Southwest can find in their claims to long-standing residency an appeal in heroic individualism. As some hard livers vacate the ranks, others may fill them.

Racial Groups: Stoic and Militant Separatism

Separatism is a long-standing American problem, and most observers would consider it the national problem—the American dilemma (Myrdal 1962). Largely, although not entirely, separatism has been a racial issue. On neither side of the barriers of race does there exist an easy avenue for assimilation. The recent Civil Rights movement embodies the mainline hope of the society for the integration of racial groups, but the subsequent emergence of nativism and the growth of racial consciousness demonstrates the tendency to use race as a basis for developing defensible styles of life.

Those who are defined and disadvantaged by the boundary of race are apt to think their case hopeless except within a society of their own. More privileged observers on the other side of the divide are inclined sometimes to agree; to recommend revolution and self-determination if they are sympathetic or outright repression if they are totally unforgiving. For those who see themselves on the unfair side of the divide, separatism in one form or another has been a persistent and understandable temptation. For the Chinese, the pre–World War II Japanese, and the American Indians the favored pattern has been to withdraw into a segregated community and bring as little attention to themselves as possible—what one might call "stoic separatism." Among blacks the strategy has been a far more outspoken demand for either a separate community or equal status for "black values"—what one might call militant separatism.

For both militant and stoic separatists, the adaptation to racial stereotypes makes especially problematic those tokens of civility that ordinarily assure others that one is sensitive to public opinion, willing to go along with convention: the handshake, the hushed presence when confronted with sacred or patriotic objects, the avoidance of loudness, the modest display of clothing and wealth, and so on. For stoic separatists, these tokens of civility become only instruments for drawing attention away from themselves. Acquiescence to their use, while insincere, nonetheless serves to show that one is harmless. Militant separatism requires something near the reverse; outright iconoclasm or a deft hand at puncturing the pretensions of respectability. The tie as a sign of affluence, "politeness" as a way of putting "ladies" at ease, a well-scrubbed exterior as a means of saying that one is both clean and moral—such patrician gestures are still frequently accepted as if only the provident and respectable could afford a tie, learn good manners, or suffer the application of soap. Sponsors of this cultural tradition—and it is a part of our cultural mainstream—are so easily offended that it is a constant temptation to do so. But there is also a temptation to adhere ardently to these nostalgic versions of mainstream culture—especially when it is to one's economic advantage and when one's cultural group is small and nearly powerless.

The choice among these forms of separatism has always been difficult for racial groups, especially for blacks. Between Reconstruction and the First World War, the idea of the dual community of blacks and whites was widely adopted and found strong support from Booker T. Washington and his followers. In the same period, however, Marcus Garvey and his Back to Africa movement began to grow. Since at least the First World War, militant separatism has gained ground among blacks, and by now the image of the "Uncle Tom" has been discredited. Among Orientals, the record is more consistently that of stoic separatism. After their first militant contact with the Irish in California, the Chinese have carefully cultivated their own separatist community and an awesome capacity for disarming anyone who might expect them to be dangerous, aggressive, or disrespectful. Militant separatists among the Japanese were pretty nearly thinned out during the Second World War when the mainland Japanese were placed in "relocation camps" and later returned to Japan if they looked "uncooperative." In the case of the American Indians, only in the last decade or so have these groups moved toward a more militant expression of their separatism.

The current pattern of adaptation of racial groups is a rather poor representation of the contortions each has gone through during the last 150 years. Despite a post–World War II rapprochement in the relations between Orientals and whites, the treatment accorded Orientals has not over the long run been so different from that accorded to blacks. The idea that one traffics in drugs, is a sexual athlete, or finds real comfort in squalor and slime has been omitted from the Oriental stereotype only since the Second World War. Public concerns about family structure especially afflict blacks at the present time. Although for the past thirty years or so, Orientals have generally been associated with filial piety and family pride, yet throughout most of their history in this country a vast number of Orientals have lived outside the steady discipline of family life, and a common living arrangement among them has been that of the all-male barracks in a dingy apartment.

Since the Second World War, stoic separatism has become all the more characteristic of the Orientals, while the blacks and the Indians have become more clearly militant separatists. For blacks this has meant a flowering of those cultural devices which puncture the balloons of civility. A loud and boisterous style which extolls extemporaneity and discounts cautiousness has become a hallmark. Included in this style is a celebration of athleticism, a primal capacity for "self-expression," and an affirmation of sensuality. Vast numbers of whites have responded with encouragement, taking up the musical forms of blacks, adopting their hairstyles, mimicking their clothing, and, in general, helping to lead an onslaught on conventional expressions of civility. The now rather widespread use of the term "mother-fucker" provides an extreme but not isolated example.

Encouraged in this manner, blacks have sought to create a culture of their own while at the same time denying that this culture contributes to their poverty or stigmatization. If one takes this argument literally, black culture becomes innocuous and inconsequential. Black culture is far more important than these liberal apologies would insist. In a peculiar way blacks have been faced with the special problem of having to disown their past and the public conception of them in order to gain social acceptance. Thus, those who have experienced a widening of opportunities have had to reassure those left behind that they have not been abandoned. One tendency, then, has been to celebrate without discrimination whatever is attributed to those left behind. Thus, in its most extreme form, all things black are beautiful.

Undoubtedly this sort of undiscriminating response to "black culture" has already slackened (Jackson 1976), and leaders of the black community are preoccupied with distinguishing between that which is worth keeping and that which is self-destructive. The cultural tradition they draw upon is unusually rich, especially in its musical forms, heroic critics, famed entertainers, and exceptional athletes. The limits of such a tradition are that its high achievements tend almost invariably to lie outside the realm of safe conventionality and provide little endorsement for the restrained caution, unglorified discipline and limited ambitions which must be the main aim of most people in a modern industrial society. Many blacks have achieved despite the odds, and in following this precedent, other blacks become high-risk gamblers.

This sort of high-risk life has achieved ritual endorsement in some urban black communities, and the growth of violence and the fragility of social relations have been of concern to even some of the most militant black leaders. Perhaps the outstanding feature is a parody of conventional norms of abstinence, individual responsibility, and the Horatio Alger myth. Muhammad Ali excels at this to the point that his abilities as a comedian are beginning to overshadow those as a boxer. Such activities are often a form of "play," and it is a widespread form of entertainment among submerged groups who are especially sensitive to the hypocracy of their "social betters." And the normative claims of these "social betters" are particularly vulnerable at the present time, with the great emphasis on consumption and the widespread corruption of people in high places.

Ritual iconoclasm of this kind, however, is apt to create uncertainty about when one is "just playing" and when one is "for real." Since it derides practically all conventions, its assurances of good intentions need constant reestablishment. Thus, over the last fifteen years blacks have had to be extraordinarily creative in manufacturing new symbols of their unity: special handshakes, flags, new hairdos, new forms of deference, and a vocabulary sufficient to fill half a dictionary. As with any dramatic change in the devices of communication, the rate at which different persons incorporate the devices into their behavior is uneven and accompanied by a good deal of anomie.

Over the long term, black culture in its stoic form has provided for an extraordinary level of self-discipline and a capacity to turn aside social stigma. In its more militant form, it has provided one of the main social criticisms of the United States. It has surfaced in our high culture—in the novels of Richard Wright, Eugene Motley, Ralph Ellison—in the extension of humanist goals in Protestant religion, and in the creation of distinctive American idiom. Above all, it has given us relief from both tedium and the bombast. The contrasting themes of self-denial and self-expression are particularly well combined in the blues, America's main contribution to musical forms.

Yet it is also clear that these contrasting themes of stoic and militant separatism have not been effectively synthesized so as to give blacks a clear "design for living." Eldridge Cleaver's shift between extremes dramatizes the dilemma produced by this cultural tradition and the persistence of the line between pessimists and optimists with respect to integration. The tension has been remarkably productive in art forms, in highlighting the predicament of blacks, and, if recent presidential politics are any indication, in welding them into a more effective political constituency.

For other racial groups, stoic separatism has been by far the dominant tradition and a fairly safe avenue of upward mobility. The Japanese, in particular, have won so much public acceptance that they are being quickly absorbed by the nation's centers of higher education, its large business firms and social groupings. The Chinese have long been accepted as good citizens, though selected segments of their community—in part reflecting recent immigrants among them—have begun to adopt the language of militant separatists (Light and Wong 1976). The Indians are even more outspoken, and the turmoil surrounding Wounded Knee is certain to figure in subsequent efforts to create a common and distinctive cultural history to which all these tribal groups can lay claim.

On balance, it is surprising how closely the small racial groups in America have adhered to the pattern of stoic separatism—the Indians on their reservations, the Chinese in their tourist centers, and the Filipinos in agricultural labor. So long as they can disappear into relatively uncompetitive niches, these groups call little attention to themselves. They have also produced surprisingly little in the way of literature, new musical forms, or a fresh statement in the American vernacular. They are really our "invisible men," our people without a literature, an American history, a dance style, or a popular music of their own. Yet as these words are being written, a major American Chinese novelist is emerging, whose preoccupation is with the stoic acceptance expected of Chinese women (Kingston 1976).

The Immigrants: Marginal Man

Of all the life styles practiced among the minority poor in the United States, that of the immigrant ethnic has received the strongest endorsement as an avenue of self-advancement for the minority poor. Since most of those making that endorsement are themselves onetime immigrants or the descendants of immigrants, their prescription for "how others could do it" is understandable. However, their model for assimilation assumes that the boundaries between all groups are as bridgeable as those that divide "ethnic" or "nationality" groups. The boundaries are seen to consist largely in "customs" which, although ingrained, could change over time.

Formative of this outlook was the assumption that foreign customs were obviously inferior to American ones and that anyone in his right mind would prefer the latter if given enough time and small increments of opportunity. The emphasis, then, was upon "waiting one's turn" and taking opportunities as they came. The search for an appropriate style of life was to be guided by the dictum "work hard, lie low, and don't look gift horses in the mouth."

For the immigrant, then, the problem was to give his foreignness a low profile and at the same time to use his ethnicity when opportunity struck. The resulting style of life was one that made it necessary to keep intact one's ethnic alliances while giving more than lip service to the claims of "Americanism." Above all this meant a "busy" style of life, keeping in touch with one's ethnic peers while striving to show that hard work was not just a native American virtue. Necessarily it was also a style of life which required the accumulation of tokens of good behavior—homeownership, fresh curtains, ironed sheets, family propriety, sobriety—along with an occasional aggressive assertion of one's power and numbers.

Ordinarily this style of life was modest and provincial, but it was always balanced by a certain opportunism and forcefulness. A substantial minority of the immigrants to the country simply went back home, some because of early disappointment and more after they had acquired some wealth. Some of the Irish, Jews, and Italians became easy recruits into organized crime. Ethnic politicians aggressively used their nationality and ethnic organizations to put themselves on the ballot to replace "natives" who insisted that the "issues" or personal integrity (generally presented as patriotism and piety) should take precedence over "sectarianism." Some immigrants attempted to beat the WASPs at their own game and insisted on excelling in the arts, in the sciences, in charity, and in industry. The early and very sizable immigration of the Irish seems to have especially promoted their visible participation in our political life, although concern for propriety (as among the "lace curtain" Irish) was strong. The large and early population of German immigrants was much more cautious, especially after the trying periods of the two world wars.

These departures from modesty and patience led to episodic expressions of outrage from the wider society, but generally the local ethnic community managed to restrain its members to the point where they would keep a low profile. The recommended pattern seemed to have been a dual one of limited but continued participation in the ethnic community while gradually gaining a larger role in the wider society. Traditional religious preferences were usually retained along with many food preferences. Within the family, distinctive age and sex roles might be continued but were not flaunted. In some places ethnic newspapers and organizations flourished, but these institutions usually made exceptional displays of patriotism. Ethnic politicians might depend upon the support of their countrymen, but they were often compelled as well to support candidates of other ethnic groups as part of a "balanced ticket."

Above all, immigrant populations quickly accepted the notion of self-help and the attendant forms of local organization. The settlement houses were greeted with enthusiasm, though sponsored largely by outsiders. Ethnic churches were turned into social centers which spent six days a week dispensing charity, citizenship classes, and practical training and on the seventh day often gave a liturgy in abridged form. Informal efforts at mutual aid were probably even more widespread, and certainly they were highly recommended as a way of advancement. Immigrants got plenty of practice at pulling themselves up by their own bootstraps.

The immigrants and their descendants managed to transform selected items in their conduct into patriotic expressions of trustworthiness and good intent. Their church going, self-help charities, voting loyalties, family solidarity, and entrepreneurial aggression became "American." By the 1960s this pattern was being given special praise because blacks, Indians, and Puerto Ricans were making public expression of a more violent, separatist strategy. In this development the blacks, Puerto Ricans, and

Indians may have done little for their own cause, but they certainly made the immigrant groups look especially good by comparison. Those who remained poor and still thought of themselves as immigrants or the descendants of immigrants were probably increasingly constrained by a widespread pride in their "patience," mixed with a good deal of resentment toward others "who were making all the noise." Their predicament was an old one: somehow to find a balance between the provincial pursuit of their own self interests and the collective display of allegiance to the wider society.

The European immigrants—at least those arriving after the Civil War—have loomed so large in our account of Americanization that their career tends to dominate our notions of what happens to minority groups once they reach this country. Indeed, they form the model from which most sociological accounts are derived. These accounts tend to emphasize generational depth (first, second and third generation) or locale and class origins among immigrants (shanty Irish or lace curtain Irish; eastern, western, or southern European, Catholic or Protestant; northern or southern Italian, etc.). Such distinctions may have been brought into relief by the European immigrants themselves because of their own concerns with respectability and the degree to which they could meet "American standards." As marginal men, they were especially inclined to make marginal distinctions which measured their approach to those standards.

Thus, American sociology has been shortsighted when it has taken the European immigrants as a model against which to evaluate the "progress" of other minority poor. The graduated distinction of their origins and culture from that of this country— and the United States is very much a fragment of European culture (Fallers 1973)—has also led to a strategy of gradualism in the achievement of citizenship. In one sense it is remarkable how successful this strategy has been, and even by 1950 (Bogue 1959) the immigrants had outdistanced the native ethnics and racial minorities in economic achievement. In another sense, however, the halo of poverty still hovers about immigrant minorities both as a kind of cultural lag and as a special claim to "represent the poor." Immigrant leaders still seem to be convinced that they represent the poor, and some like Novak (1971) are deeply offended when they are recast as members of the "overclass" rather than the "underclass." Others, especially the Jews, are reluctant to abandon their role as spokesmen for the poor, although poverty among the Jews is mainly a specialized problem of the aged. Thus, immigrant minorities seem somewhat confused by their own success, not quite able to accept their role as elites in American society nor willing to relinquish their "chosen people" role in speaking for the remaining minority poor in the country. The debate between blacks and Jews (Baldwin 1969) and the emergence of "ethnic consciousness" (Novak 1971) are high points in this transition which dramatize a more general problem. The blunt fact, of course, is that the European immigrants represent the privileged and no longer the poor.

This new level of attainment and its recognition among the immigrant poor will be difficult to accept. Their habit of thought and sociological publicity leave the European immigrant with the conception of himself as someone who is especially representative of the poor and hedged in from every side. The solid wall of WASP resistence is one of their central claims to unity. This watershed in Americanism surfaces just as those of immigrant origin are making strides in contributing to national culture. There is a long line of ethnic literature—tin pan alley, the movies, advertising, and the like to which European immigrants have contributed. The Broadway musical, the pop song, and the jingle are largely their contribution. So are many of our novels since the First World War. But, by and large, the European immigrants seem to be moving toward "high cultural" productions and away from the commercial successes of popular culture. More and more they speak to the top of society and not to its bottom.

The Transformation of Minority Cultures into "Americanism"

The divisions between regional, racial, and immigrant groups are the major boundaries in American society, but they are boundaries that have shifted from time to time, and there has been variation in relative distrust among groups. Sometimes the boundaries of race have been enlarged to include such groups as Mexicans and Jews. At other times these boundaries have shrunk, with a corresponding expansion of those considered "immigrant."

One way of addressing these variations in minority group status is to recognize that the distinctions we have been making between "hard livers," "separatists," and "marginal men" are analytical distinctions which apply to all American minority groups, although more to some than to others and more at some times than at others. We have chosen to emphasize the more durable features of the boundary which separates each segment of the minority poor from the cultural center of American society. But there have been marginal men among racial minorities, separatists among native ethnics, and hard livers among European immigrants. One need think only of the marginal status of blacks who pass as whites, of the continuing secessionist sentiment among some Southerners and the pronounced bohemianism among some second- and third-generation European immigrants. These cultural styles are not especially characteristic of the minority poor, but they are often related to a strong sense of group status in American society.

Group poverty, however, remains the force which generates a special consciousness of minority-group status and the cultural elements which provide an evaluative account of that poverty. Thus, the bearers of each of these cultural traditions—hard living, separatism, and marginal man—are likely to change. American society tends to queue up minority groups, so that as each advances another may lay claim to the status it vacates. For example, as hillbillies, Cajuns, Okies, and Arkies and others pass into respectability, older Mexican, Indian, or French Canadian residents may begin to lay claim to the "frontier tradition" of "hard living." And as the notion of racial separateness narrows to include only blacks, groups such as Cubans, Puerto Ricans, and West Indians may come to be more clearly identified as immigrants or marginal men.

All these ups and downs over the past have tended to defy our folk model of the "melting pot." The continued resurgence of the distinctions between racial, immigrant, and native ethnic groups, especially during the late 1960s, has brought some observers to the conclusion that there is no substantial long-term change going on—only alternative periods of conflict and relative peace between these populations and the wider society. This view, however, seems as short-sighted as that embodied in the melting pot model. After each period of conflict and heightened attention to these societal divisions, there has been change, although the words "assimilation," "acculturation," and "absorption" do not capture fully what has transpired.

A more useful although not very elegant metaphor may be that of a rachetlike motion—a series of discrete periods of conflict in which some minority groups, but not all, raise themselves a notch—but often only a notch. They do so first by taking some steps to legitimize themselves as "Americans," and second by increasing their participation in the wider society. This means both that ethnic, racial, and native groups are enlarging the definition of what is "American" and also that they are incorporating features of the wider society into their own self-definitions. We may recall the way in which the hard-working habits of the Slavs were rechristened as an example of the American "work ethic" during the 1960s. It was once thought that such work habits were symptomatic only of a "weak mind and strong back" among Central Europeans. Rather than rejecting this recent redefinition of their "heritage," the Slavs came largely to accept it and to use it as a basis for insisting on a somewhat greater role for themselves and their organizations in public affairs—not just as Americans but as Polish-Americans, Croatian-Americans, or Hungarian-Americans. In this instance and countless others, the boundaries between groups do not disappear. As Park recognized, "old world traits" (I would prefer the phrase "new world symbols of old world origins") do not simply disappear but become transformed as elements of the national culture. The process is not simply one of "pluralism" disguised as Americanism, for the selective pressure is great and the competition among groups is continuous. It is the hard work of the Slavs that we call "American" and not his purported anti-intellectualism and country manners. In the course of such changes both sides must give way. The minority group must swallow some of its pride and keep its skeletons closely guarded in a collective closet. The wider society must accept minority group virtues as native products while turning a blind eye to patterns of behavior and stereotypes which previously have spread distrust. Notching upward in this fashion is by no means inevitable or uniform among minority groups, for the bargaining among them and the wider society depends heavily upon their competitive advantages and the pressing sense of need which occasionally comes to make their loyalty as full citizens more valued.

Despite the continuing weakness of our national culture and the presence of submerged groups, one cannot help but be impressed with the extraordinary acceptance or inclusion of minority group culture. Since the flowering of New England literature, practically all of our literature has been dominated by minority writers or themes that dwell upon their status and way of life. Distinctive "American" dance and music is almost entirely a minority group creation. Pictorial art in America never achieved much independence from European models, but such of it as has (Bellows, Homer, Wyeth, O'Keefe) seems to dwell on the regional, ethnic, and racial character of the country. It is especially in popular culture that minority group culture seems to penetrate the mainstream and get transformed into American culture—in our comic strips, in our radio programs, in our Broadway musicals, and in our movies. Indeed one might argue that cultural integration is the leading edge of minority integration and that it is through the selective acceptance of minority group culture that other avenues of integration are opened.

Such a conclusion does not lead us to the view that American culture is only a random sampling of minority group cultures or only the "low culture" of the poor transformed into the "high culture" of the few. Some sort of competitive process is at work, and its selective principles are not simply those laid down by WASPs who have the advantage of establishing our first "effective settlement" (Zelinsky 1973). These selective principles are extremely difficult to define, as is evident from the tortured decisions of the Supreme Court which is the central arbiter of culture in our society. The full meaning of our national culture exists only in its outlines, and the broad doctrine of "equality of opportunity" shapes the process by which we meander toward its accomplishment. The minority poor and those who are sensitive enough to share in their public status have made significant contributions to this skeletal national culture. However, they are not the sole contributors to our national culture, and, in any event, the competitive process does not simply pit cultural forms against one another.

7 Status and Citizenship Among the Minority Poor

While the cultural traditions of minority groups have given poverty a separate meaning in each case, we must consider their relative competitive position in order to understand long-term patterns of minority mobility, assimilation, and acculturation. Popular debate often confuses the issues by a series of hasty assertions: that contemporary minority groups wish to preserve their culture to the exclusion of the wider American culture; that the opportunity for mobility has finally closed on the remaining poor; or that the past mobility of other minority groups is either a myth or a form of cultural genocide. These views mistake the language of minority group negotiations for an actual description of their present status or goals. Inflated statements about the separatism of minority groups are meant to pressure their opposition into acceptance, not rejection and mutual isolation. Otherwise these statements would have little rational intent, since they are usually paired with the declaration that the opposition must give way rather than insist on cultural separatism itself. In minority group negotiations one gains most by being proved wrong about all the negative assertions one makes about the opposition.

Relative competitive position must not be conceived of narrowly to include only occupational competition. Occupational competition is important, but so are geographic location, historic tests of citizenship, the struggle for internal community control, and the changing bases for participation in urban politics. What on balance is most important is the achievement of citizenship—a trusted place in American society where one's investments and achievements tie one to the nation and reduce the fragmentation that we have persistently returned to in our analysis of American welfare.

ECONOMIC NICHE

The more nearly a minority group confines itself to an uncontested economic niche, the less likely its poverty and social character will become a focus of national attention, doubt, suspicion, and distrust. The Chinese, Japanese, Greeks, and Filipinos in America have been so confined over fairly long periods of time, but the economic ledge they occupy is easily overcrowded. For example, the relatively large influx of "Hong Kong" Chinese over the last decade is beginning to overrun the small-scale tourist industry of some Chinatowns, threatening their capacity to maintain local peace and a reputation for "taking care of their own" (Light and Wong, 1975). Filipino nurses seem in no proximate danger of running into competition or much suspicion, although male Filipinos, concentrated in the more competitive positions of farm laborers in California, have frequently aroused at least local apprehensions over their respectability (Jenkins, 1975). Mexican steel workers are entering into competition with well-established Slavic workers (Kornblum 1974). Since the federal government's renewed support of affirmative action, blacks have been brought into conflict with numerous old-line ethnic groups, especially those in the construction industry (hardhats).

In an expanding economy, the more submerged minority groups tend to take the offensive in charging others with ill will, clanishness, and repression; in a retracting economy, on the other hand, it is usually the dominant groups that accuse minority groups of subversion, pleas for special treatment, and disorderliness. The claims of the aggressors center on "justice" and those of the latter center on "law and order." By no means does this mean that minority group conflict simply reflects general economic cycles. Each of the economic niches is subject to its own trends, and generally they only partially coincide with macroeconomic trends. The tourist trade for Chinatown seems to be booming despite current "stagflation," and the central problem is the influx of new immigrants, especially illegal ones. The garment industry has undergone a long term decline in the United States, largely because many of its operations can be so routinized that they can be exported to other regions (e.g., the South) or other countries (e.g., Puerto Rico). The demand for domestics has undergone a similar decline over a longer period, partly because of the growing availability of mechanical "household utilities" and partly because having a servant is no longer a mark of respectability. The Greeks are heavily dependent on the restaurant trade, the Jews on the garment industry. Haitians and West Indians are probably even more dependent on the trade of our northeastern airports. In general it appears that our smaller minority groups are concentrated in economic niches which depend on an expanding economy and a large volume of discretionary income. Large minority groups like the blacks and Hispanics seem much more heavily involved in basic industries and to depend upon long-term economic growth for employment.

The supply of labor to and from each of these minority group niches helps determine whether or not each niche become overcrowded. High immigration has continued to imperil the status of Puerto Ricans and Mexicans. After a long decline in black birthrates, a growth in black births over the last fifty years is increasing the relative supply of black labor. A very high birthrate among Mexicans tends to endanger any economic ledge they attempt to occupy. A large number of illegal immigrants, running from four to eight million, arouses vague fears that the attachment of some groups to the United States is being eroded by new entrants with little or no economic stake in the country. The political crisis concerning illegal aliens involves much more than an increase in our welfare burden or reduced job prospects for other minority groups, particularly blacks. Illegal immigrants cast a shadow over the claims to good citizenship of legal entrants to the country, especially of Mexicans, other Hispanics, and Caribbeans. In the deepest sense, illegal aliens present a moral and legal problem as well as an economic one.

While economic niche, labor supply, and economic expansion and contraction underlie most minority group conflict, that conflict is not necessarily expressed in terms of jobs, income, or security. These elements are always present, but disputes seem to center more on law and order, repression, patriotism, and justice. Material interests are at stake, but they are typically enlarged into status politics before they can enlist people into opposing sides. During periods of economic expansion, minority groups tend to make even more insistent demands and to threaten separatism and social disorder to make their case, while their opponents call for law and order, question the national allegiance of minority members, and hint at the "subversion within." During periods of economic contraction, minority group members tend to compete with one another and fall into such discord that they cannot present a united front. Then outsiders are apt to give voice to sociopathic interpretations of internal disorganization among minority groups, while minority group leaders try to work behind the glare of public attention, some seeking favors from established political officials while others threaten to unsettle these quiet trade-offs unless they are included.

Much of the time, of course, there is considerable stability in the economic niche occupied by the poorer minority groups, and people in various niches more or less ignore one another. However, very intense conflict seems to occur when a minority group attempts to enlarge its niche, as when the blacks sought to gain further access to the construction industry in the late 1960s or when a number of immigrant groups supported the union movement (Wilensky 1966). Groups such as the Jews and the Japanese have been able to extend their economic niche by the indirect route of higher education while meeting relatively little opposition. This avenue of expanding one's economic niche seems to be increasingly attractive to minority members and may turn higher education itself into "economic niche" with quotas, affirmative action, and turmoil over the relative standards for different minority students.

What is really at stake is social acceptance: as patriots, as good workers, as people committed to the "regular political process," as decent parents and sober residents—in short the whole range of features that go into the notion of citizenship in this very fragmented society.

GEOGRAPHIC NICHE AND SOCIAL VISIBILITY

Some American minority groups have been so widely dispersed or so concentrated in remote regions that their presence has scarcely been felt by the wider society. American Indians are a prime example. Not necessarily by their own choice, they come into contact with most other Americans primarily as a tourist attraction. Locally they may be the object of considerable dislike; the dirty, drunken, shiftless Indian may be the popular image. But for most Americans, the Indians are still noble savages, quaint carriers of enlightenment images of physical purity, personal dignity, and honorific warfare that have been lost to the rest of the world. We emphasize these traits in our introductory anthropology classes ("the Hopi way") and on the buffalo head nickel, and while this sort of antiquarianism may offend some Indians, it protects others from widespread hostility. The recent conflict at Wounded Knee represents both a change in their geographic niche and a widening of mutual hostilities as the Indians move off the reservations and begin to compete in the mainstream of minority group relations.

Regionally, American blacks are very widely dispersed, with many of them concentrated in the very centers of decision making in our larger cities—Washington, New York, and Chicago. Like the Jews, who are similarly concentrated, they tend to excite the suspicion that they are so near the nodes of decision making and power that they exercise undue influence. Concentration in the major urban centers, however, can work to the advantage of a minority group for the very reason it arouses suspicion: it does make a group difficult to ignore, and members of the group constitute an important electorate that must be won by city political machines that hope to have a hand in the "king making" of presidential politics.

For a long time the Mexicans were concentrated in the American Southwest and remained invisible outside that region. By the 1930s however, they had begun to reach major urban centers like Chicago, and even earlier such places as Los Angeles, Pueblo, San Francisco, and the larger cities of Texas. They have become widely dispersed and are no longer just a regional "problem." During the 1960s the reduction of the *Bracero* program increased their competitive edge as agricultural laborers and brought them to the attention of the nation. They made strong advances in unionizing their labor and in advancing into new economic niches (Jenkins 1976; Kornblum 1974). But the new competitive position of the Mexicans is in constant threat of being undermined by two other conditions: a very high birthrate and a sizable influx of illegal immigrants.

For a very large group, geographic concentration can also be of some advantage, as in the case of the Germans and Scandinavians in Wisconsin, Minnesota, and the Dakotas. Not only did these groups happen to settle in a relatively rewarding region at the periphery of the Great Lakes and the American urban heartland, but their concentration was so complete that they were allowed to carry on their own economic and political life relatively unchallenged. An occasional tendency to elect socialist mayors scarcely reached the national press, and the region has produced many blue ribbon candidates (R. M. La Follette, Hubert Humphrey, and Walter Mondale, to name only a few).

SIZE AND ELECTORAL STRENGTH

The blacks in America are a very large population, nearly 12 percent of the total. They are also probably the largest single group with a common primordial identity. While heavily concentrated in the more rural regions of the South, in uncontested economic niches (e.g., domestics), and in the least visible portions of our principal cities, their numbers are so great that they cannot help but unsettle those who see in racial discrimination and poverty a volatile mix. They are so numerous, so dispersed, and yet so distinct a group that their presence and potential power cannot be disregarded. In the 1976 presidential election they provided the winning edge.

For smaller groups, the growing solidarity of the blacks is a mixed blessing. For the Jews in a few of our larger cities, it may mean that they are being replaced as the "swing vote" in municipal as well as national elections. These two groups who have had a long history of past alliances are now at loggerheads about their relative role in at least local politics (Baldwin, 1969).

But in this respect the blacks are not especially different in American life, since large groups have always aroused more debate than small ones. Witness the case of the Germans and Italians during World War I and II; the Irish from the Civil War to World War I, and more recently, the fear that growing strength of the sunbelt will make southerners the renewed referees of national politics. In large part these shifts in national politics are expected responses to the growing strength of different electorates. After the enfranchisement of the 1960s, the United States is faced with the problem of learning how to deal with a new voting population; it is much blacker, more southern, and poorly enlisted into the organizations of party politics. Some politicians are obviously confused, while others seek to capitalize on growing, if ill-organized constituencies. This is especially evident in the efforts of national candidates to accommodate themselves to the growing voting at once of blacks, southerners, and suburbanites. For those accustomed to thinking of the New Deal as an effective coalition of cohesive interest groups, those which emerged in the 1976 presidential election must appear contradictory, and candidates for national office must appear hypocritical. Anyone who sees the New Deal as a conciliation of similar interests, however, forgets that it was mainly a national candidacy that brought together the competing interests of labor and management, and that since then it has functioned mainly as a way of brokering their division of interest to the neglect of most other groups—often regional or residential groups—and to the neglect of race or ethnicity. The FDR coalition was based on the assumption that people voted their pocket books and that an administration which could adjust the difference could win the support of both employees and employers.

As Morris Janowitz has pointed out in a recent work (1976), the American welfare state has made it progressively difficult for people to "vote their pocket books." Candidates for office cannot simply divide Americans into employees and employers and hope to capture office by offering to act as brokers between them. Class politics have been replaced by a more diffuse, special issue, the organization of constituencies. Most Americans are employees, but most of them also have some expected income from the welfare state. They are as divided by their role as public beneficiaries as by their occupational incomes: by race, ethnicity, region, or residence in the new typology of central city, suburb, or hinterland. New political aspirants, then, must consider which of these groups can be combined into a large enough constituency to promote their claim to office. Large groups, even incompatible ones, are tempting, for American politicians are brokers who seek to reconcile different interest groups rather than ideological purists who seek to satisfy a single constituency. Size of constituency especially recommends the politician who can claim to negotiate the arguments of blacks, Hispanics, suburbanites, and occupants of the sunbelt.

Because of their size, these new minorities and regional groups make their presence felt in electoral politics, particularly national politics. Their interests may be contradictory, even conflictual. What they do accomplish, however, is a shifting of national attention from old conflicts over pocketbook issues to new political aspirants and political brokers who are willing to deal in the relations between the emerging voting blocs. These new divisions are more subtle, and they center on the aspiration of more or less submerged groups to be recognized as "somebody" or to have a hand in national affairs. Group honor is as much an issue as is income. And group size is a rough index to the honor to which these groups lay claim.

HISTORIC TESTS OF CITIZENSHIP

The competitive position of different primordial groups in the United States is heavily conditioned by the extent to which their citizenship is accepted. Demonstrations of national loyalty have played an important part in establishing initial advantage in the more routine competition of party politics and the economic market. The relative advantage of these groups, then, has changed dramatically, depending on their symbolic and practical contributions to the nation state during critical periods, especially wars and periods of national dissension.

During the Revolution, descendants and settlers from England were compelled to demonstrate that their Americanism outweighed their alien loyalties. Unquestionably, New Englanders passed this test, although the South, heavily Tory and internationalist in its economic interests, was less firmly anchored to the new country and its experimental constitution. The War of 1812 went a long way toward establishing the patriotism of the South. With the election of Jackson as president thirteen years later, hordes of southerners and backwoodsmen claimed to be almost as American as the first settlers of Boston.

The Civil War reopened many wounds, and while it initiated the question of black citizenship, it did not offer blacks much opportunity to show that they were more loyal to the country than to each other. The First World War sorely tried the patience of the German immigrants. Although they did not emerge as heroic nationalists, they put to rest doubts which might otherwise have been worse during the Second World War. The Italians were treated shabbily during the later war, and the mainland Japanese were incarcerated in relocation camps. The Germans and the Italians emerged from the war with a firmer claim to citizenship than before because they had stood up well in this combat against their former compatriots. The Japanese emerged with a particularly strong claim to full citizenship, for, despite the treatment accorded them at home, Japanese-Americans manned an elite corps which put to shame most other units of our land forces in the field.

These wars represent the high points at which minority groups in the United States have been able to take major steps in placating or permanently reducing the doubts which surrounded them. There are, however, a number of smaller episodes which have provided for more or less durable tests of patriotism.

Voluntary and conscription service in the nation's land forces have progressively demonstrated willingness for national duty among many groups of relatively low social standing, particularly southerners, midwesterners and southwesterners. A widespread suspicion that Jews, college graduates, and the "city born" have avoided military duty has continued to cast doubt over the genuineness of their loyalty to the United States. The recent development of a volunteer army has been a special source of concern for those who argue that the obligations of military service must be widely and evenly distributed if the services are to continue to be a mark of citizenship for all minority groups (Janowitz 1975).

No historian has yet meticulously sought to discover how military service—particularly in the lower ranks of the country's land forces—has functioned to raise or lower doubts about the fullness of the citizenship of minority groups or their willingness to stand fast in the face of danger and privation. Many Americans have had doubts about their own loyalties to the country and about the loyalties of others (Shils 1956). During some periods of American history, vast numbers of immigrants did choose to return to their native lands after a more or less profitable stay in the United States. The "new immigrants" who came after the Second World War were widely accepted, apparently because their anticommunism was thought an insurance of their Americanism. Some immigrants, like the Cubans, are said to have made great sacrifices and to have abandoned thoroughly all hopes of returning to their native land. By contrast, the Puerto Ricans are thought to have made no hard choices in determining their national allegiances and to be commuters going regularly back and forth with the rise and fall of economic opportunity. A country which advertises itself as a "land of opportunity" cannot help but fear opportunism. A country which equally accepts utilitarianism and self-interest as guiding doctrine is bound to fear that even slight differences in economic privation will weaken the ties of patriotism.

The remarkable thing is that the United States has not broken up into racial, immigrant, regional, and nativistic territories. One reason this has not occurred is the generally good—if often unexpected—performance of minority groups when their dual loyalties and scant stake in material holdings were tested. Not all groups have been tested on such a national stage. Still, the record has, on balance, favored minority groups and has equalized their relative advantage and their competitive position as citizens. This trend toward equalizing initial advantage, of course, is subject to change, especially where there are high rates of immigration, or where international relations cast doubt over competing loyalties.

URBANIZATION AND COLLECTIVE COMPETITION

Of all the conditions affecting the competitive position of the minority poor, urbanization is one of the most complex. Some (Wilensky 1977) chose to set it aside in favor of a series of other distinguishable variables. We choose to deal with the effects of urbanization together here because they promote a collective form of group competition in the formation of interest communities in American politics. Urbanization brings minority groups into a fuller inclusion in our wage economy, into a widened visibility of their minority group status, into increased contact with a range of alternative normative outlooks, and—above all—into a competitive struggle to order life within their own local communities while also achieving a position in the power structures of metropolitan areas.

Over time, these processes have revealed a pattern. First, because of popular apprehensions, minority groups tend to be avoided as if they had some contagious disease. Sometimes the fears are mutual, so that self-segregation is joined to external avoidance. The primary form this takes is residential concentration—usually in those areas of the city which are least desirable.

Second, the management of large urban areas seems so remote, so haphazard, and so impersonal that it is difficult for minority groups to see local government as anything more than a cynical expression of established, vested interests. Everything appears to go against the newcomers to the city and to favor those who have been there longer, who are better organized, and who are most self-interested. These perceptions require a dual strategy. On the one hand, relations with the wider community appear to require a large measure of opportunism. On the other hand, relations within the segregated subcommunity seem to require maximum loyalty and public-regardingness.

The distrust minority groups share with the wider society infects them as well as the rest of us, blocking any easy avenue they might select for mutual organization. The minority groups which occupy our cities are typically strangers to one another, and their only way of understanding most of their neighbors is to accept what the wider society says about them. In addition, they bring with them a host of divisions of their own making. Ordinarily North Carolinians, for example, have nothing to do with "Sand Lappers" (South Carolinians), and the people from the western part of North Carolina often mistrust those who live in the "piney woods" (the Piedmont, true Tar Heels). Virginians often speak of North Carolinians as "white trash," a burden that Virginians believe they must bear because of the unwisdom of free movement within this country. The distinctions among Italians, Jews, and Yugoslavs in this country dwarf those that obtain among our own regional groups. Nonetheless all are cast together as a community in search of unity.

Our fears of these groups are aggregated together with their own timeworn fears of one another. The fears they share are primitive and include an apprehension for their personal safety and the security of their private property. They fear robbery, muggings, rape, physical coercion, and their own naïveté. In such a forbidding world they must withdraw to the safest enclosures they can find—natural groupings in which people are protected by the presumption that inherent proclivities make them relatively safe partners. The perimeters are those defined by kinship and family, age, sex, and territory.

These perimeters give the most evident shape to minority colonies in our cities. Newcomers tend to follow their relatives, friends, or people of whom they have heard. This pattern produces residential clusters, although not necessarily ghettos. The latter seem to originate where there is a compounding of external hostility and public suspicion which makes it judicious for minority group members to reside near areas where they are already concentrated. It is the total pattern of external hostility and internal concerns for security which produce these sizable minority group neighborhoods. However, even where both in-ternal and external fears warrant segregation, one should not overemphasize the extent of segregation and subcommunity formation. Usually the minority group establishes one or a few inner city colonies, while a sizable proportion of the population lives in dispersed clusters that do not make up a visible colony (Nelli 1970). These enclaves, nonetheless, achieve considerable importance because they provide the critical arenas within which minority group life achieves some collective forms that are widely recognized and have the potential for establishing the minority group as a collective participant in American life.

Some groups are desperately feared, and some members desperately fear persons from the wider society, while others are scarcely feared at all and have little reason to withdraw to the safe boundaries of their own people. In the last fifty years, urban blacks have found it necessary to retreat into highly segregated inner city enclaves. Over a much longer period of urbanization, the Chinese have experienced a very uneven reception, although there is little doubt that the first hundred years made self-segregation advisable. A more typical pattern may be that of the Italians. Nelli (1970) estimates that only half of the new Italian immigrants in Chicago settled in central city neighborhoods, while the remainder resided in small clusters widely dispersed in or around several neighborhoods.

Over time most minority groups seem to concentrate in our larger cities, partly no doubt because of economic advantages but also because of the city's greater tolerance and capacity to accommodate itself to multiple ethnic colonies. The Irish and German immigrants established such ethnic enclaves at the beginning of their immigration in the 1840s. At the outset of their immigration in the 1850s the Chinese were widely dispersed, but had founded urban colonies in San Francisco by the 1870s. The majority of the Scandinavians have remained widely dispersed since the major wave of their migration began in the late 1860s. The Italians, Jews, and Slavs, who started to arrive in large numbers by 1890, followed much the same pattern as the Irish: initial settlement in urban centers, with many—often most— finding their way into inner city colonies. Blacks had begun to move into major American cities by the first World War, and by 1920 they had established sizable inner city colonies.

Both economic opportunities and a range of tolerance seem to attract minority group members in disproportionate numbers to our central cities. Yet they have often become more segregated while at the same time more collectivist in their approach to the urban polity and economy. Because they are beset by rudimentary fears for life, limb, and property, their main patterns of organization are dictated by a restriction of social relations so that people associate primarily with those they consider most trustworthy. Above all, this means confining one's movements to the local neighborhood, within which one is at least known and generally of the same minority group status as one's neighbors. For numberless minority group children, the parental dictum "Stay on your own block" has been an efficient way of saying, "Stay among your own, and stay where people will know you."

The same fears warrant a further partitioning of social relations. Boys are thought of as natural rogues, and girls are warned to keep apart from them lest they be "compromised." However, this does not mean that individualism is recommended, for all age, sex, territorial, and minority group members are counseled in various ways to remain in groups. Young girls are not let out of the house unless accompanied by companions of the same age and sex. Boys are warned to stay away from older and sturdier members of their own sex who might "run over them." Adult, sexually active men and women are to remain at arm's length lest they arouse suspicion or jealousy.

The result of these simple, although almost universal, ideas is a segmental structure in which the peer group and the family are the main building blocks of social order (Suttles 1968). The most visible part of this social order is usually the adolescent street corner boy's gang. Often these groups achieve a public name and a ferocious reputation that is at least partially successful in keeping "troublemakers" (i.e., nonresidents) out of their neighborhood or block. Sometimes these groups are extended to include "midgets," "juniors," "seniors," or some similar ancillaries. But the more common association is a small unnamed clique that has a regular hangout and a narrow residential base. Such groups range from young girls clustered around a place near one of their homes to elderly ladies who regularly take up posts each evening on the front stoop. They include groups of men who regularly gather at the corner tavern or at storefronts. Within these small peer groups, there is a continual exchange of personal biographies and the construction of a social order based largely on personal loyalties. Between groups there is often a pattern of rivalry, outright antagonism, or sharp segregation. However, such groups also offer the first step toward a more secure world in which the threat of a Hobbsean disorder is lessened if not laid to rest.

These local social units also have a capacity, although a limited one, for aggregation into a larger, yet provincial order which can include the whole minority neighborhood. The hierarchy of gangs is probably the most explicit effort to enlarge the boundaries of association. A more inclusive process is the extension of a personal network among these groups so that in time a member of one group can know or be related to a member in practically all of the others. Such ties are especially significant because they make entire groups less suspecting of one another and more secure in the close juxtapositions that slum neighborhoods impose.

Such a pattern of ordered segmentation is well suited to the machine politics of our larger cities. Each segment, from the street corner group to the mother's club at the local parish house, has its formal or informal precinct captain who can deliver votes in return for favors—for jobs, for welfare, for legal exceptions and symbolic recognition. The social order of these minority enclaves makes them a serious power in American interest group politics, especially in our larger cities.

These local groups and the network among them are often accompanied by a complement of institutions that adds to minority group efforts at self-help and political mobilization. For many inner-city minority neighborhoods, the church, settlement house, union hall, ethnic association, and entrepreneural establishments provide links to the wider community and avenues for political influence and economic advancement. These institutions, of course, are not equally developed among all minority groups. Some groups, such as the Greeks, Croatians, and Jews, bring with them very exclusive forms of religious association. A few others, such as the Irish and Italians, continue to receive aid and leadership from their parent country. The Settlement House movement helped organize many minority poor communities during the period 1880–1914, but groups that entered urban areas after that time (blacks, Puerto Ricans, Indians, Southern whites) found the settlement houses relatively inactive or monopolized by their immigrant predecessors. Some groups (e.g., Slavs) were heavily concentrated in industrial employment from the start and subsequently became an important component in the labor movement (Kornblum 1974). Yet others were equally concentrated in small entrepreneurships (e.g., Jews, Chinese) and founded their own business associations (Light 1972). In general, those who involved themselves in both economic (union or entrepreneural) and local (political ward or charitable) organization achieved competitive advantage.

All of these local institutions have been significant in mobilizing minority urban communities for self-help and for the development of charitable efforts. However, their central significance was in local politics. From the 1870s to the Second World War, the big city machines dominated political life in many of our urban centers and were heavily dependent on the "ethnic vote." The union hall, church, settlement house, neighborhood association, ethnic alliance, men's club and local newspaper became critical ways of reaching and drawing that vote. Prominent politicians and lowly precinct workers sought out such groups and their leaders to put in a good word for their candidates. In exchange, jobs, favors, license renewals, and public aid flowed back to the ethnic colony.

The big city machines were an essential part of what Glazer and Moynihan (1970) have called the group relations model of urban politics, for the big city machine was the necessary jobbing agent to negotiate among ethnic and racial groups and to distribute both benefits and power. Certainly the benefits, favors, and jobs were not evenly distributed, but the big city machine offered a powerful incentive for organization at the local community level and some hope among the minority poor that they could gradually rectify their relative political and economic situation by working "within the system."

By the end of the Second World War, however, many of the big city machines were seriously weakened in their capacity to produce reliable voting majorities. Civil service legislation had eaten into the patronage available to city politicians and reduced what the machine could offer in return for the "ethnic vote." Welfare had been progressively bureaucratized with much the same consequences. By the early 1960s, the development of unionization among city employees created a new way of lining up the vote in many cities and substantially replaced local ethnic or racial communities as the key constituencies in urban politics. As Lowi puts it, these "new machines"—the teachers' unions, policemen's benevolent associations and firemen's associations— were able to make or break city administrations and city political parties irrespective of local ethnic alignments.

The result was that large numbers of the minority poor who entered American cities after 1950—primarily the blacks, Puerto Ricans, Mexicans, and American Indians—faced a different political situation than had their predecessors. As these groups developed their own residential colonies, the importance of local political organizations was greatly diminished, since about all they could do was carry out modest efforts at self-help. In most cities, the politicians were faced by the problem of placating the old-line minority groups, who rightly feared that the vote of the new minority colonies might require substantial concessions. Temporarily this predicament has produced an alliance between the new machines of city employees and old-line minority groups against the newcomers to the city. Local urban politics, then, have lost much of their capacity for improving the competitive position of the new urban minority groups.

Faced with such an unpromising urban political organization, it is not surprising that the blacks, Puerto Ricans, and Mexicans have remained rather peripheral to city politics. Standing outside of the regular political process, these new urban minorities have had to adopt a far more militant stance to draw attention to themselves and to lay claim to some political power. What does seem to have emerged is the large-scale, militant organization which is not directly linked to party politics but which does attempt to deal directly with urban political regimes. Many such organizations (e.g., Operation Breadbasket, PUSH) are confederations of smaller, local groups such as block clubs, ethnic associations, or even street corner gangs (e.g., Young Lords). To a considerable extent they represent a competitor to local parties and they have not attracted the attention of established political leaders. On occasion, however, they have been able to influence the outcome of councilman elections and local referenda and they are also able to attract the attention of the mass media to dramatize their predicament. In rare instances, as in Gary, Indiana, they have displaced the local political machine. These confederations are part of a broadly based organizational effort in which diverse residential organizations have abandoned the political parties to establish confederations concerned with specific issues: pollution, zoning, highway construction, transportation, and so on. Some are even beginning to develop national alliances (Janowitz and Suttles 1977). In these alliances the new urban minority communities may come to play a significant role if they can trade their considerable voting potential for support from other groups that are concerned with the quality of life in local neighborhoods.

Despite these emerging possibilities, the competitive position of the new urban minorities—the blacks, the Puerto Ricans and the Mexicans especially—is likely to require new institutions. Our larger cities are declining bastions of political power, although they house many of those who are poor and of minority status. The fate of our central cities, however, is closely linked to what the new American welfare state does about the minority poor. Improving their competitive position may be a requisite for supporting the capacity for urban centers to function as relatively pleasant places for others to work and play. Increasingly, the central cities have become centers of tourism, the convention trade, high culture, and consumption. As they lose their factories, the cities become spas for entertainment. Supporting these functions and making the cities safe places for such use will certainly entail some concessions to the minority poor who are so concentrated in the centers of consumption. Indeed, the financial viability of many of our older cities progressively depends upon the economic advancement of the cities' poorer residents (Suttles 1977). Unless they can become effective taxpayers, many cities will not be able to serve the large population that continues to use them as a place for consumption, entertainment, and cultural diversity. If the new minorities in the cities are to serve as its tax base, they must also be its political base.

CONCLUSION

Economic advancement may be the "bottom line" in the relative competitive position of the minority poor; yet it has been shaped by social rather than purely economic considerations. The size of minority groups, their response to national crises, the impact of continued immigration, their geographic niche and time of settlement—all of these conditions help shape their relative competitive advantage. By and large, time has worked in favor of most of the American minority poor. Economic niches have been expanded, geographic location has become less remote and less concentrated, historic tests of citizenship have been surmounted, and urban communities have been established. For the last twenty-five years, however, new minority groups have not been effectively included in our political party structure, and the old urban political machines themselves seem to be declining in a nation that is progressively suburban, issue-oriented, and disenchanted with party politics. It is the political weakness of the new minority poor which makes their situation acute and distinctive. Growing urban organizations are attempting to aggregate these aliens from party politics. They may not provide unobstructed course toward a more effective voice for these new urban minority groups. But effective advancement on any other competitive ledge probably depends on the outcome of this one.

8 *Bureaucratization, Professionalization, and the Poor*

At one time, poverty seemed so omnipresent and natural that few people thought to comment upon it. Later, affluence appeared to be so widespread that poverty for a time became invisible. Now poverty has become not merely a well-recognized reality; it is a phenomenon to be defined and redefined, classified and reclassified, counted and re-counted. Governments, university research institutes, and other agencies have come to feature bureaus of statisticians, economists, sociologists, social workers, and other white-collar employees whose task it is to calculate the varying amounts and types of poverty under a range of definitions and assumptions. Highly differentiated systems of governmental agencies minister to certain subcategories of the poor according to the particular programs and subcategories for which the agencies were devised. Additionally, some of the white-collar employees who pay attention to the poor—the authors of this volume included—have as their mission the generation of various diagnoses, pronouncements, and plans for the remediation of poverty or discussions of its presumed immutability. Such statements not only circulate through governmental, political, or academic circles but sometimes also seep through the media to the public at large, including the poor themselves. Some groups who thought of themselves as only Americans two decades ago have become acutely aware of their minority status because of the various welfare programs that disproportionately "benefit" them. To be poor in present-day America has come to mean that one has been diagnosed as poor by bureaucracies and professionals.

We contend that bureaucracies and professionals—particularly those in the fields of education and social welfare—administer and, in some cases, perpetuate poverty and more especially a sense of injustice. This process finds its clearest illustration in ways in which agencies define the roles of poor persons, as when the impecunious find it necessary to learn to play out scripts attached to such bureaucratic categories as "recipient of Aid for Dependent Children" or "participant in a work-training program." One problem with such roles is that they carry with them newly devised social labels by which poor persons become known to agencies and, at times, to the public (e.g., "ADC mother"). Once attached, such labels can be difficult to remove; the poor person may find that no matter what he does to improve his financial situation, he still is known principally by his poverty label—often an injurious, dispiriting, and stigmatizing one. Another problem with assignment and learning of poverty roles is that they may undo the person's will toward positive action. He may learn, for example, to adopt as dependent and fawning a manner toward public officials as bureaucratic procedures would seem to require; or he may come to accept as true a stigmatizing label, thus losing self-respect or reacting with self-defeating anger.

Such consequences are, of course, largely unintended by those who operate bureaucratic and professional programs. Paradoxically, reforms intended to help the poor, the undereducated, or targets of discrimination have principally changed the rules of the game under which some people come to be known as deprived and others as "normal" without altering the basic pattern of outcomes of this game. Those who are "poor" may receive additional income, but they remain in a relatively low status, perhaps one lower than they thought themselves to occupy before being helped.

Up to now, in this study, we have emphasized the fact that while various forces have coalesced in the society to make the poor visible, the United States has been unable to do anything fundamental about their situation because of its commitment to laissez-faire principles, its cultural fragmentation, and its weak political regimes. We now turn our attention to the reforms that *have* taken place, to the rather ineffective results these have had in changing patterns of inequality, to the character of the agencies and programs these reforms have helped create, and to the consequences of these efforts for the day-to-day lives of the poor.

THE BUREAUCRATIZATION OF INEQUALITY

"Bureaucratization" is a matter of degree. The sociologist Max

Weber (1946; 1947) developed the concept of bureaucracy and the hypothesis that Western institutions are moving to increasing bureaucratization. Following Weber, we think of bureaucratization as the process by which organizations come to take on rational-legal form, an arrangement that stresses efficiency, the explicit justification of activities in terms of the contributions they make to specified goals, the development of a complex division of labor and hierarchy of authority, an insistence on impersonality in decision making, and a reliance on written rules and records to guide behavior. One can think of a society as becoming bureaucratized to the extent that its central institutions come to include highly bureaucratized organizations, and, as a corollary, its citizens find their roles and statuses progressively mediated through the actions of bureaucratized organizations.

Others of Weber's ideas about bureaucratization are useful here. He was concerned with the relationship between the reduction of inequalities, or what he called social leveling, and the bureaucratization of society. He reasoned that organizations in a society having very great social distance from top to bottom could not be expected to be "fair" in applying rules impersonally to make decisions about the highly privileged and the lowly situated alike. Thus, reduction in inequalities was a prerequisite to bureaucratization. Weber suggested that once a substantial level of bureaucratization had been obtained, some kinds of social leveling would increase further, because, being fair, the bureaucratized organizations would recruit their staff members widely, incorporating skilled personnel from low as well as high social strata.

We must ask about the *limits* of this process. Does bureaucratization reduce inequalities broadly and in perpetuity? The answer must be no. First, by allocating status and rewards on the basis of achievement rather than ascription, modern society clearly alters the bases for inequalities but not always the results. Were the system to become progressively fairer, it would still allocate unequal status and rewards increasingly on the bases of differences among individuals. These would progressively come to approximate variations in inherited traits and acquired abilities. Second, the system never does become entirely fair. Persons seeking to achieve obtain many advantages by being born into better rather than poorer situations (for example, by receiving the educational benefits of birth into an upper-middle class home rather than an impoverished one). In this way, even assuming great bureaucratic fairness in rewarding persons for accomplishments, achievement perpetually confers ascriptive advantages upon the achiever's children. Third, the highly bureaucratized society is one in which achievement is not so much measured directly as gauged roughly on the basis of bureaucratic certificates—a process that seriously limits the eradication of inequalities. Finally—and this was of basic concern to Weber—such social leveling as results from bureaucratization may render large portions of the population at large relatively powerless in the face of the bureaucracy and subject to manipulation by it, thus producing a new kind of inequality altogether.

Our Hypothesis

Our hypothesis, then, is that inequality—in the last three decades, at least—is not so much being reduced as being bureaucratized. We can refer again to data on the distribution of income, which indicate that over the early decades of this century there was perhaps a very modest reduction in inequalities in this country, while recent decades have possibly seen the end to this trend. For example, information on the percentage of total income going to the poorest and second-poorest fifths of the population shows identical figures over a twenty-two-year period: in both 1944 and 1966, the lowest fifth received 11 percent (Kolko 1962).[1] Yet, over this period, bureaucratization of the public services was sweeping. It emphasized universalism and fairness and showed itself in such developments as continued civil service reforms, in belated but substantive efforts to reduce gerrymandering and racial discrimination in big city school systems, in the movement from private to public funding of welfare services, in continued extension of various social services, and in the growth of the mass system of higher education.

A major indicator of the importance of this bureaucratization of inequality can be seen in the extent to which large-scale educational and welfare organizations persistently sort and select persons in ways that result in a series of decisions that are fateful for these persons' lives. Such decisions include providing or withholding educational certificates that provide access to jobs of varying status. Americans have almost universally emphasized the positive, upwardly mobile outcomes of such decisions, but by definition these choices have another side, one described in somewhat overstated fashion by Gans:

> The legend has it, that once upon a time the public school was an effective antipoverty agency, that took poor immigrant children and taught them so well that eventually they became affluent Americans. The reality . . . was quite different: the public schools of the late nineteenth and early twentieth centuries did not help poor children, but instead, failed them in large numbers and forced them out of school. Indeed, the actual function of the public school was just the reverse of the legendary function: it certified the children of the poor as socially inferior at an early age, and thus initiated the process that made many of them economically inferior in adulthood and kept them poor. In current terminology, the school was an agency of negative credentialism. (Gans 1972)[2]

These bureaucratic decisions also involve the making of judgments on entitlement to many kinds of benefits, whether those from the U.S. Department of Agriculture rewarding farmers for not growing crops or those of county welfare departments aiding blind or disabled persons.

To say that these decisions occur increasingly through bureaucratized procedures is not simply to introduce a side issue about processes that are real but unimportant in affecting the outcome. Once set in motion, bureaucratic processes can have a substantial life of their own, as exemplified in findings of studies of hospitals, prisons, social welfare agencies, psychiatric treatment centers, and other organizations that indicate that officials, under pressure to find economical ways to get through the day, develop a set of routines for making classifications of their clientele that are "quick and dirty" but usable no matter how fateful. Thus, the agencies are likely to develop "reasonable" categorizations that embody such gratuitous assumptions about the immutability of human behavior and the persistence of social class and ethnic differences as both common sense and popularized social science may provide. The fatefulness of the categorizations may be greatly heightened as expectations, in inducing their own fulfillment, foreclose alternatives. The importance of this mechanism is argued by Rosenthal and Jacobson (1968), who report that when teachers are told that what is in reality a random sample of their pupils is likely to "bloom" academically, those so designated do indeed improve academically to an unusual degree.[3]

The bureaucratization of inequality has often been embedded in a rhetoric arguing that the elaboration of governmental services in the society would reduce inequality. The American answer to the problem of inequality has predominantly been that of extending opportunity, generally by providing additional educational, welfare, or health services and/or further procedures to open access to these services. Expansion of such services and access has, of course, been a perfectly reasonable effort to improve the lives of Americans and to let larger proportions of the population take advantage of the opportunities their society offers. Indeed, the tendency for the successful to use their rewards as facilities to protect their situations and to pass on advantages to their children is probably so great that the perpetual extension of opportunities is necessary just to keep the system from becoming less egalitarian. The justifications given for such expansion have, however, ordinarily contained a large dose of the myth that simply equalizing opportunity would produce equality itself. The idea of infinite expansion or full equalization of opportunity might have seemed reasonable in the nineteenth century before the close of the frontier could be appreciated, but not in the twentieth century. Even if the perpetual upgrading of industrial productivity seemed an unlimited way of increasing the general affluence, the upgrading of skills to man this industrial system was clearly not infinite. "Equalizing opportunities" has usually referred to policies for bringing the underprivileged to some absolutely higher levels, but whenever policies embodying this aim have been pursued, the more highly privileged groups in the society have generally been able to raise their levels as well.

A dramatic instance of the difficulties of producing greater equality of results rather than merely of opportunity has occurred over the past twenty years in education. Many resources have been devoted over this period to upgrading education for lower-class populations with the aim of substantially increasing the numbers who are able to obtain high school diplomas. At the same time, even more resources were being generated to expand institutions of higher learning, including their graduate departments, a pattern which had the general effect of raising further the educational levels (and therefore the lifetime earning levels) of the children of the middle classes. While the poor get richer, the rich get even richer. Pressure toward sustaining and enlarging inequalities through the expansion of higher education comes as this growth consumes large amounts of public funds collected through relatively regressive tax structures (Hanson and Wiesbrod 1969; Windham 1970; and Pechman 1970),[4] and as the completion of college continues to be highly correlated with family income (Bowles 1975).

There are obviously many positive aspects to the changes in the educational system after mid-century, but for the poor the results have often been extremely disappointing in the light of the expectations that the programs engendered. For example, by the time large numbers of poor minority group youth had come to attain high school diplomas, these credentials had lost some of their value on the job market. Similarly, by the time a growing minority of poor youth were able to accomplish a year or two of college training, achieving at least a bachelors' degree had become normal in many segments of the middle-class economic and social marketplace. No doubt some of these changes occurred as occupational tasks became more specialized and thus demanded higher skills. But some change also derives from "credentialism," the tendency to upgrade educational requirements so as to raise the status and perhaps narrow the competition in certain occupations, no matter what the objective demands (Hapgood 1971 and Berg 1970).

The Pseudo-Meritocracy

The meritocracy is a hypothetical, idealized system featuring a maximum equality of opportunity in which persons are to get their status solely on their merit—that is, wholly on the basis of their ability and effort (Young 1958). The concept of the meritocracy predates the rise of large-scale bureaucracy, but bureaucratization affects it too, as it provides procedures for administering, storing, and utilizing standardized test results and related indicators of merit.

In practice, American education might most faithfully be described as a pseudo-meritocracy. There is a heavy reliance on the forms of the meritocracy expressed in the "contest mobility system," in which unremitting emphasis is placed upon crossing a succession of hurdles in order to achieve in the scholastic and occupational spheres (Turner 1960). The nation has many of the trappings of meritocracy: repetitive testing, tracking systems, specialized curricula, advanced degrees, etc. Further, the educational system is steadfast in emphasizing curricula and procedures that sort students by presumed merit, despite a variety of efforts to change this emphasis. As indicated by Wilensky:

> Despite the collapse of academic standards in some departments and schools . . . , despite the egalitarian thrust of movements to increase access and reduce tracking by ability in secondary schools, technical institutes, colleges, and universities . . . , modern educational systems remain overwhelmingly meritocratic and vocational, only slightly modified by the counterculture. They admit new masses of students, but at the same time, rather than dropping standards in established curricula, they develop new hierarchies and new specialties—limited arenas of competition at every academic level, which in the end feed appropriate levels of the occupational structure; they diversify to accommodate the immensely varied genetic and cultural advantages of the individuals they process. They loosen up requirements or abolish traditional grading practices . . . but new incentives emerge, and the general emphasis on occupationally relevant performance or work habits remains. Academic credit is given for "life experiences" off campus, including social and political action or routine jobs, but that credit is ultimately honored only in the less demanding niches of the economy—in the shrinking parts of the labor force where educational entry requirements were and are low. (Wilensky 1975, pp. 3–4)

These features of American education contribute more to the appearance than to the reality of the ideal meritocracy. Despite the symbols, many traditional and ascriptive elements continue to play an important role—as in the cultural biases of IQ tests and the advantages and disadvantages that can derive from such social characteristics as socioeconomic status, race, and sex.

However "pseudo," the concept of the meritocracy can place a powerful burden upon the poor. As Michael Young, the British sociologist who developed the conception of the meritocracy, describes it, this system would have great psychic costs for the "losers." Because the system is believed to be so "fair," the losers do not have the excuse that others' success follows from what they were born into or whom they know; thus, the losers are seen not as unlucky but as deserving of their fate. Whatever the realities, this system reinforces the belief that the game at least "is supposed to" reward merit and merit alone.[5] Thus, there develops a compression of social values such that social worth increasingly comes to be defined solely in terms of academic and concomitant occupational achievement. For the children of the middle class and stable working class who are not going to succeed in the contest, the educational system develops elaborate counseling procedures to "cool out" and soften the blow for the losers (Clark 1960). For the lower classes, however, few if any cushioning procedures exist. Failures from this stratum in the pseudo-meritocracy become persons who lack the credentials to demonstrate that they are not members of the undeserving poor; they may also lack any conviction that they are deserving. Thus, the bureaucratization of inequality creates shame among members of what Marx called the surplus labor pool.[6] And the single-minded emphasis on "credentials" may detract from the genuine importance of sheer hard work which was sometimes effective for earlier generations of the poor.

Bureaucracy as a Multiplier of Disadvantage

The bureaucratization of inequality can add another problem to being poor: difficulty in knowing how to relate to the bureaucracy itself. In a study of a Brooklyn public assistance office, Gordon has demonstrated the utility of the concept of "bureaucratic competence," referring to the extent to which, from previous experience, persons have developed facility at presenting themselves convincingly to welfare officials from whom they seek help (Gordon 1972). The findings indicate that those who have greater knowledge of the jargon and procedures of the welfare department and who have had such experiences as filing their own income tax are more likely to receive a favorable decision, no matter what the merits of the case.

The need for bureaucratic competence is likely to be greater when the organizations with which one must deal are suffering from the pathologies of bureaucracy such as immersion in red tape and the flowering of the "bureaucratic personality" to whom the means or procedures of the organization have become ends in themselves (Merton 1957). Bureaucracies are not necessarily pathological, but their procedures can be applied in an extreme fashion, so "efficient" as to be inefficient, as in the Catch-22 situation of a poor person unable to receive a welfare check until she documented her housing costs by submitting her rent receipt, and unable to gain approval as a public housing tenant until she furnished proof that she was receiving welfare payments. When bureaucratic procedures are applied with little or no discretion, they can be extremely stressful and can require a considerable reservoir of both knowledge and will to cope. The poor often have a short supply of both.

Even in the absence of "bureaucratic pathology," the agencies that minister to poor persons often act in self-defeating ways through personnel policies that allocate their least qualified staff members to the poor, and through procedures which, ill adapted to many life situations, "cream off" the most "amenable" clients (Sjoberg, Brymer, and Farris 1966). The poor need not only bureaucratic competence but also great amounts of patience (as when welfare officials refuse to make appointments and keep recipients waiting interminably), high tolerance for rudeness and insult (as when indigent users of hospital emergency rooms find that no one even notices that they are trying to ask questions), and unusual readiness to make their private lives public (as when one is questioned in an open cubicle of a welfare office about one's sex life). Such demands upon the poor are exacerbated when officials are very "middle class," when there is a great shortage of resources that would make the agency's purposes attainable, and when there is much cynicism on the part of the officials—a phenomenon that grew greatly in inner city schools and welfare agencies during the 1960s. These demands are especially high for those treated as members of the "undeserving poor" (for example, people on ADC) rather than the "deserving poor" (for example, people who receive Social Security retirement benefits). It is no coincidence that the former are called "recipients" and the latter "beneficiaries."

Finally, no matter how well intended, certain standard bureaucratic procedures are simply out of gear with patterns of mutual aid that have traditionally existed among the poor. Coping with poverty has usually been enhanced by such practices as giving, borrowing, and lending money and goods in a free manner, moving about in flexible (and often crowded) living arrangements as changing circumstances require, and passing children back and forth among close and distant relatives as various persons find and lose work. Yet many such practices are formally proscribed by welfare, public housing, and school bureaucracies that are legally charged with insuring that the poor receiving public services have carefully budgeted and accountable incomes, stable residences, and unambiguous and intact family membership (Suttles and Street 1970). No doubt, bureaucratic officials rather frequently ignore minor departures from their rules, but their discretion to do so is severely limited. Efforts to increase this discretion may take the form of movements to "debureaucratize"—a term that characterizes procedures used by the Israeli government officials to relate themselves to that nation's many non-Western and therefore largely bureaucratically incompetent immigrants (Katz and Eisenstadt 1960). In the United States, such efforts to increase discretion are repeatedly halted by outcries that they would allow "laxness," cheating, and the "waste of the taxpayers' money" (the complaint of the nonpoor) or allow favoritism (the grievance of the poor).

Bureaucratization thus sustains inequality while it transforms it to some degree. The pseudo-meritocracy provides a central organizing principle distinguishing the able from the inept and justifying inequalities in the rewards obtained by each; attaching powerful stigma to the "losers." And to the exigencies suffered by the poor in terms of material rewards, social status, and personal self-esteem are added difficulties deriving from the fact that poverty must be dealt with in an impersonal, complicated, often esoteric and increasingly bureaucratic way.

The Professionalization of Reform

Parallel to the bureaucratization of inequality and linked closely to it has been the professionalization of reform. Here, "professionalization" refers to the process by which occupations work to establish a publicly accepted monopoly of expertise in dealing with some aspects of behavior that are considered to be relatively important. The most clearly professionalized occupation, of course, is medicine, in which practitioners exercise a high degree of control over health care and in which they have established an official monopoly making the practice of many kinds of health care illegal for any but qualified physicians. For self-interested along with altruistic reasons, all other white-collar and some blue-collar occupations aspire to be "more professional" by moving toward the medical model. In so doing, they unevenly work to develop theories of practice, ideologies of service, programs for designing training schools, licensing procedures, professional associations, and codes of ethics along the lines that the doctors have pursued so successfully (Hughes 1958).

By the "professionalization of reform" we mean the defining of
social problems as the exclusive province of particular occupations. Moynihan first made this term well known, pointing to the
fact that during the Kennedy and Johnson administrations,
particularly while the antipoverty program was under development, a host of specific social reforms were proposed and
implemented at the behest of various professionals—social
workers, educators, social scientists, lawyers, psychiatrists, and
others (Moynihan 1965 and 1969). In contrast to earlier periods
of reform in America, these programs were designed in the
relative absence of demands for them from deprived, liberal, or
"public-regarding" groups or from the public at large. There
were expectations at large in the society for reform at the
broadest level (the *end* to poverty!), but these expectations did
not compel any specific programs. Thus, the professionals inside
government and without, as in the Ford Foundation and other
private foundations devoted to philanthropy, emerged in the
context of generalized political demands with several heretofore
hidden but very detailed agendas for specific reforms that were
suddenly defined as imperative. As McCarthy and Zald have
argued (1973), the existence of the political demands was in large
measure dependent on the operation of "professional social
movements" for which foundations and affluent groups provided
the main support.

Our use of the term "professionalization of reform" is not
limited to the period of the antipoverty program or to Moynihan's
conception of the process. We refer to an American predilection
for developing professional ideologies—across education, social
welfare, and other occupations—that define as appropriate and
"expert" certain proposed social remedies. We can profitably
refer to aspects of what Lowi describes as the workings of
"interest group liberalism" in the design of the antipoverty
program. Lowi suggests that the principal problem to which the
antipoverty program was a response was the elimination or
reduction of injustice in the society—something that might have
been addressed directly, for example, by making racial discrimination in housing illegal. Lowi contends that the government
dealt with injustice indirectly, by "delegating good intentions"
and appropriating money. Congress allocated millions of dollars
to "eliminate poverty" without making careful specification of
the uses to which the funds could be put—money that was

thenceforth available to those professions that were competing for it in order to state and implement their own definitions of reform (Lowi 1969).

Individualistic Diagnoses and Strategies of Service

The ideologies of professional educators have beset the poor from every side. As we have indicated, in this nation problems of inequality and poverty are conventionally redefined as problems of effort and opportunity, and the corrective measures prescribed have typically involved improving the educational system. The fact that the United States developed a mass secondary school system long before the nations of Northern and Western Europe did so may be crucial to understanding why this country has been so much more reluctant to develop a welfare state than have those other countries. The United States had institutionalized a conventional wisdom in which changes in the social and economic systems were deemed unnecessary; all that was necessary was for individuals to develop the motivation to take advantage of expanded educational opportunities.

The strength of this commitment to education as *the* solution can be seen in its dominance throughout the antipoverty program. Even during the period in which community action programs were at center stage demanding "fundamental change in the system," the predominance of program resources was going to educational programs for preschool children (Headstart), manpower retraining programs, and parallel programs devoted to improving individual functioning and skills. Although it had become clear again and again that the extension of educational opportunity does not produce equality of results, its proponents continued to act as if it did.

Social work, too, acts as if it would solve problems of inequality but fails to provide a technology that can accomplish this. The principal input of social work into the solution to social problems has been to suggest the curative value of "social casework" through the provision of counseling—addressed to putting the client in contact with resources, helping him to understand "reality," and (sometimes) ministering to his psyche. However helpful this provision may be to individuals, it patently cannot address the general problem of inequality. This professional technique is, however, compatible with educational strategy: counseling people to take fuller advantage of such opportunities as are available and thereby diverting the attention of change-oriented publics from direct revisions of the system through income transfers, etc.

Education, social work, and other professions addressing social problems have shared a commitment to the service strategy, in which the prescription for change is to fund new programs that hire professionals to provide the requisite services to individuals or neighborhood residents. Educators teach about the need for more teachers, social workers counsel the provision of additional caseworkers or group workers, doctors prescribe new clinics, lawyers advocate legal aid for the poor, policemen command an enlarged patrol capacity, psychiatrists bring to consciousness the need for new "community mental health centers," and city planners construct blueprints for additional public housing projects. The universality of the service strategy is no surprise, given the dual commitment of professions to altruism and self-interest. Thus, whatever the profession making the proposal, the social reform defines the poor as clients or beneficiaries and of trained, paid practitioners as the "engine" of change. Where professions cannot prove expertise in a given area of reform, new specialties may be developed—as when "community psychology" arrives as an offshoot of psychology to compete with "community mental health" professionals from psychiatry and social work.

Competition, Coalition, and Disaccreditation

Acting in the interests of social improvement, reformers become "moral entrepreneurs" (Becker 1963); during the competition for increasing resources available in a period of high attention to reform, they can rather easily become simply "entrepreneurs." Efforts at large-scale change, no matter how grandly phrased, frequently consist only in the aggregation of existing service strategies rather than the development of new approaches. This is the case with often ballyhooed "comprehensive programs" that generally involve some combination "service package" satisfactory to each of the professions involved. As social problems gain public attention, the various professions come forward with proposals for new packages. Most dramatic in recent years has been the drug-service industry in American cities, consisting in large numbers of medical doctors, psychiatrists, social workers, clergymen (particularly black ones), and others who seek legitimacy and money for new "drug programs" (whatever these are).[7] Symptomatic of the process was a newscast in the early 1970s showing reactions of a highly placed New York City public school official to a study which showed high use of drugs within the city's schools. The official asserted that the study proved the need for immediate state or federal action to provide the "necessary millions" to set up "major drug programs" within the schools. What the content of the programs would be, or (given the paucity of knowledge of what to do about the drug crisis) how they might in some sense alleviate this situation, were matters unaddressed.

Despite the frequent willingness of the various competing professions to compromise by including themselves into comprehensive programs, the ideologies of these professions often act so as to discredit reformist claims of the other professions. This has nowhere been seen more dramatically than in the school controversies of the late 1960s in New York City between those who sought to decentralize the system (often led by social workers who, dissatisfied with the casework approach, had become "community organizers"), and the teachers who, through their union, fought mightily to preserve the prerogatives of their profession against parent groups, community groups, and the social workers (Street 1967a). This example also shows how disaccreditation of reformist claims can occur within a single profession—in this instance social work. At various times, social work has differentially emphasized each of the three world views that Lofland and Stark (1965) propose as basic to any individual defining his life problems: religious, psychological, and political. Nineteenth-century social work showed a mix of the religious and political world views, professional social work has emphasized the psychological view to the present day, and the community organizers of the 1960s came to stress the political view once again. To some proponents of the latter perspective, the concept of "help" becomes anathema; an individual in difficulty is not to be helped but must be taught to understand that he is "screwed by the system"—information about as helpful to the poor as the earlier doctrine that poverty was self-inflicted.

Across professions, disaccreditation wreaks havoc. The proponents of community control see the practitioners of community mental health as naïvely apolitical; the community mental health people in turn see the mental health "establishment" as tied to an obsolescent medical model; the members of that establishment see the others as unprofessional—and such circles surround each profession until it becomes a laughing stock. Mutual disaccreditation of reformist ideologies among professions no doubt heightens general apathy and cynicism about the potential for change among legislators, government officials, and the public at large. Paradoxically, the effort to improve the society beyond what could be expected on traditional laissez-faire assumptions induces a competition that is strikingly capitalist in character. To many of the poor as well as to other Americans, the reformers become understandable only when their zeal is seen as marketing technique. Americans have little grounds for trusting the altruism of others, even the reformers among them. Indeed, America's reformers often show an unrealistic position and a tone that seems arrogant. As Novak puts it, important publics resent "the prejudice of the enlightened against the unenlightened, the animosity of the educated against those less educated. It is the moral self-righteousness of those who regard themselves as 'liberated'" (1971). This lack of trust for those who espouse public improvement, expressed in the invidious use of the term "do-gooder," is found among professionals as well, and embodies a self-reinforcing prophecy that may be inimical to genuine reform.

Competition and pork-barreling of programs also adds to the disaccreditation of the poor themselves. Professional competition to define their situations often serves to multiply stereotypes in such a fashion that the situation of the poor is seen as even more hopeless and deviant. As Friedson says, "In the course of defining and classifying the universe which they claim needs their services, all control agencies in effect become responsible for drawing clearer lines than in fact exist in every day life or in the processes by which people were originally led into their services, and agencies may come to define people as deviant who would not ordinarily have been so defined. Both professionalism and bureaucratization objectify deviance and reify diagnostic categories" (n.d.). Consider the case of poor black school pupils, as the schools came to seek additional resources for "innovation" to help these pupils and to work with other professions in comprehensive service strategies during the 1960s. The schools and cooperating agencies and professions proliferated categories for describing the pupils' problems. Thus while it is difficult to be *poor* and difficult to be *black*, the problems of these pupils became defined also as those of being "culturally deprived," "emotionally handicapped," "from a broken home," "resident of a slum," "subject to gang pressures," "a child of a junkie community," etc., etc., etc. Diagnoses, however well-intended, can multiply to create a powerful stereotype that makes Claude Brown's heroic escape from the ghetto seem the only exit route possible (Brown 1965). Such stereotyping can be particularly pernicious when one social scientific approach to understanding the poor, that of the "culture of poverty," is selected as an explanation to the public of why the stereotype holds. According to the "culture of poverty" theory, the poor really *want* to live as they do, or at least they know no other way to live. This theory is uniquely suited to a contemporary reinforcement of laissez-faire and the service strategy, for while seeming to take "structural explanation" (socioeconomic forces and the larger culture) as the heart of the problem, the individual receives the blame in practice, for he is thought to require resocialization if he is redeemable at all (Ryan 1971).

Definitions of the problems of inequality that challenge the individualist service strategy recurrently emerge within the various professions but lose their force as they come to be discredited as more "political" than "professional." During the period of the antipoverty programs, various efforts to break out of the standard services model—particularly by social workers not oriented to casework—fell prey to the opposition of established political, union, business, and civil service groups. The opposition came not only from the traditional "opponents of change," however; it also came from *within* the reform-oriented professions. Once it is agreed that the solution to a social problem is a professional matter, processes of disaccreditation between and within professions arise, and the usual victor—understandable given its strong entrenchment in the culture—is the standard professional model embodying the individual service strategy. Professions are probably incapable of anything other than a service orientation and certainly they discredit themselves when they adopt a political orientation. This service model is supported by the commonsense American assumption, made by both professional and lay persons, that the people's distrust of their bureaucracies can be made manageable through face-to-face communication between individuals who come to know each other personally. In the absence of such relationships, the poor would have few grounds for sympathy for those who claim to speak in their behalf.

The Weakness of Reform

The bureaucratization and professionalization of inequality and social problems are only partial; the bureaucracies and professions that relate to the poor are weak. This assertion will be illuminated below when we discuss problems of reform in the urban school systems, in the nation's public welfare programs, and in the antipoverty efforts of the 1960s. In each of these settings a variety of conditions tended to weaken the agencies seeking reforms. The following conditions have been especially debilitating:

1. *The multiplicity and ambiguity of the goals with which these agencies are charged,* conditions that make it difficult to set priorities and often lead to a bifurcated organizational structure in which the "right hand doesn't know what the left is doing." Examples of difficulties with goals are suggested by the diffuse set of meanings attached to the words "to educate" and by the contradictions that the public welfare agency faces because it is charged on the one hand with helping the poor and on the other with exercising surveillance over them.

2. *Problems the agencies have in recruiting adequate levels of support, legitimacy, and freedom to act.* Like prisons, public welfare agencies have a low status simply from the fact of working with a disesteemed clientele, and this disables them in obtaining resources and support for genuine reform. Both public welfare organizations and public schools are often caught between conflicting political groups and left with little autonomy.

3. *Weakness of internal structures of decision making and command.* This is largely a result of fragmentation into a variety of agencies, each of which is "incomplete," and of statutory requirements that circumscribe certain practices and roles in such a way that the organizations can make little change.[8] While public agencies can affect thousands of individuals, and in this sense are powerful, they are not thereby in control of themselves or of their own actions. Relating to America's bureaucracies that serve the poor is more like sleeping with a comatose dinosaur than with an insomniac gorilla.[9] Further, the growth of large public bureaucracies seems to create its own limits or countervailing forces. A clear example is provided by the civil servants' unions in New York City which, up to the period of fiscal crisis, recurrently used the threat to strike to bring themselves very favorable

pension settlements (allowing, for example, retirement with full pension at age 50). The upshot is that very large proportions of the city's budget for decades are earmarked into these pension payments, freezing organizational flexibility fatefully.

4. *Various outcomes of the professionalization of reform.* Within the public bureaucracies, professional groups tend to be given little autonomy. Concomitantly, they most often use what autonomy they do have to safeguard prerogatives of status—thus reducing further the scope of bureaucratic command without focusing on professional discretion over tasks. Public school teachers usually are given little say over matters of curriculum, but their status as "professionals" is used to place strong protective barriers around their being shifted around in a flexible manner or being asked to serve in flexible roles. Whereas in Europe the professionalization of the public services has had to do with the development of a policy-oriented "higher public service," in the United States it has tended to have more to do with growth of a "civil service mentality" and protectionist, trade-unionist behavior.

The Failure of Educational Innovation in the Sixties

The 1960s in America were a period of great hopes, followed by frustration, in an attempt to end racial discrimination in the schools of and for the poor. It was also a period of raised expectations, followed by disappointment and then cynicism, about the provision of high-quality education to the poor. Much of the change, to integrate and to improve education, came from a recognition that the schools had not been living up to the universalistic standards long proclaimed as their ideal. The outrageousness of the operation of the schools at the beginning of the 1960s is perhaps nowhere better illustrated than in Sexton's findings (1961) on the Detroit public schools. She demonstrated that better facilities, materials, and teachers were furnished to schools in higher-income areas. Free school lunches, in fact, were more often provided in schools in wealthier neighborhoods.

Civil rights protests and other forces led to a recognition that such inequalities had to be altered. A great period of effort at reducing racial and economic discrimination (e.g., reducing gerrymandering of school attendance boundaries) then occurred in the city schools. In parallel fashion, educators, other professionals, the foundations, and the federal government became excited about new avenues of opportunity for minorities and the poor. There, their efforts spawned great professional competition and also resistance on the part of educators to outsiders' efforts and ideologies. Ultimately, however, what Trow refers to as the traditional conception of opportunity, wherein the school simply tries to be fair to one and all, changed to the "radical" definition of opportunity, wherein the schools attempt to provide compensatory education to those who had lost out in the past (Trow 1966). For blacks, it was recognized that the schools would have to do more than conduct "business as usual" in the ghetto, and that it would be necessary to experiment with new modes of teaching, new curricula, nongraded programs, and a variety of other innovations if the deprived populations were really to be reached (Street 1967b).

The upshot was, in the words of one analyst, "a great deal of innovation and very little change" (Janowitz 1969). With regard to desegregation, racial reshuffling of neighborhoods and the emergence of powerful backlash groups prevented all but a few token instances, if dramatic ones, of stable racial integration of schools in Northern cities. With regard to educational innovation for the underclass, a variety of bureaucratic processes inhibited change. The schools proved to be too inflexible to change creatively for the benefit of the disadvantaged. Among key processes inhibiting change was what earlier had been a major accomplishment in American education: the development of the school's fundamental commitment to universalism. Operationally, this principle implied that schools must be administered by formula, with numerically determined ratios of teachers, administrative personnel, and specialists—a formula of standardization that made it difficult for individual principals to innovate within their own schools.

Further, innovations in education for the poor were defeated by the very propaganda used to justify them. To justify funds needed for innovations, educators and others working with them fell into the proliferation of stereotypic diagnoses (e.g., "multiple-problem family") that can be so disabling. They also, reflecting the American emphasis upon immediate results, adopted the policy of continuously conducting researches aimed at demonstrating that instantaneous improvements in educational performances resulted from their innovations. When the seven-day-wonder experiments failed to produce anything other than inconclusive results, the innovations were discarded forthwith.[10] Even when results were promising, they were so overwhelmed by further innovations, results, claims, and counterclaims that they tended to get lost in the shuffle or to perish through immediate but superficial adoption.

This failure contributed to a cult of pessimism about the schools of the minority groups and the poor, pessimism fed also by the educators' inability to gain the consensus necessary for integration programs, the rapid social change occurring in many urban neighborhoods, and the development of demands for community control and separatism not only in white but also in Black neighborhoods. The pessimism was fed most dramatically by the publicity attached to findings of the Coleman report, a national study of integration and education. This report indicated that integration (so difficult to accomplish) was more important in affecting the school performance of black children than were variations in school quality—as measured by such items as teacher-pupil ratio, graduate education of teachers, and availability of libraries and science laboratories (Coleman et al. 1966). Important to understanding such a conclusion is the fact that school quality is so highly correlated with socioeconomic characteristics of communities that the effects of variations in schools cannot easily be unscrambled from those of social status. Because the latter are presumed to be more "basic," variations in school quality can come to be seen as almost irrelevant. Worse, critics of the schools came to forget the fact that Coleman studied not the experimental or the possible but only the normal variations in quality that one sees in a sample of ordinary American school systems. The critics were thereby unjustified in their pessimism about the ability of schools to deflect pupils in any substantial way from the educational performance that is "natural" to their social class backgrounds (Jencks et al. 1972).

As a result, educational experimentation for the poor had almost come to a halt by the 1970s. Both the school system as a bureaucracy and education as a profession had been too weak to formulate and implement a coherent set of strategies that might have brought substantial change in schooling in the ghetto. The professionalization of education in America had never developed a satisfactory ideology to defend itself against the gratuitous as well as reasonable demands of laymen speaking in the name of the community, and across the nation's cities educators were simply trying to defend themselves and play a delaying game against ghetto residents demanding "community control," "black education," and key jobs in the school system. The ideology that education is a cure-all for all problems of American society was so broad as to be indefensible. The educators could not defend themselves satisfactorily against professional social scientists ready to discredit educational innovation with the notion, in effect, that the poor are naturally—socially or culturally—stupid.

Frustration in Reforming Public Assistance

Like the schools, the public welfare system demonstrates that magnitude does not bring mastery of one's operations. The size of the public welfare enterprise has escalated with the growth in the numbers of recipients of public assistance. Welfare is administered in a confused and fragmented fashion across federal, state, and local levels, and it operates in omnipresent political squalor. With the system's growth has come a proliferation of policy manuals, memoranda, rulings, procedures, and paperwork forms, all designed to demonstrate to the public that the welfare system makes judicious rulings on each and every case. This proclivity often slides into "bureaucratic pathology," and at the extreme it becomes a nightmare, as seen in Forbes's research (1973) on public aid caseworkers in Chicago. Bureaucratic formalism is necessary not only for public relations but also as a way of achieving some consistency of action, given the weak organizational commitments of staff members that usually obtain in public welfare agencies. These organizations depart substantially from the ideal bureaucracy, since only small proportions of the officials—at least in the cities—perceive employment in public welfare as a career. Most caseworkers see themselves as in between other occupations or units of higher education, and high turnover rates reflect this fact. Further, few employees see public welfare as an arena for professional social work or have the credentials for such work.

The first major reform of public assistance, as we have seen, came during the Great Depression, when substantial sums of federal money were channeled to lower levels of government for the provision of case and services to the poor. The programs produced by this reform turned out to be much more substantial and lasting than originally intended. The need for public assistance has continued to grow, leading to the recognition that for some classes of persons this program would require it permanently. This fact guaranteed permanent public unpopularity too, for while social insurance was intended positively and in perpetuity for the "deserving poor," public assistance seemed inadvertently to give tenure to the status of the "undeserving poor."

A second major reform sought to address the question of permanence on the public assistance rolls through an upgrading of the provision of "services"—an ambiguous term denoting on the one hand professional help and on the other manipulative assistance in getting persons off the rolls—an assistance that can become coercive (e.g., by pushing recipients into "manpower training programs," regardless of their situation). The reform came in the 1962 Amendment to the Social Security Act, when the federal government sought to clarify support for the provision of services. The caseworker had always served a dual function, checking eligibility and enforcing the rules as one task and providing information and advice as another. Under the new legislation the federal government moved to provide additional subsidies to states that would insure that their welfare workers routinely provided substantial services to recipients. This reform capped the professional social workers' long advocacy of individual casework.

The potential for social work to alleviate poverty has been recurrently limited by the promulgation of *casework* services as the professional model, whereas *income distribution* was the critical problem. This problem was exacerbated in public assistance by the difficulty of reconciling the provision of help with the authoritative role of surveillance and determination of eligibility. The centrality of the casework model is understandable, for in searching for a legitimizing scientific theory the profession seized upon psychology. Clearly the social worker can help the poor person in many of the same ways that the psychotherapist can aid the affluent, but, just as clearly, the treatment will not raise his income or provide him with employment.[11]

The individual casework model has perhaps its least useful although widespread application in legislation that mandates substantial individual services. The realities of agency operation, including the shortage of resources and the high caseload sizes of the 1960s, meant that this service model would simply become superficial or symbolic and thus the object of derision. In several

American cities, the services consisted solely in the caseworker routinely indicating on a form that he had indeed provided services (completely undefined) during the preceding month. This "reform" only exacerbated the conflicts and ambiguities of goals that haunted the public welfare organization, especially the strain that exists among the multiple goals of providing financial resources, services, and surveillance.

The upshot was that by the late 1960s the public welfare system seemed unworkable and ready for another round of reform. It had an elaborate number of unmanageable programs. It lacked resources to provide sufficient help for people, and those working in the system largely knew this. Staff spoke of the "double standard," wherein the middle-class employees came to recognize that they were enforcing standards of living upon welfare recipients that would be unthinkable for themselves. Caseworkers showed some short-run enthusiastic do-gooderism, but also displayed the extremely high turnover already mentioned. Among those who remained, many were "bureaucrats" in the sense that they are identified only with the agency, or were "apathetics" who identified with neither agency nor client. Given the bureaucratic realities, it is not surprising that the bureaucrats and apathetics were sometimes more effective with clients than those who were identified with the recipients (Kroeger 1971). In addition, the public assistance agencies showed a great deal of expressive behavior. Constrained by their multiple goals and audiences, the agencies were continuously involved in the pursuit and announcement of new self-congratulatory studies of the effectiveness of service, new procedures for cracking down on "welfare cheaters," and new programs. Indeed, the case can be made that beyond the substantive benefits provided with money and certain services allocated to persons in such categories as blind and disabled, the public aid organization functioned largely as a "symbolic bureaucracy"—providing ritual public demonstrations of universalistic routines (Jacobs 1969).

Yet the reforms of the late 1960s and early 1970s meant relatively little for the welfare bureaucracy. By mid-decade the public assistance agencies were essentially the same as they had been after implementation of the legislation of 1962, except that (1) the dilemma of combining determination of eligibility of service had often been addressed—however unstably and briefly —by splitting the two roles between separate personnel, (2) certain of the non-AFDC categories of recipients had been removed from the agencies' purview, destigmatized by inclusion with the social security beneficiaries, and (3) a variety of judicial opinions had restricted several of the surveillance procedures and rules making people ineligible.[12] The organizations' principal technology remained the allocation of money; the subsidiary and "window dressing" procedure remained the provision of services —casework or labor-compelling, depending upon the audience to be impressed. Interlarded in the services provided were programs involving such matters as job training and literacy—utilizing the traditional educational strategy once again. The professional claims for casework services have been generally discredited in public assistance, but they have not been replaced or reformed.

Indeed, the big news about public assistance and about the poor in general in the early 1970s was the failure of welfare reform—this time rather basic reform. The change proposed— in Nixon's Family Assistance Plan or in other versions (guaranteed annual income in its various forms) had offered to eliminate the "social work middleman" and the public assistance bureaucracy by moving to an impersonal system mailing out checks on a universalistic basis. Congress at length failed to adopt such a plan. Despite support from some bureaucrats, many economists, some social workers, and some other professionals, it was basically a plan seeking to eliminate bureaucracy and reduce professional claims. Thus the lack of backing—especially professional backing—sufficient to insure passage is hardly surprising.

The Rise and Fall of the Antipoverty Program

The most dramatic failure of contemporary reform directed at inequality was of course the rise, the peaking, and the falling off of the "War on Poverty," signified by the passing of the Equal Opportunity Act of 1964, the implementation of hundreds of programs in the years immediately following, and a drastic reduction of programs preceding a dismantling of the Office of Economic Opportunity in 1973.[13]

A complex series of explanations can be offered for the ultimate failure of the poverty program. Fundamentally the program sought both bureaucratization and professionalization of inequality, attempting to create a federal agency that could develop a rational ordering of programs emphasizing a total strategy for the elimination or at least the dramatic reduction of poverty. In its bureaucratic aspects it is obvious that the program suffered from the familiar weakness that its command of expenditures and programs was too weak to control decision making from the top.

It is in its "professionalization of reform," however, that the antipoverty program is most intriguing. It is useful to think of the professionalization of reform as becoming, during the anti-poverty program, the repoliticization of reform. Contrasting the earlier period, in which the specifics of reform were the proper subject of legislative debate, with the War on Poverty period, in which reforms become professional prerogatives, one sees that latter era as one in which high levels of professional competition ultimately transformed and repoliticized reform. While the air was filled with glowing pronouncements that the federal government was directing a comprehensive and integrated attack upon poverty, in reality an array of public and private agencies and groups were engaged in fierce political in-fighting to gain resources and public support.

To understand the repoliticization of reform, it is useful to make use of and extend Lowi's analysis of "interest group liberalism" (1969). Lowi suggests that American history shows that the New Deal did not lead to the end of capitalism but to its salvation. Capitalism was saved, Lowi asserts, by the acceptance of the necessity of statism, or large-scale governmental interven-tion, and of pluralism as the conventional wisdom of politics. Interest group liberalism thus becomes the dominant form of politics, following pluralist philosophy in assuming that all relevant interest groups should be party to political decisions. Further, where there are not identifiable interest groups, these must be created. As a result, those practicing interest group liberalism acquiesce in or even honor the compromise of the traditional distinction between administrative agencies, includ-ing regulatory units, and the interest groups to which they are to relate. In Lowi's terms, interest group liberalism elevates conflict of interest from a criminal act to a principle of government. Thus, log-rolled decisions are defined as legitimate so long as their production involves all of the relevant parties. The formula of involving all interested parties to bargain out lines of action becomes a recurrent solution to all kinds of problems, ranging from inflation and antipollution to "community programs" for race riot prevention.

The antipoverty program provided an example par excellence

of interest group liberalism. A host of programs were developed at different levels and in varying jurisdiction on the basis of the negotiations of groups of professors, social workers, public school officials, lawyers, ministers, and some members of the poor themselves—all said to "represent" or "speak for" the poor. It was in such a fashion that competing professions and agencies repoliticized reform during the War on Poverty. Agencies came to be seen not merely as bureaucracies administering certain programs, but as agencies *identified* with certain parties (e.g., professions) or interest groups (e.g., ethnic constituencies) that were instrumental in getting those programs approved. Rather than being seen as rational Weberian bureaucracies and impersonal instruments of policies that were either right or wrong, the agencies came to be identified with certain interest groups. As with federal regulatory agencies like the Federal Communications Commission that treat those they regulate as constituencies, the departments of Health, Education, and Welfare and of Housing and Urban Development came to be seen as providing a necessary partisan element in drawing the poor into pluralistic politics. Thus, the poverty program came to be identified with the poor, and employees of the poverty program came to see themselves in this way, too. The agencies tended to become interest groups in themselves. They became parties to the political decisions, seeking to "get theirs." To do so, they programmatically become chameleons: during the War on Poverty, an array of agencies lined up to get whatever kinds of resources they could for whatever kinds of programs were marketable to the federal government. Community-oriented organizations would become interested in individual counseling, and counseling agencies would develop an interest in community organization—keying their pitch to the market of antipoverty funds.

Further, in becoming interest groups, the agencies often lost sight of long-run accountability, looking only to day-to-day success. The result was to undercut whatever prospects these agencies had for being granted a professional mandate. As with reform in the schools, the agencies came to accept the popular version of pragmatism requiring immediate demonstration of successful effects on client populations. The *New York Times* reported, on the same day and on the same front page, that (1) the Office of Education had decided that experiments in bringing in American businesses to run ghetto schools were a failure, and

(2) the new head of the New York City Welfare Department had a master's degree in business administration from Harvard and was planning, with the aid of a new business-oriented staff, to completely revitalize the welfare operation along efficient lines. The loss of long-run accountability was inimical to the autonomous operation of the bureaucracy as well as to professional integrity. Neither bureaucracy nor professionalism can be implemented given the day-to-day changes required by political bargaining with external publics and continuing expressive conflict.

The dramatic failure of the antipoverty program of the 1960s must be understood not simply as a whistling of reform against the wind of laissez-faire, but also as a prime example of the weakness of the American conception of reform and of the inadequacies of the bureaucratization of inequality and of the professionalization of reform. The government sought to eradicate poverty through programs of giving funds to a great array of bureaucratic organizations but without the authority to change, rather than merely subsidize, these agencies. The variety of competing and coalescing professional groupings nowhere produced a consensus of purpose much more specific than endorsement of change.

EFFECTS

Although the bureaucratization and professionalization of inequality may improve the position of certain subclasses of poor persons, their general effect is less to reduce inequality than to transform the ways in which men become and live as unequals. The attempts in recent years at reform in education and public welfare, together with the carnival of changes attempted under the antipoverty program, merely exacerbated the problems of the poor. To the economic disadvantages and general social stigma attached to poverty were added the tasks of comprehending and relating oneself to the bureaucracies that administer inequality and the professions that seek to reform it and to the social categories that are produced. The pseudo-meritocracy produced an additional set of invidious categories, legitimized as the fair results of open opportunity but compounding the difference between "normal" and "poor." Fortunately, the structural weakness of the public bureaucracies and the strong processes of competition and mutual discreditation among the professions that deal with the poor serve as strong limits upon their accretion of power or the plausibility of their pronouncements.

Perhaps the most important effect is the plethora of competing bureaucratic, professional, political, and social definitions of the poor. This becomes especially problematic for the way in which the poor come to view themselves. What may have been most difficult for the poor was the fact that within less than a decade reform efforts could produce such high levels of optimism and such apparent failure. It is no wonder that various groups of poor persons reacted at various points of time in that same period with high levels of obsequiousness, enthusiasm for rioting, feelings of stigmatization, involvement in instrumental self-help activities, politicalization and "militance," self-aggrandizement and "mau-mauing," and general apathy.

The various diagnoses made of the poor have had multiplying negative effects, as we earlier indicated. Professional labels, however, sometimes make little difference, for they are quickly translated back to traditional terms—as when "culturally deprived pupils" becomes a euphemism for "black pupils." Despite elaborate terminology, both poor and nonpoor groups often know who is "really" being talked about and who is "really" to benefit from a given program. Generally, professional labels are likely to be more useful for warnings they imply than for clarification—as when residents of a poor neighborhood become more wary of street crime rather than less once they learn that a methadone maintenance clinic has opened in their area. Some labels may have the intended effects—as when members of a generation of Americans raised after the Great Depression learn the notion of structural poverty signified by the term "underemployment."

The public definition of the bureaucracies and professions that are engaged with the poor is mixed as well. They are seen simultaneously as trying to help and as ready to "cater" to the poor, to give universalistic aid but also to provide benefits to certain favored minority groups, to design new programs but also to bootleg support for tired ones, to recruit talented staff but also to furnish jobs to old buddies. In practice as well as image, the agencies and professions do all of these things. Reform has both a "genuine" side and an "appearance" side. Reform efforts do indeed seek to "do something" about the poor, and thus they tend to meet and exhaust the demands of those genuinely interested in

change. Simultaneously, the professionalization and politiciza-
tion of reform tend to discredit notions of change, thus feeding
cynicism about these efforts in the public at large and among the
poor and the professionals themselves.

The result is stalemate. Ultimately, reform is largely symbolic;
it stands for doing something about the poor while hardly
challenging—and sometimes reinforcing—the gap between poor
and nonpoor.

9 Change, Continuity, and Prospects

REFORM AS OLD WINE IN NEW BOTTLES

The War on Poverty illustrates the cyclical and ephemeral quality of reform in America. Much activity during the poverty program consisted of the marketing of old wine (e.g., the idea of motivating the poor through self-help) in new bottles (e.g., "maximum feasible community participation"). Reform often has merely changed the way things are done, without producing significant change in outcomes. For all the discussion of the growth of the welfare state in America, the nation still lags behind many modern industrial nations in the size of its welfare effort and especially in the coherence of this effort and its attention to amelioration of greatest need. Reforms made in the name of the poor often benefit mainly the not-so-poor. About 90 percent of our federal welfare expenditure aids people who have been employed most of their lives—through OASDHI (Old Age Survivors Disability Health Insurance), Medicare, railroad retirement, and veterans benefits. Only about 10 percent goes to the chronically unemployed—through AFDCU (Aid for Dependent Children—Unemployed), GA (General Assistance), OAA (Old Age Assistance), and Medicaid programs. The big winners in the American welfare state are persons seasonally unemployed in selected high-wage industries (e.g., construction), the elderly who have nonwage incomes in addition to their pensions, the veterans, and some retired municipal employees. The big losers are those who are persistently unemployed (the partially disabled, the unskilled, and those with heavy family responsibilities), and the working poor—those performing work that is not included in the current programs and who earn just enough to make them ineligible for other benefits. Insurance programs such as social security function largely to relieve the middle class and stable working class of the financial burdens they previously had to assume for their elderly parents. Such functions may be meritorious, but they can obscure the fact that the problems of many of those who are unambiguously poor are the least addressed.

The continuing growth of our categoric programs has perplexed both those who favor and those who fear the welfare state. Those critical of welfare have frequently attributed increased expenditures to the willful improvidence of the very poor, while those who favor welfare have encouraged increased expenditures on the assumption that they will invariably aid the very poor. Neither viewpoint is correct. Further growth in our present welfare system may only bring into relief the injustices of current income transfers.

Widespread complaints and malaise over "welfare cheaters" and "government giveaways" must be taken seriously. When welfare expenditures have reached the level of more than $1,000 per capita of the entire population, and when numerous people still remain very poor, a deep distrust of the welfare system and its recipients is bound to occur. If these observations are coupled with the knowledge that numbers of people who are not that badly off receive benefits, public confidence in all welfare programs is undermined. For this reason, the liberal view that any increase in welfare expenditures is beneficial to the poor can be self-defeating.

It can also be self-serving. Professionals and workers in the welfare industry have a vested interest in seeing that new programs are not too dissimilar from old ones. It is not just that the welfare industry employs a significant number of reasonably well-paid professionals and semi-professionals, but also that current programs "package" welfare into solutions that fit easily into the existing framework of available experts and organizational arrangements. Additional programs emphasizing social casework, the extension of opportunity, and community action fit the training and career aims of those in ongoing bureaucracies. New programs can be implemented simply by adding another organization or "department," whereas a concerted reform of the welfare system might require considerable efforts to reassemble speciality roles and reduce organizational boundaries among welfare bureaucracies. Similarly, the categoric approach makes it possible for a variety of groups and organizations to engage in self-congratulation for their willingness to "aid the poor" while in no way disadvantaging themselves. The administrative overhead for all of our welfare programs is high, usually over 50 percent, and it continues to grow as a percentage of total expenditures (Rein and Heclo 1973, and Derthick 1975). Liberal support for no tuition or low tuition payment to places of higher learning remains an outspoken plea for the poor, while in the aggregate the universities serve mainly the better-off.

The pattern of changing the means of distributing income without altering its basic consequences is expressed in the generalization that American governmental activities have less reduced inequality than they have bureaucratized and professionalized it. Under these processes, the operations of the system of inequality become more sophisticated, definitions of poverty become more precise, policies for defining eligibility become more complicated, and programs of help receive greater expert attention. As a result, the system becomes somewhat more generous to those both motivated and fortunate, but in the aggregate it operates mainly as a treadmill. Reforms in the name of expert professional opinion may even stand in the way of change, the reform becoming largely an expressive act. In the War on Poverty the hiring of large numbers of welfare professionals was thought of as "doing something" about poverty. The poor were mainly impecunious bystanders.

Expanding the welfare state without substantially changing the distribution of income increasingly invites strident public demands for further reform. As funds for the expansion of the welfare state become less available—and there must be a limit (Janowitz 1977)—it becomes less possible to address the needs of the very poor without reducing income transfers to the less poor. Such a rearrangement in the disposition of public funds is certain to be opposed. Yet so long as the American welfare state simply repeats or enlarges existing income inequities, it is bound to arouse a sense of social injustice and the potential for social disorder—or, since public aid repeats the inequities of the existing market place, to amplify old claims. It is likely, then, that the American welfare state will contribute to a chronic social malaise which centers both on "government giveaways" and gross inequalities. Stalemate and cynicism are the most likely outcomes unless new leadership and new ideas can inspire the individual sacrifices required.

Persistence of American Beliefs and Structures

Significant aspects of American society persist in somewhat altered fashion to limit reforms and to give basic shape to poverty in the country. The persistence of a large underclass within the capitalist system receives new justifications. Such rationalizations permit understanding of, and even a modicum of kindness toward, the members of this class. Edward Banfield—one of the strongest advocates of capitalism, competition, and individualism—finds room in his heart for a dole for those he sees as already losers in the competition.

Stereotyping can induce a self-fulfilling prophecy in which those assumed to be headed nowhere are accorded less attention and support and consequently suffer reduced life chances. This is largely true of the stereotype of the black mother of illegitimate children on ADC. The multiplicity of categories for describing the poor (disadvantaged, from broken homes, discriminated against, culturally deprived, from the ghetto or the hills, "on welfare," etc.) results in large part from the professionalization of reform and serves to rationalize the persistence of laissez-faire.

Also disabling to genuine reform is the continuing cultural fragmentation of the United States (a fragmentation that does not necessarily coincide with bureaucratic and professional categories.) Many commentators on America, including sociologists, are so enamored of the popular image of American cultural homogeneity that when they rediscover persistent culture variety they are prone to explain it as a secondary and subsequent form of differentiation.[1] Yet the huge rural-to-urban migrations of the last two decades have brought the message of cultural fragmentation and heterogeneity home even more directly, despite predominating theories of subcultural adaptation in the debate over public welfare. The primordial groups continue to have a life of their own, to affect our political processes vitally, and to delimit the extent of mutual trust in the management of the national budget—as witnessed in the mid-seventies' resurgence of regionalism in the resistance to providing federal aid to ease the fiscal crises of New York City.

Fragmentation is omnipresent on the national scene, where the incrementalism of the New Deal programs is joined by sporadic legislation creating additional agencies and subagencies, administering and funding programs on a variety of levels, and generating thousands of regulations and accounting procedures.

The development of national standards in welfare has been a long and uneven struggle, and standards continue to vary substantially from state to state. Weak government affects the poor profoundly as the cities lose their power through the outflow of populations and resources, and authority is turned over to the newer minority populations. As the old political machines recede, new technocratic machines emerge.

Prospects

The idea of the welfare state has gained a considerable if grudging currency in America. No coherent welfare state has yet been established, however, nor have its ideological justifications gained informed public acceptance. Instead, Americans have commonly come to expect that the government should "do something" about what was formerly seen as personal difficulties that might befall themselves, their aging kin, or their friends struck by sudden illness or economic dislocation, etc. However inarticulate this counter-ideology—it is often only an aggrieved demand—definitions of financial need faced by Americans have moved impressively toward a social-structural explanation.

Changing expectations about life chances are likely to contribute to crises in legislating and administering welfare programs. Heightened expectations are bound to collide with the reality of limited resources. Thus the usual liberal propensity to favor whatever expansion of welfare expenditures seems presently marketable—for example, supporting programs for blacks and Lockheed Aircraft at the same time—is doomed to frustration. A general depression and/or of energy shortages could generate economic squeezes at many levels of society— not only among the poor but among such middle-class groups as businessmen, farmers, and "consumers." *All* are likely to demand government action if not "welfare." Crises will occur where remediation turns out to be prohibitively expensive although its provision seemed implicit in the extension of existing welfare programs—for example, adequate nursing home care for millions of aged under Medicare and social security pensions, full aid for veterans, or dialysis for victims of kidney disease under the proposed national health insurance.

The general idea that the government should "do something" to put a floor under incomes may have to be joined to the idea that there is also a ceiling to the collective responsibilities of the welfare state. Universalism can run in both directions—it must define both rights and responsibilities. With the advantages of hindsight, one can note that the much maligned 1972 McGovern plan of a bloc grant of $1,000 per person accompanied by progressive income taxation would probably have reduced current welfare expenditures by as much as 25 percent if it had been adopted and were our only welfare program today. Even if accompanied by a national health insurance program, the McGovern plan would probably have cost about the same as current programs.

As resources and demands run on a collision course, American welfare programs will certainly require further federalizing and universalization. Universalization is less problematic than Americans have been led to believe. Either the Workfare Program of Richard Nixon (FAP) or the grants favored by George McGovern would have been significant advances if accompanied by more genuinely progressive income taxation. In accounting for the failure of such programs or enactments, disputes among proponents of the negative income tax and guaranteed income plans are trivial by comparison with the wellsprings of support for a categoric system that fits too easily into the logrolling habits of the American Congress and welfare bureaucracies. The inveterate enemy of welfare reform in the United States is not a power elite or primitive ideology but the irresolution of the federal government. The response to the Work Fair program made obvious the absence of a resolute political regime having a clear sense of direction and public support.

Federalizing welfare programs is more complicated. Some formula for adjusting aid to the cost of living in various regions must be adopted, but it cannot be allowed to vary much if it is to avoid raising suspicions of regional favoritism and interference with the mobility of labor. There are grave problems here, because the American population is moving away from the old centers of concentration in the Northeast, and there is redistribution elsewhere as well. Further, large numbers of dependent persons now concentrated in the central cities of the "northern triangle"—the region described roughly by lines drawn between Washington, D. C., Milwaukee, and Boston—must be slowly resettled through providing a set of attractive incentives as well as some humane response to the problems of living in America's newest depressed area. Specific grants for seeking employment in another region—the type of support that Cubans and some other immigrants have already received—may have to be expanded and kept as a part of our welfare economy.

Federalizing and universalizing the welfare system will clearly require increased support and management from Washington. This step might be widely favored in the face of a fiscal crunch facing the cities and states. It could also give the system a legitimacy sufficient to counteract the widespread view of welfare programs as but favoritism to one group or another. The other side of the coin is that certain valued attributes of the present welfare system would have to be foregone. Painfully, at least the following steps would have to be taken:

1. *Giving up the masking of the means test.* Americans have been so ambivalent about poverty that they have often supported programs for aiding the poor but have been unwilling to stigmatize them by making explicit their deprivations. Masking of the means test has served the admirable function of reducing the extent to which the state could enforce gratuitous standards of respectability upon the poor by probing into the details of their lives. Under a universal system, invasion of privacy would be reduced as criteria for allocating aid became limited to a few pieces of information (e.g., annual income and family size) that were presumed essential. On the other hand, falsification of those limited pieces of information would have to be defined as illegal and publicly sanctioned as such. Under the present system, with the means test masked and welfare programs addressed to the health of the larger community, more benefits go to the haves than to the have-nots. Losing in the new system would be both the nonpoor who have previously been beneficiaries and the "fortunate poor," those whose geographical location and situation relative to the overlapping of welfare programs has granted them many more benefits than is the norm.

2. *Giving up the myth of group self-help.* Americans have glorified the notion of self-help, and the pluralistic conception has celebrated the idea that the various ethnic and racial groups would automatically organize themselves collectively to handle problems of welfare on their own. This conception has had a real

but uneven utility, for some groups have been sufficiently settled in residential areas and have possessed enough commitments and resources to provide substantial intragroup support, while others have not. Blacks, in particular, have been so mobile, so poor, and so uncertain of their own ethnicity that self-help schemes have seldom worked well among them. The problem faced by blacks is shown dramatically in New York City through recent challenges to governmental subsidy of the private system of child welfare. It has been observed that Catholic and Jewish agencies receive the lion's share of resources despite the fact that a larger and larger share of the client population consists of black children, who receive little attention from these private agencies because they are routinely classified as Protestant. Because Protestant agencies are small and poorly organized in that city, needy black children go by default to public programs, leading to the suspicion that any governmental subsidy of the child welfare system expresses favoritism to advantaged groups. The movement to further universalization of welfare could recognize as unfortunate any losses that might come through the reduction of private and group self-help, but would require that the principal private programs, while often admirable, must not receive governmental subsidy. Otherwise, the pattern of dealing away welfare resources into the hands of competing ethnic and religious groups seen in the War on Poverty would continue, leading to heightened accusations of favoritism and to general distrust inimical to the welfare system.

3. *Giving up reliance on state and local government.* Reliance on national standards, even with aid adjusted to address regional variations, would move welfare toward the federal level, putting the issue of guns (or highways) versus butter more squarely on the national agenda than it has been in the past. This action obviously would reduce reliance on such benefits of state and local initiative as still obtained—although it should be recognized that the demands made on state and local government in welfare and other areas have lately so far outrun the resources of these units that little in the way of innovation has been possible at these levels. Indeed, one is hard pressed now to speak of "progressive" states or cities. Further, it has become apparent that welfare programs are so national in scope, involving such highly mobile populations in an interdependent economy, that decentralization

to fifty states and their constituent local units becomes increasingly impractical. Perhaps in a society where a small number of regional units encompassed stable populations and distinct ethnic or racial units, continuation of decentralization would make sense—as in the British Isles, where the Scots can be appropriately somewhat free to have different programs than the English. In America, decentralization to jurisdictions involving shifting polyglots of ethnically organized and nonorganized poor has lost its utility and purpose.

4. *Giving up the myth of the helping person.* The movement to further universalization based on need would undercut as well the provision of governmental programs that involve activities other than the allocation of cash or of objectively specifiable services or resources such as medical care or housing. In so doing, it would reduce the governmental support accorded programs normally carried out by welfare professionals, such as personal counseling, job training, and community organizing, except insofar as these obtain resources in the free market from those who are benefiting from cash subsidies. One result would be a diminution in governmental attention to the image of the helping person, a view that derives from the concept of the philanthropic lady bountiful and from romantic socialist thinking in which each is helped in accordance with his individual need. Professional helping would continue in the society, but could no longer be justified as a direct response to poverty. Universalization would require the somewhat unpalatable acceptance of impersonal bureaucratization—of administration of help through clerk, computer, and check-cashing. This, too, would constitute a hard reality: in a society deeply scarred by intergroup distrust, it becomes impossible to administer a fair program with an air of "niceness" or, one fears, even "good will."

There is no guarantee that a solution to the welfare crisis will be found. We assume that the problems of the poor must ultimately be seen as moving toward a zero-sum game requiring, first, that welfare be something beyond capitalism-with-piecemeal-reform and, second, that groups become willing actually to give up something. We further assume that a program of universalization based on objective need constitutes an unexciting but potentially effective way to legitimize the sacrifices a fair welfare system would entail. Whether or not there will emerge a political leadership attuned to and able to market a program demanding such costs remains to be seen.

Despite the great need for welfare reform along these lines, it would constitute only one step in facing the problems that confront American society. During the 1960s it was fashionable in some circles to say that all our social problems—urban problems, racial problems, social conflict, and the like—were only problems of income distribution in various guises. The urban fiscal crises, the energy crisis, and stagflation have served to refocus attention on the general problems of national development and have brought into question conventional views that we have an automatically increasing economic pie and that our only true problem is how it is to be divided. Certainly many of the problems that currently face the nation will remain even if we achieve universalization and nationalization of welfare programs. These larger problems will demand unity and concerted effort, and the fragmentation and distrust engendered by the present welfare system can only obstruct effective attempts to approach the general problems of national development.

Appendix

CHRONOLOGY OF LEGISLATION, PUBLICATIONS, AND OTHER EVENTS CONNECTED WITH WELFARE IN THE UNITED STATES AND SELECTED NATIONS

Key

European Continent	Selected events and legislative acts concerning social welfare on the Continent of Europe (through 1901).
Great Britain	Selected events and legislative acts concerning social welfare in Great Britain (through 1963).
U.S. federal	Legislation concerning social welfare in the United States on the federal level.
U.S. state	Legislation concerning social welfare in the United States on the state level (through 1946).
Selected events	Selected events in the development of social welfare and government functions.
Publications	Publications, government reports, and surveys pertaining to social welfare.
Charities and social work	Private charities and professional social work.
Supreme Court	Advances and reversals pertaining to social welfare in Supreme Court rulings.

THE PRE–CIVIL WAR PERIOD

800 **European Continent**
Statute of Charlemagne prohibits mendicancy and fines those giving alms to able-bodied beggars.

1349 **Great Britain**
Statute of Labourers: first poor law in England (following the Black Death and consequent shortage of laborers). Orders able-bodied workers to accept employment for any master willing to hire them, and forbids them to leave their parish.

Most of the information in this Chronology is taken from Bremner 1956; Axinn and Levin 1975; Trattner 1974; Breul 1965; Davis 1967.

1520   **European Continent**
Martin Luther appeals to princes to forbid begging and to organize in all parishes a "common chest" for receipt of money, food, and clothes to assist the needy.

1526   **Publications**
Vives' *De Subventione Pauperum* (The Collection of the Poor and Their Classification) in England.

1531   **Great Britain**
Statute of Henry VIII: first constructive measure by the government for relief of the poor. Mayors and Justices of the Peace are to investigate applications of the aged and paupers unable to work and maintained by the parish.

1536   **Great Britain**
Act for the Punishment of Sturdy Beggars and Vagabonds: first plan of poor relief; residency requirement (three years). "Impotent Poor" are to be maintained by voluntary contributions. Able-bodied beggars are to be forced to work. Children aged 5–14 are to be removed from their parents and indentured.

1562   **Great Britain**
Statute of Artificiers regulates wages and hours of work. Apprentice system.

1563   **Great Britain**
Compulsory measures are introduced to finance poor relief.

1572   **Great Britain**
Statute of 1572: a general tax to provide funds for poor relief. Final recognition that the government is responsible for providing aid to people who cannot maintain themselves. Overseers of the poor.

1576   **Great Britain**
"Houses of Correction" supplied with raw materials established. Forced work, particularly with regard to young people.

1597   **Great Britain**
Statute of 1597: Justices of the Peace to appoint the churchwardens and four substantial householders as overseers of the poor. Relatives are held to be responsible for poor people. Establishes "Almshouses" for the impotent poor.

1601   **Great Britain**
The Poor Law of 1601 ("43 Elizabeth"): a codification of preceding poor relief legislation. New feature: responsibility for grandparents as well as for parents and children.

1619   **U.S. state**
Idle persons bound to compulsory labor in Virginia.

1624   **U.S. state**
Colony of Virginia adopts measures for relief of soldiers.

1630s **European Continent**
Father Vincent de Paul organizes lay order "Ladies of Charity," the members visit the poor, distribute food and clothing.

1633 **European Continent**
Father Vincent de Paul founds "Daughters of Charity," young women of peasant class who are trained in visiting the poor. Forerunners of social workers.

1642 **U.S. state**
Plymouth Colony adopts provisions for the poor, with taxing powers.

1657 **Charities and social work**
First almshouse at Rensselaerswyck, New York.

"Scots Charitable society," first American "friendly society" founded in Boston, reorganized in 1864.

1662 **Great Britain**
Law of Settlement and Removal: Justices of the Peace allowed to turn away and return any newcomer who might become a public charge.

1675 **U.S. state**
Massachusetts provides relief for frontier settlers who were victims of King Philip's War. This was a departure from the principle of relying exclusively on local provisions.

1676 **U.S. state**
Massachusetts makes provisions for the special care of the insane.

1682 **Charities and social work**
William Penn's "Holy Experiment."

1686 **Great Britain**
Stricter enforcement of the *Law of Settlement.*

1691 **Great Britain**
Announcement of newcomers to be posted in the church to facilitate enforcement of the *Law of Settlement.*

Selected events
Boston employs four full-time overseers of the poor.

1696 **Great Britain**
Workhouse Act of 1696, in Bristol and other places.

Report of John Locke to the Board of Trade, proposing work schools for employing the poor.

1699 **U.S. state**
Massachusetts: vagabonds, beggars, and disorderly persons forced to work in houses of correction.

1704 **Great Britain**
Daniel Defoe responds to Locke in "Giving Alms, No Charity and Employing the Poor. A Grievance to the Nation," opposing workhouses as being destructive to trade.

1718   **U.S. state**
The Province of Pennsylvania requires every person receiving poor relief to wear the letter "P" on the shoulder.

1719   **Selected events**
Forty-nine Irish paupers not allowed to disembark from the ship Elizabeth in Boston.

1722   **Great Britain**
Overseers are given authority to make contracts with private manufacturers who employed paupers. Relief refused to anyone not willing to enter workhouses.

1729   **Charities and social work**
First orphan home in the United States at New Orleans.

1730   **Charities and social work**
"Saint Andrew's Society" in Charleston, S.C., assists people in distress.

1736   **Selected events**
New York City establishes its Public Workhouse and House of Correction.

1739   **Selected events**
The Great Awakening, 1739–41.

1751–   **Charities and social work**
52   Pennsylvania Hospital opens, the first general hospital in the United States.

1754   **Charities and social work**
"Episcopal Charitable Society" of Boston founded. Distributes private charity to needy church members.

1760   **Charities and social work**
"The Society for Encouraging Industry and Employing the Poor" established in Boston.

1761   **Great Britain**
All infants in workhouses to be registered in order to combat the high infant mortality rate of 82 percent.

1767   **Great Britain**
Children ages 0–6 years removed from workhouses and placed with foster parents.

1772   **Publications**
Mandeville, *Fable of the Bees, or Private Vices and Public Benefits.*

1773   **U.S. state**
The insane removed from almshouses for the first time: Virginia.

1774   **Charities and social work**
"Society for Innoculating the Poor Gratis" established by Philadelphia doctors.

U.S. federal
The Continental Congress prohibits the importation of slaves.

1775 **U.S. state**
State responsibility (financial) for state paupers, i.e., newly arrived
paupers: Massachusetts.

1776 **Publications**
Smith, *The Wealth of Nations.*

The United States *Declaration of Independence.*

Charities and social work
"Society for Alleviating the Miseries of Public Prisoners" in Philadelphia,
reactivated in 1787.

1782 **Great Britain**
Poor Law Amendment ("Gilbert Act") abolishes the contractor system,
establishes salaried "guardians of the poor." Persons able and willing to
work to be maintained at home until employment is obtained.

1786 **Publications**
Townsend, *A Dissertation on the Poor Law. By A Well-Wisher to
Mankind.*

1787 **Charities and social work**
"Philadelphia Prison Society" founded.

1788 **European Continent**
Hamburg, Germany: district system of investigation and distribution of
relief to individual paupers through volunteer committees appointed
by the Senate.

1789 **European Continent**
The French Revolution starts.

1790 **European Continent**
Munich, Germany: system similar to that of Hamburg initiated.

U.S. state
The first orphan asylum under government auspices is established in
Charleston, S.C.

Charities and social work
Free mulattoes of Charleston, S.C., organize Brown Fellowship Society.

1792 **Selected events**
The cotton gin is invented.

Publications
Paine, *Rights of Man.*

1794 **Charities and social work**
Massachusetts: "Charitable Fire Society."

1795 **Great Britain**
Speenhamland Act: relief allowances in home given according to size
of family.

Amendment to *the Law of Settlement:* newcomers cannot be returned to
parish of previous residence until after they have actually applied for
relief in the new parish.

1798   **Publications**
Malthus, *Essay on the Principle of Population.*

Charities and social work
"New York Society for Relief of Poor Widows with Small Children."

1799–   **Great Britain**
1800   The *Combination Law* prohibits workers from forming trade unions in order to obtain higher wages or better working conditions.

1800s   **U.S. state**
Soldiers and Sailors Relief initiated in several states.

1802   **Great Britain**
Health and Morals Act restricts working hours of "pauper apprentices" to twelve hours and forbids night work for children (on the insistence of Robert Peck).

1809   **Publications**
First recorded investigation of unemployment relief situation in New York, by the Humane Society.

Charities and social work
"Sisters of Charity of Saint Vincent de Paul," concentrates on hospitals and orphan homes.

1814   **Great Britain**
Reverend Thomas Chalmers organizes a program of private charity on the principle of neighborly aid: Glasgow.

1817   **Charities and social work**
"New York Society for Prevention of Pauperism" concentrates on penitentiaries and juvenile delinquencies and determines the causes of poverty; emphasis on different means of rehabilitation.

1818   **U.S. state**
"New York Institution for the Instruction of the Deaf and Dumb" established.

1820s   **U.S. state**
School for the deaf in Kentucky.

1821   **Publications**
Quincy Report of 1821 on the Pauper Laws of Massachusetts.

1823   **Publications**
Yates's survey of poor relief in New York.

1824   **Great Britain**
Combination Law repealed.

U.S. state
County Poor House Act, New York, transfers management of the almshouse from the township to the county.

1825   **Charities and social work**
New York House of Refuge established.

1826 Selected events
"American Society for Promotion of Temperance."

1827 Selected events
Mechanics' Union Trade Association is established in Philadelphia. The first crafts union in the United States.

1831 Great Britain
Trade unions begin to pay benefits to unemployed members.

1832 Great Britain
"Royal Commision for Inquiring into the Administration and Practical Operation of the Poor Laws."

Publications
Reverend Joseph Tuckerman surveys the conditions of the poor in Massachusetts.

Charities and social work
New England Asylum (later Perkins Institution): leading American institution for the blind established.

1833 Great Britain
Factory Act prohibits employment of children under nine years of age in textile industry; limits children's working hours.

Publications
Carey, *Appeal to the Wealthy of the Land, Ladies as Well as Gentlemen, on Character, Conduct, Situation and Prospects of Those Whose Sole Dependence for Subsistence Is on the Labour of Their Hands.* Sees poverty as related to malfunction of economic system.

1834 Great Britain
New Poor Law, based on 1832 report.

1835 Great Britain
The Chartist Movement (1830s–1848).

1836 Charities and social work
The first maternity home and hospital is opened in Boston.

1837– Publications
38 De Tocqueville, *Democracy in America.*

Dickens, *Oliver Twist*

1840 Great Britain
Free public vaccination against cholera, typhus, and smallpox (on the insistence of Edwin Chadwick).

Publications
Dickens' writings in Great Britain and that of his imitators in the United States.

Charities and social work
"Little Sisters of the Poor," dealing with the aged poor.

1842   **Great Britain**
"The Metropolitan Association for Improving the Dwellings of the Industrious Classes."

Chadwick's study of health and sanitary conditions of the working class.

1843   **U.S. state**
First state law for establishing special facilities for the mentally ill under the influence of Dorothea Dix: Massachusetts.

Charities and social work
"New York Association for Improving the Conditions of the Poor."

1844   **Great Britain**
The Chartists open a cooperative store.

Publications
Griscom, *The Sanitary Condition of The Laboring Population of New York.*

1845   **Charities and social work**
First American conference of the "Society of Saint Vincent de Paul."

1846   **Great Britain**
Fatal Accident Act, which proves to be insufficient.

1847   **Great Britain**
Factory Act, maximum of ten hours of work per day for women and children under eighteen.

U.S. state
State Reform School is established in Massachusetts as an institution for juvenile delinquents.

1848   **Great Britain**
"Christian Socialism": Ludlow and others.

Public Health Act: General Board of Health established.

1850   **European Continent**
France and Belgium: voluntary old age pensions.

U.S. state
Massachusetts School for the Idiotic and Feebleminded Youth.

Charities and social work
"Society of Saint Vincent de Paul" founded.

1851   **Charities and social work**
"Travelers' Aid" founded.

"The Young Men's Christian Association" founded.

Adoption being used as permanent substitute care for dependent children.

1852   **Great Britain**
Outdoor Relief Regulation Order upholds principle of less eligibility (relief to be less attractive than work).

1853 **European Continent**
Elberfeld system, similar to those operating in Hamburg and Munich. Financed exclusively from public taxation. Volunteers live in areas served. The plan is widely adopted in European cities.

Charities and social work
"Children's Aid Society," New York.

1854 **European Continent**
Austria: compulsory social insurance system.

Charities and social work
The first day care centers are opened in the United States.

Selected events
President Pierce declares that the federal government cannot become the "great almoner of public charity throughout the United States."

Dorothea Dix's mental hospital bill vetoed by President Pierce.

Supreme Court
Dred Scott v. Sanford, 19 U.S. 393: "beyond the competence of the national legislation to ban slavery anywhere."

1850s **Great Britain**
Florence Nightingale: reform of nursing, hospitals, and medical practice.

1858 **Charities and social work**
"Young Women's Christian Association," in New York.

THE CIVIL WAR

1860 **Charities and social work**
"Boy's Club" in Connecticut established.

1861– **Charities and social work**
66 "United States Sanitary Commission"; becomes "Red Cross" in 1881.

1861 **U.S. state**
Ohio institutes mandatory removal of all children from poorhouses.

1862 **U.S. federal**
A pension system is instituted for disabled Union soldiers and their survivors.

Morrill Act: first grants to states for public education—land grant colleges.

Homestead Act.

Charities and social work
"Freedmen's Relief Association," in the North, provides teachers and relief supplies for former slaves.

1863 **U.S. state**
State Board of Charities and Correction in Massachusetts.

Charities and social work
"Catholic Protectory" (child care) in New York.

1864   **Great Britain**
Octavia Hill rebuilds slum tenements in London.

Charities and social work
Sanitary Fairs in Northern cities to support the "United States Sanitary Commission," 1863–64.

1865   **Great Britain**
The Salvation Army is established in England.

U.S. federal
Bureau of Refugees, Freedmen and Abandoned Lands. Extended 1869. Terminated 1872.

Thirteenth Amendment to the *U.S. Constitution*, abolishes slavery.

The Period of Social Concern, 1870–1915

1867   **Great Britain**
Reform Bill: suffrage to urban workers.

U.S. state
Board of State Charities in New York, also in Ohio.

Publications
Marx, *Das Kapital;* in English in 1906.

1869   **Great Britain**
"Society for Organization of Charitable Relief and Repressing Mendicity," Charity Organization Society.

U.S. state
Massachusetts establishes a State Board of Health.

Selected events
"American Woman Suffrage Association."

1870   **U.S. federal**
Amendment to the *U.S. Constitution:* the right to vote cannot be denied on the basis of race.

1872   **Selected events**
From 1872 to 1877 public outdoor relief increased 100 percent in Brooklyn

Publications
Brace, *Dangerous Classes of New York.*

Charities and social work
"New York State Charity Aid Society."

1874   **Charities and social work**
"Conference of Boards of Public Charities"; later becomes "National Conference of Charities and Correction," "National Conference on Social Work" and "National Conference on Social Welfare."

1875   **Great Britain**
First trade unionists enter Parliament.

U.S. federal
Civil Rights Act; declared unconstitutional in 1880.

Supreme Court
Minor v. Happersett, 21 Wall. 162. The Fourteenth Amendment does not require the extension of the electoral franchise to women.

1877   **Selected events**
Brooklyn cuts off all public relief as result of increase in expenditures in 1872–77. The result: no difference.

Publications
Dugdale, *The Jukes: A Study in Crime, Pauperism, Disease, and Heredity.*

Charities and social work
"The Charity Organization Movement" spreads to the United States (Buffalo).

1878   **Charities and social work**
The first meeting of the National Conference of Charities and Corrections is held. *Proceedings* are published.

1879   **Publications**
George, *Progress and Poverty.*

1880   **Great Britain**
Employer's Liability Act; proves insufficient.

Supreme Court
Ex Parte Virginia, 100 U.S. 339. Civil Rights Act of 1875, which purported to make it illegal for private persons to discriminate in making public facilities available, is held unconstitutional.

1881   **Charities and social work**
"The American Red Cross" is founded.

1880s   **European Continent**
Social insurance begins to appear widely, especially in Germany under Bismarck.

1882   **U.S. federal**
Federal act restricting immigration of the mentally ill.

1883   **European Continent**
Bismarck: compulsory insurance against illness.

Great Britain
The "Fabian Society" is founded.

1884   **European Continent**
Bismarck: national plan of workmen's accident insurance.

Great Britain
Toynbee Hall Settlement House in London (Samuel A. Barnett).

U.S. federal
The Bureau of Labor Statistics is established.

Charities and social work
"Hebrew Sheltering and Immigrant Aid Society" in the United States.

1886   **Great Britain**
Booth's study of the living conditions of people by trades (30 percent of London's population was on, or below, the poverty line).

Selected events
Haymarket bombing in Chicago; organized labor is accused of anarchism.

Publications
U.S. Commissioner of Labor, *Industrial Depressions.*

Charities and social work
Neighborhood Guild Settlement House in New York (Coit).

The Salvation Army is established in the United States.

1887   **Publications**
Campbell, *Prisoners of Poverty: Women Wage Earners, Their Trade and Their Lives.*

Bellamy, *Looking Backwards*

Charities and social work
"Associated Charities of Denver" is established, the first federated fund drive.

1888   **Publications**
McCulloch, "The Tribe of Ishmael" sees degeneracy of the individual as the causes of pauperism.

1889   **European Continent**
Germany: compulsory disability and old age insurance.

Publications
Carnegie, *Wealth*

Charities and social work
Hull House Settlement in Chicago (Jane Addams).

College Settlement House in New York (Scudder).

1890   **U.S. federal**
Pension Act provides pensions to veterans, their widows and orphans, based on need only.

The *Sherman Anti-Trust Law.*

Publications
Riis, *How the Other Half Lives.*

1891   **European Continent**
Denmark: Program of "pensions" to the needy over age sixty.

Publications
"Concerning New Things," Encyclical Letter of Pope Leo XIII, accepting unions and family allowances.

Carnegie, "The Advantages of Poverty."

Charities Review, periodical; becomes *Charities* in 1901 and *Charities and the Commons* in 1905.

1892 **Selected events**
"The People's Party" organized at Saint Louis.

The Homestead Steel Strike, there are pitched battles between strikers and Pinkerton detectives.

Publications
Riis estimates that 20–30 percent of New York's population lives in poverty.

Betts, "Some Tenement House Evils."

Charities and social work
South End House Settlement in Boston (Woods).

1893 **European Continent**
Berne, Switzerland: limited unemployment insurance program.

Charities and social work
Henry Street Settlement House in New York (Wald).

1894 **Great Britain**
Poor Law Amendment: makes members of the boards of guardians which administered poor relief elected officers.

Selected events
The Pullman Strike over cut in wages with no cut in rent or profits.

"General" Coxey's army of unemployed marches on Washington, D.C.

Publications
Crane, *Maggie, a Girl of the Streets.*

U.S. Commissioner of Labor, *The Slums of Baltimore, Chicago, New York, and Philadelphia.*

Warner, *American Charities*, examines the causes of poverty.

1895 **Publications**
Report of the Tenement House Committee (New York).

American Journal of Sociology is started.

Addams, "A Belated Industry"; about domestic work.

Supreme Court
Pollock v. Farmer's Loan and Trust Co., 157 U.S. 429, 158 U.S. 601. Federal income tax declared unconstitutional.

1896 **Selected events**
William Jennings Bryan runs for president, supported by the Populists. This signals the high point of the Populist movement.

Publications
Kelley, *Third Annual Report of the Factory Inspectors of Illinois.*

The Commons, a journal for settlement workers. Becomes *Charities and the Commons* in 1905.

Moore, "A Day at Hull House."

Supreme Court
Plessy v. Ferguson, 163 U.S. 537 accepts the separate but equal doctrine.

1897 **Great Britain**
Workmen's Compensation Act.

Selected events
Beginnings of the Progressive movement.

Outdoor public relief outlawed in New York City Charter.

Publications
MacLean, "Factory Legislation for Women in The United States."

U.S. Commissioner of Labor, *Work and Wages of Men, Women and Children.*

1898 **New Zealand**
Pensions for the needy aged.

U.S. state
Pensions for the blind introduced in Ohio.

Selected events
New City Charter in Baltimore prohibits all public relief to adults except in almshouses.

All allotments of relief to poor in the U.S.A. to be distributed through a central private agency in Washington D.C.

Charities and social work
New York School of Philanthropy inaugurates six-week formal training courses in social work; expands to full-year program in 1904.

1899 **U.S. state**
Juvenile Court Law in Illinois.

Publications
Addams, "Trade Unions—a Public Duty."

MacLean, "Two Weeks in Department Stores."

Richmond, *Friendly Visiting among the Poor.*

Charities and social work
"National Consumers League" organized by Florence Kelley.

1900 **Publications**
New York Tenement House investigations, model for later social surveys.

Peabody, *Jesus Christ and the Social Question.*

1901   **European Continent**
Ghent, Belgium: subsidized unemployment funds of labor unions.

Publications
R. S. Rowntree, *Poverty: A Study of Town Life* (published in Great Britain). Finds that 28 percent of the population of York lives in poverty.

Charities, absorbs *Charities Review* and becomes *Charities and the Commons* in 1905.

Hunter, *Tenement Conditions in Chicago.*

Bushnell, "Some Social Aspects of the Chicago Stock Yard."

Münsterberg, "Poor Relief in the United States."

1902   **Charities and social work**
"Goodwill Industries" organized.

1903   **U.S. state**
Illinois establishes the first child labor law.

Selected events
The National Women's Trade Union League is established.

Publications
Riis, *The Making of an American.*

Addams, "Child Labor and Pauperism."

De Forest and Veiller, *The Tenement House Problem.*

U.S. Commissioner of Labor, *The Cost of Living and Retail Prices of Food.*

1904   **Selected Events**
National Child Labor Committee, provides guidelines and policy.

Publications
MacLean, "The Sweatshop in Summer."

Hunter, *Poverty*, estimates of poverty in New York City.

Spencer, *The Principles of Ethics.*

Charities and social work
"National Tuberculosis Association."

1905   **Great Britain**
"Royal Commission on the Poor Laws and Relief of Distress" (reported in 1909).

Unemployed Workmen Act: relief by local distress committees, aid in finding employment.

Selected events
The "Ash-can School," realistic art portraying the poor.

Publications
Ryan estimates that 60 percent of the adult male wage earners receive

less than $600 annually (in large cities it is estimated that an annual income of $650–800 is needed to support a family of "normal" size); *A Living Wage* (published 1906).

Kellor, *Out of Work: A Study of Employment Agencies.*

The "Charities Publications Committee" is established to sponsor social investigations.

Charities and the Commons is established; becomes *Survey* in 1909. The new journal reflects the merging of settlement (*The Commons*) and charity (*Charities Review*) publications. *Survey* ceases publication in 1952.

Charities and social work
"Boy's Clubs of America" (Boston).

Supreme Court
Lochner v. New York 198 U.S. 45. A state law fixing maximum hours of employment is held unconstitutional.

1906   Great Britain
Provisions of Meals Act: free school lunches in elementary schools.

U.S. federal
Hepburn Act regulates some big businesses.

Food and Drug Act, in part a response to Sinclair's *The Jungle.*

Publications
Sinclair, *The Jungle.*

Alger, "Industrial Accidents and their Social Cost."

1907   Great Britain
Education Act: medical examination of school children.

Selected events
Russell Sage Foundation organized.

Publications
Rauschenbusch, *Christianity and The Social Crises.*

Kelley, *Obstacles to the Enforcement of Child Labor Legislation.*

More, *Wage-Earner's Budget: A Study of Costs of Living in New York City.*

1908   Great Britain
Old-age Pensions Act: five shillings per week to deserving poor over seventy years of age.

Publications
The Pittsburgh social survey (1907–8). Economic and social conditions.

Supreme Court
Muller v. Oregon, 208 U.S. 412. Legislation fixing maximum hours of employment for women held constitutional (Brandeis's brief).

Adair v. U.S., 208 U.S. 161. Federal law making it illegal for interstate carrier to discharge an employee because of his union membership held unconstitutional.

1909 **Great Britain**
Labor Exchange Act: Board of Trade to increase mobility of labor.

Selected events
"White House Conference on the Care of Dependent Children," leading to the establishment of a "Children's Bureau."

Publications
Chapin, *The Standard of Living among Workingmen's Families in New York City.*

MacLean, "Life in The Pennsylvania Coal Fields with Particular Reference to Women."

Charities and social work
"Community Welfare Councils."

"National Association for the Advancement of Colored People."

1910 **Selected events**
The Russell Sage Foundation establishes a "Committee on Women's Work," in 1916 becomes the "Division of Industrial Studies."

The first city department of welfare is established in Kansas City, Missouri.

Publications
U.S. Bureau of Labor, *Report on The Condition of Women and Child Wage Earners in the United States*, 13 Volumes, 1910–13.

Addams, *Twenty Years at Hull House.*

Butler, *Women and the Trades.*

Charities and social work
"Boy Scouts of America," founded in Chicago.

"National Urban League."

"Campfire Girls."

1911 **Great Britain**
National Insurance Act: health and unemployment benefits.

U.S. state
Workmen's Compensation, Wisconsin.

Mother's Pension, Illinois and Missouri.

Selected events
Carnegie Corporation.

Publications
Bosworth, *The Living Wage of Women Workers.* Survey of 450 women in Boston.

1912   **U.S. federal**
Children's Bureau established.

Selected events
Bull Moose Convention, high point of the Progressive movement.

Publications
Preliminary Report of the Factory Investigating Commission, New York State. Full report in 1913.

Goddard, *The Kallikak Family*; on feeblemindedness.

Charities and social work
"Girl Scouts of the U.S.A."

1913   **U.S. federal**
Sixteenth Amendment to the *U.S. Constitution:* federal income tax.

Federal Reserve System; reforms banking.

Selected events
Rockefeller Foundation formed.

Publications
Rubinow, *Social Insurance.*

Charities and social work
"American Cancer Foundation."

Modern Community Chest movement in Cleveland.

"Intercollegiate Bureau of Occupations" in New York City establishes a special department for social work as a unique field.

"Federation of Charity and Philanthropy," founded in Ohio, later becomes "Community Chest."

1914   **U.S. federal**
Federal Trade Commission Act.

Clayton Act: Workmen's Compensation Act.

Clayton Antitrust Act.

U.S. state
Bureau of Health Education in New York.

Charities and social work
Red Cross "Mercy Ship" to Europe at start of World War I.

"The Cleveland Foundation," i.e., "Community Chest."

1915   **Selected events**
"National Conference on Charities and Corrections" emphasizes public relief.

Supreme Court
Weber v. Freed, 239, U.S. 325. Congressional supremacy in fixing maximum hours for employees engaged on carriers in interstate commerce upheld.

Coppage v. Kansas, 238, U.S. 1. State cannot prevent an employer from refusing to employ a union member (reversed in 1949).

1916 **U.S. federal**
Child Labor Act forbids interstate shipment of goods produced in violation of age and hour standards, declared unconstitutional in 1919.

WORLD WAR I

1917 **U.S. federal**
War Risk Insurance Act covers death and disability due to war injuries.

Smith-Hughes Act: federal grants to states for vocational training in agriculture, industry, and home economics.

National Employment Service established.

Selected events
Julius Rosenwald Fund is established; concentrates on Negro education.

Publications
Richmond, *Social Diagnosis.*

Charities and social work
"National Social Workers Exchange" takes over the work of "The Intercollegiate Bureau of Occupations." Becomes "American Association of Social Workers" in 1921, "National Association of Social Workers" in 1955.

"American Friends Service Committee."

Red Cross Collects $100 million.

Supreme Court
Women's Minimum Wage Law held unconstitutional.

1918 **Great Britain**
Representation of People Act abolishes disenfranchisement for recipients of poor relief.

U.S. federal
U.S. Railroad Administration, 1918–20, takes over the administration of the railroads during the war.

National War Labor Board.

Charities and social work
"American Association of Hospital Social Workers"; later becomes "American Association of Medical Social Workers."

"United War Work Campaign" raises $200 million for international war relief agencies.

"Community Chests and Councils of America," first founded as "American Association for Community Organizations."

Supreme Court
Hammer v. Dogenhart, 247 U.S. 251. Congress cannot ban interstate

transportation of goods produced by child labor in violation of the act of 1916; reversed 1946.

1919   **U.S. federal**
Restriction on child labor in *Revenue Act;* declared unconstitutional in 1922.

Eighteenth Amendment to the *U.S. Constitution:* prohibition.

Selected events
The Red Scare and the Palmer Raids.

Twentieth Century Fund established.

"The Children's Bureau Conference on Child Welfare Standards."

Charities and social work
"American Association of the Visiting Teachers."

"The Easter Seal Society."

"American Association of Psychiatric Social Workers."

"Association of Training Schools of Professional Social Workers;" in 1952 becomes "Council on Social Work Education."

THE INTERLUDE OF THE 1920s

1920   **U.S. federal**
Nineteenth Amendment to the *U.S. Constitution*: women's suffrage.

Selected events
Sacco-Vanzetti case, 1920–1927.

Publications
Social Casework journal begins

Charities and social work
"Child Welfare League."

Homemaker services start in the United States.

1921   **U.S. federal**
Quota System Act: basis for Immigration Act of 1924.

Maternity and Infancy Act provides for services; expires 1929.

Selected events
"National Conference on Unemployment."

Publications
Dos Passos, *Three Soldiers.*

Charities and social work
"American Foundation for the Blind."

"National Social Workers Exchange" becomes "American Association of Social Workers." (Four sister organizations established by 1949).

1922   **Publications**
Child Welfare journal starts.

Charities and social work
"Section of Psychiatric Social Workers of the American Association of Hospital Social Workers."

Supreme Court
Bailey v. Drexel Furniture, 259 U.S. 20. Revenue Act of 1919 with clauses for child labor held unconstitutional.

1923 **U.S. state**
Old-Age Pensions in Montana.

Supreme Court
Adkins v. Children's Hospital, 261 U.S. 525. Congress' attempt to establish minimum wages for women in Washington D.C. held unconstitutional.

1924 **U.S. federal**
The *Immigration Act*, highly restrictive.

1925 **Great Britain**
Widow's, Orphans' and Old-Age Contributory Pension Act.

Selected events
The Scopes trial.

Supreme Court
Gillow v. New York, 261 U.S. 652, sustains the conviction under state law of the publisher of the *Communist Manifesto*.

1926 **U.S. federal**
Railway Labor Act; later becomes *U.S. Board of Mediation*, which becomes the *National Mediation Board*.

Charities and social work
"American Association of Psychiatric Social Workers," independent of "American Association of Hospital Social Workers."

1927 **Publications**
Social Service Review journal is founded.

1928 **Charities and social work**
Philanthropic peak of the 1920s: 500 lump sum gifts of $1 million or more.

Supreme Court
Ribnik v. McBride, 277 U.S. 350, denies state power to license and regulate employment agencies; reversed 1934, 1941.

1929 **Great Britain**
Local Government Act: fundamental reform of the public relief structure, now organized on the county level.

Selected events
Stock market crash.

Supreme Court
U.S. v. Schwimmer, 279 U.S. 644, sustains denial of citizenship to a pacifist; reversed 1946.

THE GREAT DEPRESSION

1930   **Selected events**
The Kellogg Foundation.

"White House Conference on Child Health and Protection."

"Emergency Committee for Employment"; recommendation not acceptable to the President.

Publications
Robinson, *A Changing Psychology in Social Case Work.*

1931   **Great Britain**
National Economy Act: unemployment assistance to those who have exhausted or are ineligible for unemployment insurance benefits.

U.S. state
Temporary Emergency Relief Administration in New York State, assisting local communities in financing unemployment relief.

Selected events
"The President's Organization on Unemployment Relief Committee" advises against federal aid to the unemployed.

Publications
Steffens, *Autobiography.*

Abbott, *Social Welfare and Professional Education.*

Supreme Court
Stromberg v. California, 283 U.S. 697: statute which bans the mere display of a communist flag is held unconstitutional.

1932   **U.S. federal**
Reconstruction Finance Corporation, terminated under Truman.

March: Federal Farm Board authorized to give 40 million bushels of wheat to the Red Cross for distribution; similar measures in June.

July: *Emergency Relief and Construction Act.*

Norris-La Guardia Act restricts the use of injunctions against union strikes.

U.S. state
Wisconsin, *Unemployment Insurance.*

1933   **Great Britain**
Children and Young Persons Act, comprehensive system of child care.

U.S. federal
Twenty-First Amendment to the *U.S. Constitution:* repeals the *Eighteenth Amendment* (prohibition).

March: *Civilian Conservation Corps;* expires 1935.

May: *Federal Emergency Relief Act:* expires 1935.

Tennessee Valley authority Act.

Emergency Banking Relief Act.

Agricultural Adjustment Act, farm price support; expires 1935.

Emergency Railroad Transportation Act; expires 1936.

Public Works Administration; becomes *Federal Works Agency* in 1939 when former act expires.

Securities Act.

National Recovery Administration; declared unconstitutional in 1936.

National Industrial Recovery Act; declared unconstitutional in 1935.

Home Owners Loan Corporation.

Wagner-Peyser Act: establishes a U.S. employment service.

Civil Works Administration; expires 1934.

Federal Housing Administration.

1934 **Great Britain**
Unemployment Act: administration of assistance placed in unemployment assistance boards.

Special Areas Development and Improvement Act, to alleviate immediate unemployment problem.

U.S federal
Securities Exchange Act.

U.S. state
New York: *Unemployment Compensation.*

Selected events
"Committee on Economic Security" and "Advisory Council on Economic Security" established.

Charities and social work
"Community Fund."

1935 **U.S. federal**
National Labor Relations Act (Wagner Act) recognizes labor's right to bargain collectively. In 1947 becomes the "National Labor Management Relations Act."

Public Utility Holding Company Act.

Work Progress Administration; expires 1939, continues as *Work Projects Administration,* which expires in 1943.

Social Security Act.

Publications
Sherwood, *The Petrified Forest.*

Supreme Court
Railroad Retirement Board v. Alton Railroad Co., 295 U.S. 330; *Railroad Retirement Act* held unconstitutional.

Schechter Poultry Corp. v. U.S., 295 U.S. 495; *National Industrial Recovery Act* held unconstitutional.

Louisville Joint Stock Land Bank v. Radford, 295 U.S. 515; the Frazier-Lemke *Farm Bankruptcy Act* held unconstitutional.

1936 **Great Britain**
Special Areas Reconstruction Agreement Act; same as Act of 1934

U.S. federal
Washington Job Protection Agreement; protection of workers with regard to mergers, acquisitions, and consolidations.

George-Deen Act, vocational training.

Federal Contracts Act (Walsh-Healy Act) contracts with the federal government for over $10,000 carry requirement for compliance with minimum wage and maximum hour standards.

Selected events
The Ford Foundation (not in operation until 1950).

Supreme Court
Morehead v. New York ex. rel. Tipaldo, 298 U.S. 587, strikes down a New York minimum wage law.

U.S. v. Butler, 287 U.S. 1; the *Agricultural Adjustment Act* held unconstitutional; act expired in 1935.

1937 **Great Britain**
Barlow Commission: "Royal Commission on The Distribution of The Industrial Population"; studies the causes of localized unemployment.

Selected events
Federal Social Security Administration in conflict with Illinois regarding compliance with mandatory financial and accounting procedures, with requirements for a fair hearing and with "other essentials of adequate administration."

Supreme Court
Helvering v. Davis; upholds the old-age benefits part of the *Social Security Act.*

National Labor Relations Board v. Jones and Laughlin Steel Corp. 301 U.S. 1, holds the *National Labor Relations Act* constitutional.

Steward Machine Co. v. Davis, 301 U.S. 548, holds the *Social Security Act* constitutional.

1938 **U.S. federal**
Railroad Unemployment Insurance.

Agricultural Adjustment Administration Act.

Federal Wage and Hours Law (Fair Labor Standards Act): minimum wages, overtime pay, and child labor provisions.

Selected events
Federal Social Security Administration in conflict with Oklahoma regarding exposure of padding of OAA rolls (157 corpses and 12 inmates of insane asylums received OAA) and regarding adequate records of eligibility.

Federal Social Security Administration in conflict with Ohio (Governor Daney) regarding inclusion of state merit system in the federal act.

Charities and social work
"National Foundation for Infantile Paralysis."

"March of Dimes."

Supreme Court
Missouri ex. rel. Gaines v. Canada, 305 U.S. 337; state cannot close doors of its university's law school to a qualified Negro applicant.

1939   **Great Britain**
"Unemployment Assistance Board" becomes "National Assistance Board"; deals also with war victims allowances.

U.S. federal
Amendment to the *Social Security Act*, inclusion of survivors and disability insurance.

Work Projects Administration; expires 1943.

Federal Works Agency, expires 1943.

Selected events
"Bureau of Employment Security" established.

Publications
Steinbeck, *Grapes of Wrath*.

Supreme Court
Mulford v. Smith, 307 U.S. 38, sustains the right of legislature to use taxing power to regulate commerce.

1940   **Great Britain**
Old-age Pensions Act; additional pensions based on individual needs, especially medical care.

U.S. federal
Amendment to the *Social Security Act*, the merit system to be used in the administration of the Social Security Act.

Selected events
"White House Conference on Children in a Democracy."

Federal Social Security Administration in conflict with Ohio concerning whether the state should be reimbursed for loss sustained during period of suspension. (Ohio lost.)

World War II

1941   **Publications**
The Beveridge Report published in Great Britain.

U.S. federal
Office of Price Administration: rationing, price ceilings, rent controls, family budgets; terminates in 1947.

"Fair Employment Practices Committee" by executive order. Not effective; strengthened in 1943.

Secretary of agriculture takes over functions later granted to War Foods Administration.

Community Facilities Act gives federal aid to defense-impacted communities.

Charities and social work
"United Service Organizations."

Supreme Court
Child labor restrictions of the *National Recovery Act*, which were declared unconstitutional in 1935, are now upheld.

Olsen v. Nebraska, 313 U.S. 236; state maximum price regulation is held properly to extend to employment agencies.

Mitchell v. U.S., 313 U.S. 80; Negro passengers cannot lawfully be segregated into unfavorable railroad accommodations.

1942   U.S. federal
War Shipping Administration.

War Manpower Commission, control over allocation of labor.

War Production Board; terminates 1946.

National War Labor Board, mediation and arbitration; supercedes the *National Defense Mediation Board;* terminates 1946.

Publications
National Resources Planning Board, *Security, Work and Relief Policies*, evaluating and summarizing the policies and legislation of the 1930s.

Charities and social work
"National War Fund" established.

1943   U.S. federal
Office of War Utilities; terminates 1946.

"Fair Employment Practice Committee," to encourage and enforce non-discrimination against blacks (by executive order).

Emergency Maternity and Infant Care Program provides health care for servicemen's dependents.

Smith-Connely Act empowers government to take over plants during strikes.

Charities and social work
"United Nations' Relief and Rehabilitation Administration."

1944   Great Britain
White Paper on postwar unemployment.

Disabled Persons' Act, industrial or commercial enterprises with regular working force of twenty or more workers required to employ disabled persons (usually to constitute 3 percent of working force).

U.S. federal
Servicemen's Readjustment Allowances Program (the G.I. Bill of Rights): vocational training, unemployment benefits, aid for further education; expires 1952, reenacted.

1945   **Great Britain**
Distribution of Income Act.

Family Allowance Act: families with two or more children eligible.

Publications
Beveridge, *Full Employment in A Free Society.*

Charities and social work
CARE food packages to Europe.

THE INTERLUDE OF THE LATE 1940s AND THE 1950s

1946   **Great Britain**
National Health Service Act, program of public health.

National Insurance Act, old-age invalidity and health.

National Injuries Act, workmen's compensation.

U.S. federal
Amendment to the *Social Security Act,* extended coverage.

National School Lunch Program.

Employment Act, creates "Council of Economic Advisors" for providing guidance for the President's fiscal and monetary policies and establishes full employment as a government goal.

Produce and Marketing Administration of the U.S. Department of Agriculture.

George-Barden Act, vocational training.

U.S. state
Open Occupancy Act in Massachusetts.

Charities and social work
"American Association of Group Workers."

"Association for the Study of Community Organizations."

Supreme Court
Morgan v. Virginia, 328 U.S. 373, disposes of a state law requiring segregation of white and Negro passengers on interstate carriers.

1947   **Great Britain**
Town and Country Planning Act.

U.S. federal
Taft-Hartley Act, (Labor Management Relations Act), restricts discretion of unions to strike.

1948   **Great Britain**
Children's Act establishes a children's committee in each county as authority for child care (ages 0–18).

National Assistance Act: public assistance.

Children's and Young Person's Act Amendment: supplementation by professional personnel, preventive services, modern child care methods.

U.S. federal
Amendment to the *Social Security Act:* benefits increased over presidential veto.

Supreme Court
Shelley v. Kraemer, 334 U.S. 1, and *Hurd v. Hodge,* 334 U.S. 24; neither state nor federal courts can enforce covenants restricting the sale of property on the ground of race.

1949   **U.S. federal**
Housing Act.

Charities and social work
"Social Work Research Group."

1950   **Great Britain**
Adoption Act: protection of child, mother, and adopting parents.

U.S. federal
Amendment to the *Social Security Act:* adult benefits included in the ADC category.

NOLEO Amendment to the *Social Security Act:* "Notice to Law Enforcement Officials" regarding cases of desertion in the ADC category.

Amendment to the *Social Security Act,* to include "Aid to the Permanently and Totally Disabled" (APTD).

McCarran Internal Security Act, registration of Communist organizations.

Selected events
"Mid-Century White House Conference on Children and Youth."

Supreme Court
American Communication Association v. Donds, 339 U.S. 382, gives sanction to the requirement that officers of labor unions file affidavits with the National Labor Relations Board.

McLauring v. Oklahoma State Regents, 339 U.S. 639, segregation of Negro students within state law school is invalid.

Sweatt v. Painter, 339 U.S. 629, state law admitting only Negro students is unconstitutional.

1951   **U.S. federal**
Jenner Amendment to the *Social Security Act,* welfare data should be available to the public, but not to be used for political or commercial purposes.

Selected events
The Bureau of Labor Statistics ceases publication of standard family budgets.

Charities and social work
U.S.O. reactivated.

Supreme Court
Dennis v. U.S., 341 U.S. 494, holds *Smith Act*, which made it illegal to teach or advocate the overthrow of the government by force or violence, constitutional as applied to leaders of the Communist party.

1952   **U.S. federal**
Amendment to the *Social Security Act:* benefits increased.

Defense Manpower Policy No. 4, revised 1953, channels government contracts to surplus labor areas.

Charities and social work
"Council on Social Welfare Education" absorbs "American Association of Schools of Social Work" and "National Association of Schools of Social Administration."

1953   **Publications**
Clough, *The American Way: The Economic Basis of Our Civilization*, praises the American system of economy and its success in establishing a wealthy society.

1954   **U.S. federal**
Amendment to the *Training and Rehabilitation Act* puts new emphasis on rehabilitation.

Milk Program for needy children.

Selected events
Senate censures McCarthy tactics.

Publications
Bureau of Employment Security: sample survey of six states on the adequacy of unemployment benefits; survey terminated 1958; finds that benefits are inadequate, especially for married workers.

Supreme Court
Brown v. Board of Education of Topeka, 347 U.S. 483; segregated schooling, even at the elementary level, is held unconstitutional.

1955   **Selected events**
U.S. Congress establishes "Senate Subcommittee to Investigate Unemployment of the Committee on Labor and Welfare."

Charities and social work
"National Association of Social Workers" replaces seven old organizations.

1956   **U.S. federal**
Amendment to the *Social Security Act:* benefits increases, and federal government assumes a share of administrative costs of social services.

Supreme Court
Gayle v. Board of Commissioners, 352 U.S. 903, extends ruling in the school segregation cases to other municipal facilities, such as bus lines.

1957   **Great Britain**
Rent protection abolished.

U.S. federal
Voting Rights Act for federal elections.

Charities and social work
"Community Fund" and "Red Cross" join in "Crusade of Mercy."

1958   **U.S. federal**
Amendment to the *Social Security Act:* benefits increased.

National Defense Education Act.

Temporary Unemployment Compensation Act (TUC) extends coverage of unemployment insurance exhaustees during state's recessionary period.

Publications
Galbraith, *The Affluent Society.*

Charities and social work
"National Foundation," including efforts on behalf of rheumatic diseases, birth defects, and disorders of the central nervous system.

Supreme Court
National Association for the Advancement of Colored People v. Alabama ex. rel. Patterson, 357 U.S. 449, prohibits states from demanding membership lists from NAACP in the absence of good cause.

An Era of Social Unrest: The 1960s

1960   **Great Britain**
Local Employment Act.

U.S. federal
Civil Rights Act, voting provision.

Amendment to the *Social Security Act:* medical assistance included in benefits given to OAA recipients (*Kerr-Mills Act*).

Food Stamp Program introduced on temporary basis. Becomes permanent in 1964.

Selected events
Senate rejects first Medicare bill.

First sit-in in Greensboro, N.C.

"White House Conference on Children and Youth."

1961   **U. S. federal**
"Suitable Homes" clause in Louisiana clarified so that children have to be given other adequate help before any aid can be cut off—"Fleming Ruling."

Amendment to the *Social Security Act:* benefits increases and aid provided to families with unemployed fathers in the ADC category on experimental basis.

Area Redevelopment Act: $394 million is allocated for economically depressed areas.

Amendment to the *Fair Wage and Hours Law* (Fair Labor Standards Act): increases coverage, and minimum wage increases from $1.00 to $1.25 per hour.

Temporary Extended Unemployment Compensation Act (TEUC).

Selected events
Newburgh, N.Y.: welfare crisis concerning conditions of relief.

"White House Conference on Aging."

House and Rules Committee bottles up bill for $2.5 billion for school construction and teachers' salary.

Interstate Commerce Commission issues rules forbidding racial discrimination in interstate buses and terminals.

Martial law imposed in Montgomery, Ala., after racial violence.

Union of American Auto-Workers and American Motors start first profit-sharing program in the United States.

Supreme Court
Upholds internal security laws against Communist organizations.

Burton v. Wilmington Parking Authority, 365 U.S. 715, forbids the exclusion of Negroes by private owners of restaurants located on public property.

1962   **U.S. federal**
Public Works Acceleration Act.

New controls over farm production.

Amendment to the *Social Security Act*, "Aid to the Aged, Blind, and Disabled" (ADB), new emphasis on social service all but mandatory for states. Aid in ADC-UP category extended to include benefits for the unemployed person on a permanent basis.

Trade Expansion Act.

Manpower Development and Training Act: retraining the unemployed.

Selected events
Relief funds withheld in Illinois 1962–63.

"Interstate Conference of Employment Security Agencies."

New depreciation allowances allow $1.5 billion saving in taxes to businessmen.

Senate rejects second attempt to include health care for the aged in the *Social Security Act.*

Troops enter University of Mississippi to quell racial riots.

Publications
Friedman, *Capitalism and Freedom.*

Harrington, *The Other America.*

Keyserling, *Poverty and Deprivation in the United States,* indicates that two-fifths of the U.S. population live in poverty and deprivation.

Senator Byrd of West Virginia examines eligibility of ADC cases in the District of Columbia; 60 percent are found to be ineligible.

Bureau of Labor Statistics: intensive study of unemployment.

1963   **Great Britain**
Amendment to the *Children's Act of 1948:* strengthening of preventive services, improvement of juvenile court procedures.

U.S. federal
Vocational Training Act.

Selected events
Michigan: controversy about definition of "unemployment" in AFDC-UP cases. Federal administration rejects state plan.

Social Security Administration develops its low-income level which is adopted as the official poverty index.

Racial violence in Montegomery, Ala.

March on Washington, D.C., by 150,000 blacks and 50,000 whites led by Martin Luther King.

Nationwide Civil Rights demonstrations.

Senator Byrd repeats investigation of District of Columbia welfare department.

Publications
Caudill, *Night Comes to the Cumberlands,* describes poverty and exploitation in Appalachia.

Theobald, *Free Men and Free Markets,* discusses automation, unemployment and the need for adequate income.

Gordon, *The Economics of Welfare,* an international comparison of welfare expenditures.

McDonald, *Our Invisible Poor.*

Schorr, *Slums and Social Insecurity.*

Supreme Court
Petersen v. City of Greenville, 373 U.S. 244, forbids the exclusion of Negroes from privately owned restaurants and stores not located on public property.

1964   **U.S. federal**
Economic Opportunity Act, the War on Poverty.

Amendment to the *Social Security Act:* public assistance social workers must have B.A. degrees; AFDC benefits available to some older students; services to former, present, and potential recipients encouraged.

Twenty-fourth Amendment to the *U.S. Constitution:* prohibits the use of poll tax to deny the right to vote.

Civil Rights Act, establishes the "Equal Employment Opportunity Commission," to oversee implementation.

Elementary and Secondary Education Act.

Food Stamp Program extended on continuing basis.

Selected events
Nobel Peace Prize goes to Martin Luther King.

Publications
Bagdiken, *In the Midst of Plenty.*

May, *The Wasted Americans.*

Miller, *Rich Man, Poor Man.*

Charities and social work
"National Association of Social Workers" delegate assembly endorses the notion of "income as a matter of right, in amounts sufficient to maintain all persons throughout the nation at a uniformly adequate level of living."

1965   U.S. federal
Amendments to the *Social Security Act:* Medicare and Medicaid (Title IXX, medical assistance to the needy); more students eligible for AFDC benefits; some earnings are disregarded for public assistance recipients.

Economic Development Act, provides aid to several depressed regions.

Appalachian Regional Development Act.

Older Americans Act. Social services to persons over 60 years of age.

New standards for overtime pay.

Voting Rights Act, includes provisions for all elections, extended for five additional years in 1969.

Selected events
Civil Rights march on Selma, Alabama.

First nationwide teach-in on Vietnam policy.

Watts riot.

Nationwide demonstrations against the Vietnam war.

Publications
Theobald, *The Guaranteed Income.*

Ferman, Kornbluh and Haber, *Poverty in America.*

1966   U.S. federal
Child Nutrition Act, provides milk and breakfast for needy children at school.

Model Cities, coordinates federal and state and local programs at local community level.

Publications
Elman, *The Poorhouse State.*

Advisory Council on Public Welfare, *Having the Power We Have the Duty.*

Lewis, "Culture of Poverty."

1967   **U.S. federal**
Amendment to the *Social Security Act* provides for work incentives, earnings disregards and the WIN program; puts a freeze on the number of AFDC recipients. Freeze is lifted in 1969.

Selected events
Riots in Newark, N.J.

Wiley forms "National Welfare Rights Organization."

California Supreme Court rules that a public assistance worker cannot be fired for refusing to participate in "midnight raids" on AFDC homes. Most states terminate the "midnight raids."

Publications
National Committee against Discrimination in Housing, *How the Federal Government Builds Ghettos.*

1968   **U.S. federal**
Housing and Urban Development Act.

Selected events
Martin Luther King assassinated; widespread rioting.

Robert F. Kennedy assassinated.

"Poor People's Campaign" marches on Washington, D.C.

Violent demonstrations following the Democratic National Convention in Chicago.

Publications
President's National Advisory Commission on Civil Disorders reports its findings. Blames prejudice and discrimination.

Citizens Board of Inquiry into Hunger and Malnutrition in the United Sates reports on *Hunger U.S.A.*

Supreme Court
Housing Act of 1968 upheld.

King v. Smith, 392 U.S. 309; "substitute father" cannot be held responsible for the support of AFDC children, and his income may not be assumed to be available to AFDC children.

1969   **Selected events**
Nixon proposes *Family Assistance Plan* (Workfare). Would provide for a minimum guaranteed income for all families.

Largest anti-war demonstrations in U.S. history.

National Welfare Rights Organization occupies office of HEW Secretary Finch.

Publications
President's Commission on Income Maintenance Programs, *Poverty amid Plenty: The American Paradox.*

Supreme Court
Shapiro v. Thompson, 394 U.S. 618; holds durational residency requirements for public assistance unconstitutional.

1970 **Selected events**
Nationwide student demonstrations.

Resignation of Robert Finch, Secretary of the Department of Health, Education and Welfare.

Terrorist bombings in several U.S. cities.

Family Assistance Plan bottled up in committee.

Supreme Court
Goldberg v. Kelly, 397 U.S. 254; rejects the right to minimum subsistence as a basic entitlement under the Constitution.

Dandridge v. Williams, 397 U.S. 417; upholds the right of Maryland to impose absolute ceilings on welfare assistance payments regardless of family size and needs.

1972 **U.S. federal**
Amendment to the *Social Security Act:* establishes *Supplementary Social Insurance* as a replacement to the adult categories of public assistance, administered by the Social Security Agency. Automatic cost of living increases in social security benefits.

1973 **Selected events**
Wiley establishes "Movement for Economic Justice" for a broader coalition of lower-income people.

1974 **U.S. federal**
Federal regulations requires the separation of money payments and social services in the administration of public assistance.

Amendment to the *Social Security Act:* Title XX provides for state determination of social services with substantial federal support for services to public assistance recipients and "other needy" persons.

Notes

CHAPTER 2

1. By U.S. welfare programs we usually mean the following: Old Age, Survivors, Disability, and Health Insurance (OASDHI); Old Age Assistance (OAA); Aid to the Permanently and Totally Disabled (APTD); Aid to the Blind (AB); General Assistance (GA); Aid to Families with Dependent Children (AFDC); Unemployment Insurance (UI); and Medicare and Medicaid.

CHAPTER 3

1. These conclusions are based on a new calculation of the Cutright index (Cutright 1965, 1967a, b) which is simply the combined number of years that a country has had any law on the books dealing with the five major areas of social security (old age and invalidity, sickness and maternity, unemployment, work injury, and family allowances; these are the categories used by the United States Department of Health, Education, and Welfare in its periodical reports on *Social Security Programs throughout the World*, see United States Department of Health, Education, and Welfare 1976b). Using the Cutright index for 1977, the United States scored a low of 165 compared to East Germany's 352, Denmark's 345, Great Britain's 313, and a median index of 299 (same as that of Sweden) among twenty-two rich, industrialized nations studied by Wilensky (1975, 1976). These scores were calculated from United States Department of Health, Education, and Welfare 1976b, various pages.

2. See the Appendix for a chronology of specific historical events related to these trends.

3. The Humane Society in 1809, and J. V. N. Yates's survey in 1823. In Massachusetts, the Reverend Tuckerman undertook a survey of the poor in 1832. Much of the following discussion is based on Bremner 1956 and Breul 1969.

4. It is apparent that there were serious problems with poor children, and it is estimated that close to 10,000 "street arabs," i.e., homeless children, primarily boys, roamed the streets of New York in 1852. The population of New York County (Manhattan) in 1850 was 515,546, and the corresponding population of white and "free colored" males, aged 5-14 was 49,831 (Pickett 1969; United States Bureau of the Census 1972).

5. Some states had begun relatively early to remove certain groups from the almshouses. The insane were placed in special institutions beginning in 1773 in Virginia. Felons were removed to state prisons following the example of Philadelphia in 1790. Schools for the deaf were also established beginning with Kentucky in 1822. Later some states established schools for the blind, delin-

quents, and dependent children. For a discussion of the use of special institutions for such population groups see Rothman 1971. See also Pickett 1969.

6. For further discussion of the Freedman's Bureau, see DuBois 1965, pp. 212–39.

7. The following section on social workers is based on Lubove 1965. Differential casework means that the treatment given to a case is systematically varied according to the characteristics and needs of persons receiving treatment.

8. See, for example, Addams 1895, 1898; Kelley 1896, 1897; Moore 1896; MacLean 1897; Busnell 1901; Münsterberg 1901.

9. The following discussion of the Settlement movement is based in part on David 1967 and Hofstadter 1955.

10. One of the most colorful individuals who did involve himself in social reform during this period was LaGuardia. See Mann 1959.

CHAPTER 4

1. Although this program was designed eventually to pay its own way, it hasn't yet, and without major revisions in its financial structure will not do so in the future. Quite to the contrary, current estimates are that the social insurance funds will be exhausted by the late 1980s.

2. Actually, the unemployment rate increased from 1937 until the war economy developed.

3. This is not meant to imply that attempts at redistribution of income necessarily have been very successful in Western European countries. In general, most studies conclude that, with the possible exception of Norway, there has been no measurable redistribution of income in industrialized nations (Miller 1977, pp. 112–15). However, Paglin (1975) and Zald (1977) argue that if changes in population composition are taken into account, there has been a substantial redistribution of income downward, at least in the United States. See also Danziger and Plotnick 1977.

4. These ambivalences are amply illustrated in the mixed responses to survey questions focusing on individual responsibility for economic success, attitudes toward welfare programs, policies, and recipients, and the "fairness" of the system of mobility. See Schiltz 1970; Alston and Dean 1972; Feagin 1972; Kallen and Miller 1971; Williamson 1973, 1974; Ossowski 1963; Wrong 1969.

5. The craft unions (AFL) had obtained some legitimacy earlier.

6. Although the situation of American Indians is worse than that of blacks, the former are so few in number and so dispersed that blacks in fact do represent the largest low-status group in the United States, closely followed by Mexican-Americans and Puerto Ricans.

7. "Notice to Law Enforcement Officials" regarding the desertion of husbands in the ADC category. For a discussion of the issues underlying this amendment see Bell 1965 and Steiner 1966.

8. See the several articles by Mollie Orshansky in the *Social Security Bulletin* after 1963, describing the demographic characteristics of the poor.

9. Thus, in 1950 the United States ranked fifth in the world in infant mortality (i.e. only four nations had lower rates). By 1970 it was estimated that the United States ranked eighteenth, just above Hong Kong (Heilbroner 1970).

10. Recent proposals for a universal health insurance program in the United States are tailored to laissez-faire conceptions. The most viable proposal for a

national health care system would have the program administered by private insurance companies rather than by the government itself. It is also likely that the program itself would be seen as a further strengthening of the laissez-faire system by equalizing individual opportunities also in the area of health.

11. And it might be noted that there has long been a school of thought among businessmen who accept not only extensive government involvement in the economy, but also social welfare as long as it does not interfere with the supply of labor. For more on this "managerial branch" among businessmen, see Sutton et al. 1956.

CHAPTER 5

1. In 1910 women ever married had on the average given birth to 5.08 children by the time they were 50–59 years of age. In 1974, the corresponding group of women on the average had given birth to only 2.7 children, about half as many as their sisters in 1910 (United States Bureau of the Census 1975).

2. See Downs 1970 for the comparison of these poverty levels. The levels reported here have been adjusted for increases in the Consumer Price Index (CPI) until January of 1977. See also United States Department of Health, Education, and Welfare 1976a.

3. United States Bureau of the Census 1976b, p. 146, adjusted for changes in the CPI between 1974 and January of 1977. A more detailed description of the low-income level will be provided below.

4. Calculated from table A, p. 48 of United States Bureau of the Census 1976c. These data for 1975 were obtained from the revised procedure instituted by the Bureau of the Census in 1976. See also note 16 below.

5. United States Social and Rehabilitation Service 1977. The standards are reported in terms of monthly income. The annual figures presented here are simply the monthly standards multiplied by 12.

6. A similar picture emerges when we consider a retired couple. The Social Security Administration's budget for a family of two with a nonfarm residence and headed by a male sixty-five years of age or older was $3,260 in 1975 (United States Bureau of the Census 1976c, p. 33). The United States Department of Labor thought that $4,501 was necessary to provide a retired couple with a modest but adequate standard of living in an urban area in 1975 (McCraw 1976). Excluding gifts and contributions, that budget is lowered to $4,307, still about $1,035 above the poverty level as defined by the Social Security Administration during the same year.

7. We are talking here only about legitimate income. Income obtained illegally may itself be an attempt to escape poverty or replace employment income. However, by its very nature it is difficult to get any estimates of illegally obtained income and its contribution to overall levels of economic well-being.

8. United States Bureau of the Census 1976b. This report is the basis for all poverty statistics in this chapter, unless otherwise stated. More recent data was not available in sufficiently detailed form when this volume went to press.

9. In a society which places great value on children, it would seem out of order to ask the poor to forsake children as well as income, since there is no guarantee that they will not be poor if they do not have children.

10. United States Bureau of the Census 1973, p. 1–712. Of the noninstitutional

population aged sixteen to sixty-four with a work disability in 1970, 40.6 percent were too disabled to work. Of those able to work, although disabled, only 70.4 percent were actually working. All other disability data in this chapter from President's Commission on Income Maintenance Programs 1970.

11. In 1974, a person aged sixty-five to seventy-two could earn up to $2,100 a year without any reduction in social security benefits. There would be a reduction in monthly benefits of $1 for each $2 of annual earnings over $2,100. Since 1974 this earnings limit has been adjusted according to changes in the cost of living index; in 1976 it stood at $2,760 (*Social Security Bulletin Statistical Supplement 1974*, p. 29).

12. Bixby, Murray, and Belmore 1967. Very little information on this subject has been compiled since then. The *Social Security Bulletin Statistical Supplement 1974*, p. 81, indicates that of those eligible for social security benefits, 50 percent of those aged sixty-two to sixty-four, 87 percent of those aged sixty-five to seventy-one, and 99 percent of those aged seventy-two and over received some form of benefit.

13. This information has not been included in any of the reports on low-income population since 1970. Consequently, the data on union membership among the poor were obtained from United States Bureau of the Census 1971, pp. 59–60.

14. An income deficit is the amount of income needed to bring a particular family or individual up to the low-income level as determined by the Social Security Administration.

15. United States Bureau of the Census 1976c, p. 3, indicates that there was an increase in the poverty population between 1974 and 1975 to 25.9 million poor persons. The increase in the poverty population is actually more dramatic than these figures indicate, since the 1975 estimate was obtained using the revised procedure which reduced the poor population. The 1974 revised poverty population was 23.4 million persons. The following analysis of changes over time is based on the unrevised 1974 figures to prevent problems of comparability of data quality.

16. Adjusted for increases in the CPI, the average deficit for families in 1974 is still $43 larger than the average deficit in 1970. This was especially true of families headed by white males. There is considerable evidence that the CPI is not an adequate guide in evaluating the changing economic position of the poor. Recent estimates indicate, for example, that the cost of the type of food bought by the poor has increased more than twice as much as that food bought by more affluent Americans in recent years. Furthermore, the cost of health care, which constitutes a much larger proportion of the expenses of the aged than of any other age group, has increased much more than most of the other items included in the CPI. It may therefore be more appropriate to compare these deficits without adjusting for inflation to get a more accurate impression of changes in the economic well-being of the poor.

CHAPTER 8

1. There is some recent disagreement over the widely accepted conclusions and figures on inequality. Paglin (1975) standardizes the data for age in order to remove variations in income accompanying life cycle, and concludes that there has likely been some lessening of inequality over the decades. Zald (1977) echoes

this conclusion. However, an analysis of data on changes in income inequality from 1965 to 1974 (Danziger and Plotnick 1977) finds some increase in inequality over that period, and discovers that the increase can be only partially explained by changes in age and sex composition.

2. We quote such a cynical view not to endorse it totally. It is incorrect to conclude that educational opportunity in America is largely myth, for English did continue to serve as the principal language of the nation despite the many languages of its immigrants and the multilingual patterns that have developed in some other countries. In order adequately to evaluate the extreme critical view of educational opportunity, one must conduct the mental experiment of asking what would have happened, given the heterogeneity of the population, if the United States had not developed a mass public school system but instead a private or highly mixed one.

3. Their conclusions are disputed on methodological grounds. See also Brophy and Good (1974) and Rubovits and Maehr (1971).

4. Witness also the experience with "open enrollment" in the City University of New York: although substantial numbers of Blacks and Puerto Ricans were enabled to come into the system, the principal beneficiaries of broadened access seemed to be academically undistinguished, white, lower-middle-class and working-class students who heretofore had enrolled in private institutions or had foregone higher education. Examination of the beneficiaries of CUNY open enrollments in the context of the results of the great parallel expansion of the state system (SUNY) might be especially revealing.

5. Some analysts fear any challenge to the assumption that the system truly lives up to its meritocratic ideology, seeing demands for broadening the access of deprived groups to elite positions as dangerous to the central achievement values of the society. See Daniel Bell (1972). Such demands seem to receive little continued and serious attention in industry or elsewhere other than academia, however. In higher education, the use of quotas for the recruitment and retention of minority group members and women as students and faculty has had considerable vogue. However quotas rather easily become "targets for affirmative action" once the pressure of the moment has passed. As such, they have come to have partly a symbolic value and partly the meritocratic effect of making it more likely that minority group members and women are given the universalistic attention they might otherwise have failed to receive. Contrary to Bell's perspective, the hiring of a few black professors at abnormally high salaries and the belated appointment of a number of talented women to the positions they deserve at the end of the 1960s have not transformed American society.

6. For a portrait of losers, largely unable to deny their acceptance of midstream society's views that persons who hold the jobs they do can never really succeed, see Liebow (1966). A finely graded system of rating people by merit is in discord with an occupational system which sharply differentiates between primary (stable) and secondary (unstable) markets. See Reich, Gordon, and Edwards (1973).

7. The importance of this pattern regarding drug programs, and of various aspects of the professionalization of reform, has been conveyed by Joseph Helgot in conversations and in his paper (1974).

8. This derives in substantial manner from the federalized nature of the government. On the fragmentation and difficulties of coordinating administra-

tion in America, together with some of the advantages of this open system, see Crozier (1964), pp. 235–36.

9. Inspired by the remark of Prime Minister Trudeau that, in matters economic, Canada's situation vis-à-vis the United States was like "sleeping with an elephant—one feels every grunt and twitch."

10. A typical example here comes from an American teacher heard to say "I'm going to try the open classroom approach next Monday." Contrast this with the situation in Great Britain, where the development of informal education has involved a long history of organization and professional development. On this, see Featherstone (1971).

11. That the poor might not benefit as much from individual casework, which assumes readiness to verbalize and motivation, as middle-class people do is suggested in Cloward and Epstein (1965). The selection of "good" patients for psychiatric care is documented in Ross (1974).

12. The progress in the legal rights of recipients is important and results from social movement activities in and around the legal profession and by persons speaking for the poor. See Martin (1972).

13. The antipoverty program failed in its specifics, particularly with regard to the widespread reduction of poverty and enlargement of community participation. This generalization does not deny the success of occasional antipoverty programs. Efforts directed at community enrichment may have been most successful not in the cities, where the poor often fail to participate in already existing developed social and political networks, as in the rural areas not yet modernized and therefore lacking such networks. An example of partial success in such a location is provided in Street (1973). Comprehensive assessment of the War on Poverty requires seeing it as closely related to and in some ways indistinguishable from the nation's Civil Rights movement. This movement accomplished major changes, including a massive incorporation of blacks into the political mainstream, and improvement of the positions of Chicanos and American Indians, a massive change in the legal status of the poor, and the beginning of greater rights for inmates of correctional institutions.

CHAPTER 9

1. In the midst of the depression, Merton (1938) was arguing that Americans were so overtaken by the goals of pecuniary success that all other cultural variations could be regarded as forms of reconciliation to a career of failure. Only a short trip across the Hudson River could have demonstrated to Merton the size and significance of the American periphery, however.

Bibliography

Abbott, Edith. 1931. *Social welfare and professional education.* Chicago: University of Chicago Press.

Addams, Jane. 1895. A belated industry. *American Journal of Sociology* 1:536–50.

———. 1898. Trade unions and public duty. *American Journal of Sociology* 4:448–61.

———. 1903. Child labor and pauperism. In *Proceedings of the National Conference of Charities and Correction*, pp. 114–21.

———. 1961. *Twenty years at Hull House.* New York: New American Library.

Advisory Council on Public Welfare. 1966. *Having the power we have the duty.* Washington, D.C.: U.S. Government Printing Office.

Alberts, Robert C. 1974. Catch 65. *New York Times Magazine*, August 4, p. 11.

Alger, George W. 1906. Industrial accidents and their social cost. *Charities and the Commons* 27:791–844.

Alston, Jon P., and Dean Imogene. 1972. Socioeconomic factors associated with attitudes towards welfare recipients and the causes of poverty. *Social Science Review* 46 (March): 13–23.

Anderson, Nels. 1923. *The hobo.* Chicago: University of Chicago Press.

Arieli, Yehoshua. 1964. *Individualism and nationalism in American ideology.* Baltimore, Md.: Penguin Books.

Axinn, June, and Levin, Herman. 1975. *Social welfare: A history of the American response to need.* New York: Dodd, Mead, and Co.

Bagdiken, Ben H. 1964. *In the midst of plenty: The poor in America.* Boston: Beacon Press.

Baldwin, James, et al. 1969. *Black anti-semitism and Jewish racism.* New York: Schocken Books.

Banfield, Edward C. 1961. *Political influence.* New York: Free Press of Glencoe.

———. 1970. *The unheavenly city: The nature and future of our urban crisis.* Boston: Little, Brown and Co.

——. 1974. *The unheavenly city revisited.* Boston: Little, Brown and Company.

Banfield, Edward C., and Wilson, James Q. 1963. *City politics.* Cambridge, Mass.: Harvard University and M.I.T. Press.

Becker, Howard. 1963. *Outsiders.* New York: Free Press.

Bell, Daniel. 1972. On meritocracy and equality. *Public Interest* 29 (fall): 29–68.

Bell, Donald R. 1973. Prevalence of private retirement plans in manufacturing. *Monthly Labor Review* 96 (September): 29–32.

Bell, Winifred. 1965. *Aid to dependent children.* New York: Columbia University Press.

Bellamy, Edward. 1951. *Looking backward: 2000–1887.* New York: Random House.

Berg, Ivar. 1970. *Education and jobs: The great training robbery.* New York: Praeger.

Bernstein, Merton C. 1974. Federal standards and social welfare. *Monthly Labor Review* 97 (April): 41–43.

Betts, Lillian. 1892. Some tenement house evils. *The Century* 45: 314–16.

Beveridge, William H. 1945. *Full employment in a free society.* New York: W. W. Norton and Co.

Bixby, Leonore Epstein; Murray, Janet H.; and Belmore, Gidman. 1967. The aged population's economic status. In *Old age income assurance II. A compendium of papers on problems and policy issues in the public and private pension system,* ed. U.S. Congress, Joint Economic Committee. Washington, D.C.: U.S. Government Printing Office.

Blau, Thomas. 1969. Organizing participants for socal change: The poverty case. Unpublished paper, University of Chicago.

Bluestone, Barry. 1974. The poor who have jobs. In *The sociology of American poverty,* ed. Joan Huber and Peter Chalfant, pp. 141–54. Cambridge, Mass.: Schenkman Publishing Co.

Bogue, Donald. 1959. *The population of the United States.* New York: Free Press.

Boorstein, Daniel J. 1953. *The genius of American politics.* Chicago: University of Chicago Press.

——. 1965. *The Americans: The national experience.* New York: Random House.

Bosworth, Louise M. 1911. *The living wage of women workers: A study of incomes and expenditures of 450 women workers in the city of Boston.* New York: Longmans, Green and Company.

Bowles, Samuel. 1975. Unequal education and the reproduction of the social division of labor. In *Schooling in corporate society*, ed. Martin Carnoy. New York: David McKay (2d. edition).

Brace, Charles Loring. 1872. *The dangerous classes of New York and twenty years' work among them*. New York: Wynkoop and Hallenbeck.

Brackett, Jeffrey Richardson. 1903. *Supervision and education in charity*. New York: Macmillan Co.

Bremner,. Robert H. 1956. *From the depths: The discovery of poverty in the United States*. New York: New York University Press.

—————. 1960. *American philanthrophy*. Chicago: University of Chicago Press.

Breul, Frank R. 1965. Early history of aid to the unemployed in the United States. In *In aid to the unemployed*, ed. Joseph M. Becker, S.J., pp. 6-23. Baltimore, Md.: The Johns Hopkins Press.

Brown, Claude. 1965. *Manchild in the promised land*. New York: Macmillan.

Brophy, Jare, and Good, Thomas. 1974. *Teacher-student relationships: Causes and consequences*. New York: Holt, and Winston.

Bushnell, Charles J. 1901. Some social aspects of the Chicago stock yards. *American Journal of Sociology* 7:145-70, 289-330, 433-74, 687-702.

Butler, Elizabeth Beardsley. 1910. *Women and the trades*. New York: Charities Publication Committee.

Campbell, Helen. 1887. *Prisoners of poverty: Women wage-earners, their trades and their lives*. Boston: Roberts Brothers.

Carey, Matthew. 1833. *Appeal to the wealthy of the land, ladies as well as gentlemen, on character, conduct, situation and prospects of those whose sole dependence for subsistence is on the labour of their hands*. Philadelphia: Stereotyped by L. Johnson, No. 6 George Street.

Carnegie, Andrew. 1889. Wealth. *The North American Review* 148:653-64.

—————. 1891. The advantages of poverty. *Nineteenth Century Magazine* 29:370-71.

Caudill, Harry M. 1963. *Night comes to the Cumberlands*. Boston: Little, Brown.

Chapin, Robert Coit. 1909. *The standard of living among workingmen's families in New York city*. New York: Charities Publications Committee.

Citizens Board of Inquiry into Hunger and Malnutrition in the United States. 1968. *Hunger U.S.A.: A report*. New York: New Community Press.

Clark, Burton. 1960. The 'cooling-out' function in higher education. *American Journal of Sociology* 65 (May): 569–75.

Clough, Sheppard B. *The American way: The economic basis of our civilization.* New York: Thomas Y. Crowell Co.

Cloward, Richard A. 1964. Social class and private agencies. In *Education for social work 1963,* ed. Council on Social Work Education, pp. 123–36. New York: Council on Social Work Education.

Cloward, Richard, and Epstein, Irwin. 1965. Private social welfare's disengagement from the poor: The case of family adjustment agencies. In *Proceedings of the Annual Social Work Day Institute.* Buffalo: New York State University at Buffalo, School of Social Welfare.

Coleman, James, et al. 1966. *Equality of educational opportunity.* Washington: U.S. Office of Education.

Coll, Blanche D. 1969. *Perspectives in public welfare: A history.* Washington, D.C.: U.S. Government Printing Office.

Crane, Stephen. *Maggie, a girl of the streets.* New York: Newland Press, n.d.

Crozier, Michael. 1964. *The bureaucratic phenomenon.* Chicago: University of Chicago Press.

Cutright, Phillips. 1965. Political structure, economic development, and national social security programs. *American Journal of Sociology* 70 (March): 537–50.

———. 1967a. Inequality: A cross-naitonal analysis. *American Sociological Review* 32 (August): 562–78.

———. 1967b. Income redistribution: A cross-national analysis. *Journal of Social Forces* 46 (December): 180–90.

Dahl, Robert A. 1961. *Who governs? Democracy and power in an American city.* New Haven: Yale University Press.

Danziger, Sheldon, and Plotnick, Robert. 1977. Demographic change, government transfers, and income distribution. *Monthly Labor Review* 100 (April): 7–11.

Davis, Allen F. 1967. *Spearheads of reform: The social settlements and the progressive movement 1890–1914.* New York: Oxford University Press.

Davis, Harry E. 1973. Pension provisions affecting the employment of older workers. *Monthly Labor Review* 96 (April): 41–45.

De Forest, Robert W., and Veiller, Lawrence, eds. 1903. *The tenement house problem, including the report of the New York State Tenement House Commission of 1900.* 2 vols. New York: Macmillan Co.

Derthick, Martha. 1975. *Uncontrollable spending for social services grants.* Washington, D.C.: Brookings Institution.

Dickens, Charles. *The works of Charles Dickens.* National Library Edition, 20 vols. New York: Bigelow Brown and Company, n.d.

Dos Passos, John. 1921. *Three Soldiers.* New York: George H. Doran Co.

Downs, Anthony. 1970. *Who are the urban poor?* Supplementary paper no. 26. New York: Committee for Economic Development.

DuBois, William E. B. 1965. *Three negro classics.* New York: Avon Books Division, Hearst Corp.

Dugdale, Robert L. 1910. *The Jukes. A study in crime, pauperism, disease, and heredity.* Fourth edition. New York: G. P. Putnam's Sons.

Elder, Jr., Glen H. 1974. *Children of the Great Depression: Social change in life experience.* Chicago: University of Chicago Press.

Elman, Richard M. 1966. *The poorhouse state.* New York: Pantheon Books.

Fallers, Lloyd A. 1973. *Inequality: Social stratification reconsidered.* Chicago: University of Chicago Press.

Feagin, Joe R. 1972. America's welfare stereotypes. *Social Science Quarterly* 52 (March): 921–23.

Featherstone, Joseph. 1971. *Schools where children learn.* New York: Liveright.

Ferman, Louis A.; Kornbluh, Joyce L.; and Haber, Alan, eds. 1965. *Poverty in America: A book of readings.* Ann Arbor, Mich.: University of Michigan Press.

Forbes, Richard. 1973. Socialization of the public caseworker: Resolution of uncertainty. Ph.D. dissertation, University of Chicago.

Friedman, Milton. 1962. *Capitalism and freedom.* Chicago: University of Chicago Press.

Friedson, Eliot. N.d. Disability as social deviance. In *Sociology and rehabilitation,* ed. Marvin B. Sussman. Washington: American Sociological Association.

Fuchs, Victor. 1965. Toward a theory of poverty. In *The concept of poverty,* ed. Task Force on Economic Growth and Opportunity. Washington, D.C.: U.S. Chamber of Commerce.

Galbraith, John Kenneth. 1958. *The affluent society.* Boston: Houghton Mifflin.

Gans, Herbert. 1972. Foreword to *The great school legend: A revisionist interpretation of American public education* by Colin Greer. New York: Basic Books.

Garfinkel, Irving. 1977. Welfare, what's right and wrong about it. Paper presented at the Center for the Study of Democratic

Institutions, Chicago (November 22).

George, Henry. 1911. *Progress and poverty*. Twenty-fifth anniversary edition. Garden City, N.Y.: Doubleday, Page and Co.

Glaab, Charles N., and Brown, A. Theodore. 1967. *A history of urban America*. New York: The Macmillan Co.

Glazer, Nathan, and Moynihan, Daniel Patrick. 1963. *Beyond the melting pot*. Cambridge, Mass.: M.I.T. Press.

Goddard, H. H. 1912. *The Kallikak family*. New York: Macmillan.

Goode, William J. 1962. Marital satisfaction and instability. *International Social Science Journal* 14:507–26.

Gordon, Laura. 1972. The intake process: Application and decision in public welfare bureaucracy. Ph.D. dissertation, State University of New York at Stony Brook.

Gordon, Margaret S. 1963. *The economics of welfare policy*. New York: Columbia University Press.

Greeley, Andrew. 1974. Political participation among ethnic groups in the United States: A preliminary reconnaissance. *American Journal of Sociology* 80:170–204.

Greenstone, John David. 1969. *Labor in American politics*. New York: Knopf.

Greenstone, John David, and Peterson, Paul. 1968. Reformers, machines and the war on poverty. In *City Politics and Public Policy*, ed. James Q. Wilson, pp. 278–86. New York: Wiley.

Griscom, John H. 1845. *The sanitary condition of the laboring population of New York with suggestions for its improvement*. New York: Harper and Brothers.

Gronbjerg, Kirsten A. 1977. *Mass society and the extension of welfare, 1960–1970*. Chicago: University of Chicago Press.

Gusfield, Joseph. 1963. *Symbolic crusade: Status politics and the American temperance movement*. Urbana, Ill.: University of Illinois Press.

Hammerman, Herbert. 1972. Minority workers in construction referral unions. *Monthly Labor Review* 95 (May): 17–26.

Hansen, W. Lee, and Wiesbrod, Burton A. 1969. *Benefits, costs, and finance of public higher education*. Chicago: Markham.

Hapgood, David. 1971. *Diplomaism*. New York: Donald W. Brown.

Harrington, Michael. 1962. *The other America*. New York: Macmillan Press.

Heclo, Hugh. 1974. *Modern social politics in Britain and Sweden*. New Haven: Yale University Press.

Heilbroner, Robert L. 1968. *The economic problem*. Englewood Cliffs: Prentice-Hall.

———. 1970. Benign neglect in the United States. *Transaction* 7 (October): 15–22.

Helfgot, Joseph. 1974. Professional reform organizations and the symbolic representation of the poor. *American Sociological Review* 29 (August): 475–91.

Henle, Peter. 1972. Recent trends in retirement benefits related to earnings. *Monthly Labor Review* 95 (June): 12–20.

Henle, Peter, and Schmitt, Raymond. 1974. Pension reform: The long, hard road to enactment. *Monthly Labor Review* 97 (November): 3–12.

Hofstadter, Richard. 1955. *The age of reform.* New York: Random House.

Howell, Joseph T. 1973. *Hard living on Clay Street.* Garden City, N.J.: Anchor Books.

Huber, Joan. 1974a. Political implications of poverty definitions. In *Sociology of American poverty,* ed. Joan Huber and Peter Chalfant, pp. 71–80. Cambridge, Mass.: Schenkman Publishing Co.

———. 1974b. The war on poverty. In *The Sociology of American poverty,* ed. Joan Huber and Peter Chalfant, pp. 300–323. Cambridge, Mass.: Schenkman Publishing Co.

Hughes, Everett C. 1958. *Men and their work.* New York: Free Press, 1958.

Hunter, Robert. 1901. *Tenement conditions in Chicago: Report by the investigating committee of the City Homes Association.* Chicago: City Homes Association.

———. 1965. *Poverty: Social conscience in the progressive era,* ed. Peter d'A. Jones. New York: Harper and Row.

Jackson, Jesse. 1976. Give the people a vision. *New York Times Magazine,* April 18.

Jacobs, Jerry. 1969. Symbolic bureaucracy: A case study of a social welfare agency. *Social Forces* 47 (June): 413–22.

Janowitz, Morris. 1969. *Institution-building in urban education.* New York: Russell Sage Foundation.

———. 1975. The all-volunteer military as a "sociopolitical" problem. *Social Problems* 22 (February): 432–49.

———. 1976. *Social control and the welfare state.* New York: Elsevier.

Janowitz, Morris, and Suttles, Gerald D. 1977. The social ecology of citizenship. Paper presented at Conference on Issues in the Administration of Human Service Organization. The Johnson Foundation, Racine, Wis. (June).

Jefferson, Thomas. 1964 [1781] *Notes on the state of Virginia.* New York: Harper and Row.

Jencks, Christopher, et al. 1972. *Inequality: A reassessment of the effect of family and schooling in America.* New York: Basic Books.

Jenkins, J. Craig, and Perrow, Charles. 1977. Insurgency of the powerless: Farm labor movements (1946-1972). *American Journal of Sociology* 42:249-68.

Kallen, David J., and Miller, Dorothy. 1971. Public attitudes toward welfare. *Social Work* 16 (July): 83-90.

Katz, Elihu, and Eisenstadt, S. N. 1960. Some sociological observations on the response of Israeli organizations to new immigrants. *Administrative Science Quarterly* 5 (June): 113-33.

Kelley, Florence. 1896a. The working boy. *American Journal of Sociology* 2:358-68.

———. 1896b. *Third annual report of the factory inspectors of Illinois.* Springfield, Ill.: Ed. F. Hartman, State Printer.

———. 1897. The Illinois child-labor law. *American Journal of Sociology* 3:490-501.

———. 1907. *Obstacles to the enforcement of child labor legislation.* New York: National Child Labor Committee.

Kellor, Frances A. 1905. *Out of work. A study of employment agencies: Their treatment of the unemployed, and their influence upon homes and business.* New York: G. P. Putnam's Sons.

Kingston, Maxine Hong. 1976. *The woman warrior: Memoirs of a girlhood among ghosts.* New York: Knopf.

Kolko, Gabriel. 1962. *Wealth and power in America.* New York: Frederick A. Praeger.

Kolodrubetz, Walter W. 1973. Private retirement benefits and relationship to earnings: Survey of new beneficiaries. *Social Security Bulletin* 36 (May): 16-37.

Kornblum, William. 1974. *Blue collar community.* Chicago: University of Chicago Press.

Kroeger, Naomi. 1971. Organizational goals, politics, and output: The dilemma of public aid. Ph.D. dissertation, University of Chicago.

Lewis, Oscar. 1966. The culture of poverty. *Scientific American* 215, no. 4, pp. 19-25.

Liebow, Elliot. 1966. *Tally's corner: A study of negro streetcorner men.* Boston: Little, Brown and Co.

Light, Ivan H. 1972. *Ethnic enterprise in America.* Berkeley: University of California Press.

Light, Ivan, and Wong, Charles Choy. 1975. Protest or work: Dilemmas of the tourist industry in American chinatowns. *American Journal of Sociology* 80 (May): 1342-68.

Lofland, John, and Stark, Rodney. 1965. Becoming a world-saver: A theory of conversion to a deviant perspective. *American Sociological Review* 30 (December): 862-75.

Lowi, Theodore. 1969. *The end of liberalism: Ideology, policy, and the crisis of public authority.* New York: W. W. Norton and Co.

Lubove, Roy. 1965. *The professional altruist: The emergence of social work as a career, 1880–1930.* Cambridge, Mass.: Harvard University Press.

MacLean, Annie M. 1897. Factory legislation for women in the United States. *American Journal of Sociology* 3:183–205.

———. 1899. Two weeks in department stores. *American Journal of Sociology* 4:721–41.

———. 1904. The sweat-shop in summer. *American Journal of Sociology* 9:289–309.

———. 1909. Life in the Pennsylvania coal fields with particular reference to women. *American Journal of Sociology* 14:329–51.

Malthus, Thomas Robert. 1816. *Essay on the principle of population.* 7th ed. London: J. M. Dent & Sons Ltd.

Mandeville, Bernard. 1772. *Fable of the bees or private vices, public benefits.* Edinburgh: Printed for W. Gray and W. Petz.

Mann, Arthur. 1959. *La Guardia: A fighter against his times, 1882–1933.* Chicago: University of Chicago Press.

Marshall, T. H. 1964, 1977. *Class, citizenship, and social development.* Chicago: University of Chicago Press.

Martin, George. 1972. The emergence and development of a social movement organization among the underclass: A case study of welfare rights. Ph.D. dissertation, University of Chicago.

Marx, Karl. (1867) 1906. *Capital.* Chicago: C. H. Kerr.

May, Edgar. 1964. *The wasted Americans: Cost of our welfare dilemma.* New York: Harper and Row.

McCarthy, John D., and Zald, Mayer N. 1973. *The trend of social movements in America: Professionalization and resource mobilization.* Morristown, N.J.: General Learnings Press.

McCraw, M. Louise. 1976. Retired couple's budgets updated to autumn 1975. *Monthly Labor Review* 99 (October): 36–39.

McCulloch, Oscar C. 1888. The tribe of Ishmael: A study in social degradation. In *Proceedings of the National Conference of Charities and Correction,* pp. 154–59. Boston: George H. Ellis.

McDonald, Dwight. 1963. *Our invisible poor.* New York: Sidney Hillman Foundation.

Merton, Robert K. 1938. Social structure and anomie. *American Sociological Review* 3 (October): 672–82.

———. 1957. Bureaucratic structure and personality. In his *Social theory and social structure.* New York: Free Press.

Miller, Herman P. 1964. *Rich man, poor man.* New York:

Thomas Y. Crowell.

Miller, S. M. 1977. Affecting the primary distribution of income in industrialized market economy countries. *Labour and Society* 2 (April): 111–44.

Miller, S. M., and Roby, Pamela. 1970. *The future of inequality.* New York: Basic Books.

Mills, C. Wright. 1956. *The power elite.* New York: Oxford University Press.

Monahan, Thomas P. 1955. Divorce by occupational level. *Journal of Marriage and Family Living* 17 (November): 322–24.

Moore, Dorothea. 1896. A day at Hull House. *American Journal of Sociology* 2:629–42.

More, Louise Bolard. 1907. *Wage-earners' budgets. A study of standards and cost of living in New York city.* New York: Henry Holt and Co.

Morrill, Richard L., and Wahlenberg, Ernest H. 1971. *The geography of poverty in the United States.* New York: McGraw Hill.

Moynihan, Daniel Patrick. 1965a. *The negro family.* Washington, D.C.: Office of Policy Planning and Research, U.S. Department of Labor.

———. 1965b. The professionalization of reform. *The Public Interest* 1 (fall): 6–16.

———. 1969. *Maximum feasible misunderstanding.* New York: Free Press.

Münsterberg, E. 1901. Poor relief in the United States. *American Journal of Sociology* 7:501–38, 659–86.

Murray, R. K. 1955. *Red scare: A study in national hysteria, 1919–1920.* Minneapolis: University of Minnesota Press.

Myrdal, Gunnar. 1962a. *An American dilemma: The negro problem and modern democracy.* New York: Harper.

———. 1962b. *Challenge to affluence.* New York: Random House.

National Committee against Discrimination in Housing. 1967. *How the federal government builds ghettos.* Washington, D.C.: U.S. Government Printing Office.

National Resources Planning Board. 1942. *Security, work and relief policies.* Washington, D.C.: U.S. Government Printing Office.

Nelli, Humbert S. 1970. *Italians in Chicago: 1880–1930.* New York: Oxford University Press.

New York State Factory Investigating Commission. 1912. *Preliminary report of the Factory Investigating Commission,* 3 vols. Albany: Argus Company.

Novak, Michael. 1971. *The rise of the unmeltable ethnics*. New York: Macmillan.

Orshansky, Mollie. 1965a. Counting the poor: Another look at the poverty profile. *Social Security Bulletin* 28 (January): 3–29.

———. 1965b. Who's who among the poor: A demographic view of poverty. *Social Security Bulletin* 28 (June): 3–32.

———. 1969. How poverty is measured. *Monthly Labor Review* 92 (February): 37–41.

Ossowski, Stanislaw. 1963. *Class structure in the social consciousness*. New York: Macmillan.

Paglin, Morton. 1975. The measurement and trend of inequality: A basic revision. *American Economic Review* 65 (September): 598–609.

Paine, Thomas. 1942. *The rights of man*. Reprinted in *Basic writings of Thomas Paine*. New York: Wiley.

Peabody, Francis G. 1900. *Jesus Christ and the social question*. New York: Macmillan.

Pechman, Joseph A. 1970. The distributional effects of public higher education in California. *Journal of Human Resources* 5 (Summer): 361–70.

Pickett, Robert S. 1969. *House of refuge: Origins of juvenile reform in New York State, 1815–1857*. Syracuse, N.Y.: Syracuse University Press.

Piven, Frances Fox, and Cloward, Richard A. 1971. *Regulating the poor: The functions of public welfare*. New York: Random House.

Pope Leo XIII. 1891. *Rerum novarum*. Encyclical letter.

President's Commission on Income Maintenance Programs. 1969. *Poverty amid plenty: The American paradox*. Washington, D.C.: U.S. Government Printing Office.

———. 1970. *Background papers*. Washington, D.C.: U.S. Government Printing Office.

President's National Advisory Commission on Civil Disorders. 1968. *Report of the national advisory commission on civil disorders*. Washington, D.C.: U.S. Government Printing Office.

Quincy, Josiah. 1821. *Report of the committee to whom was referred the consideration of the pauper laws of this Commonwealth*. Reprinted in *Poverty, U.S.A.: The almshouse experience*. New York: Arno Press. 1971.

Rauschenbusch, Walter. 1907. *Christianity and the social crisis*. New York: Macmillan.

Reich, Michael; Gordon, David M.; and Edwards, Richard C. 1973. A theory of labor market segmentation. *American Economic Review* 63 (May): 359–65.

Rein, Martin, and Heclo, Hugh. 1973. What welfare crisis?—
A comparison among the United States, Britain, and Sweden.
Public Interest 33 (fall): 61–83.

Richmond, Mary Ellen. 1899. *Friendly visiting among the poor:
A handbook for charity workers.* New York: Macmillan.

————. 1917. *Social diagnosis.* New York: Russell Sage Foundation.

Riis, Jacob. 1890. *How the other half lives.* New York: Charles
Scribner.

————. 1903. *The making of an American.* New York: Macmillan.

Rischin, Moses, ed. 1965. *The American gospel of success: Individualism and beyond.* Chicago: Quadrangle Books.

Robinson, Virginia Pollard. 1930. *A changing psychology in
social case work.* Philadelphia: University of Pennsylvania,
Ph.D. dissertation.

Rose, Arnold. 1967. *The power structure.* London: Oxford University Press.

Rosenthal, Robert, and Jacobson, Lenore. 1968. *Pygmalion in the
classroom: Teacher expectation and pupils' intellectual development.* New York: Holt, Rinehart and Winston.

Ross, Doris Byrd. 1974. The social organization of a psychiatric
clinic. Ph.D. dissertation, University of Chicago.

Ross, Heather L., and Sawhill, Isabel V. 1975. *Time of transition: The growth of families headed by women.* Washington,
D.C.: Urban Institute.

Rothman, David J. 1971. *The discovery of the asylum: Social
order and disorder in the new republic.* Boston: Little, Brown
and Co.

Rowntree, B. Seebohm. 1901. *Poverty: A study of town life.*
London: Macmillan and Co.

Rubin, Leonard. 1974. Economic status of black persons: Findings from the survey of newly entitled beneficiaries. *Social
Security Bulletin* 37 (September): 3.

Rubinow, I. M. 1913. *Social insurance, with special reference to
American conditions.* New York: Henry Holt and Co.

Rubovits, Pamela, and Maehr, Martin. 1971. Pygmalion analyzed: Toward an explanation of the Rosenthal-Jacobson findings. *Journal of Personality and Social Psychology* 19 (August):
197–203.

Ryan, John A. 1906. *A living wage: Its ethical and economic aspects.* New York: Macmillan.

Ryan, William. 1971. *Blaming the victim.* New York: Random
House.

Scanzone, John A. 1970. *Opportunity and the family: A study of the conjugal family in relation to the economic-opportunity structure.* New York: Free Press.

Schiller, Bradley R. 1973. Empirical studies of welfare dependency: A survey. *Journal of Human Resources* 81 (September): 19–32.

Schiltz, Michael E. 1970. *Public attitudes towards social security, 1935–65.* Washington, D.C.: U.S. Government Printing Office.

Schlesinger, Arthur M., Jr. 1945. *The age of Jackson.* Boston: Little, Brown and Co.

Schorr, Alvin L. 1963. *Slums and social insecurity: An appraisal of the effectiveness of housing policies in helping to eliminate poverty in the United States.* Washington, D.C.: U.S. Government Printing Office.

Schumpeter, Joseph. 1942. *Capitalism, socialism, and democracy.* Cambridge, Mass.: Harvard University Press.

Sexton, Patricia Cayo. 1961. *Education and income.* New York: Viking Press.

Sherman, Sally R. 1973. Assets on the threshold of retirement. *Social Security Bulletin* 36 (August): 3–17.

Sherwood, Robert E. 1935. *The petrified forest.* London: Scribner's.

Shils, Edward. 1956. *The torment of secrecy.* New York: Free Press.

Sinclair, Upton. 1946. *The jungle.* New York: Viking Press.

Sjoberg, Gideon; Brymer, Richard A.; and Farris, Buford. 1966. Bureaucracy and the lower class. *Sociology and Social Research* 50 (April): 325–37.

Smith, Adam. 1937. *An inquiry into the nature and causes of the wealth of nations,* ed. Edwin Cannan. New York: Random House.

Social Security Administration. 1971. *Social Security Bulletin Statistical Supplement.*

Social Security Administration. 1974. *Social Security Bulletin Statistical Supplement.*

Spencer, Herbert. 1904. *The principles of ethics.* New York: D. Appleton and Company.

Stead, William T. 1964. *If Christ came to Chicago.* New York: Living Books.

Steffens, Lincoln. 1931. *The autobiography of Lincoln Steffens.* New York: Literary Guild.

Steinbeck, John. 1939. *The Grapes of wrath.* New York: Viking Press.

Steiner, Gilbert Y. 1966. *Social insecurity: The politics of welfare.* Chicago: Rand McNally.

Street, David. 1967a. Educators and social workers: Sibling rivalry in the inner city. *Social Service Review* 41 (June): 152–65.

———. 1967b. Public education and social welfare in the metropolis. In *Organizing for community welfare*, ed. Mayer N. Zald. Chicago: Quadrangle Books.

Street, W. Paul. 1973. *What is the impact of the indigenous paraprofessional community developer?* Lexington, Ky.: Bureau of School Services, University of Kentucky.

Suttles, Gerald D. 1968. *The social order of the slum.* Chicago: University of Chicago Press.

———. 1972. *The social construction of communities.* Chicago: University of Chicago Press.

———. 1978. New priorities for the old urban heartland. In *Handbook on urban life*, ed. David Street. San Francisco: Jossey-Bass.

Suttles, Gerald D., and Street, David. 1970. Aid to the poor and social exchange. In *The logic of social hierarchies*, ed. Edward O. Lauman, Paul M. Siegel, and Robert W. Hodge. Chicago: Markham.

Sutton, Francis X.; Harris, Seymour E.; Kaysen, Carl; and Tobin, James. 1965. *The American business creed.* Cambridge: Harvard University Press.

Tannenbaum, Frank. 1946. *Slave and citizen.* New York: Random House.

Theobald, Robert. 1963. *Free men and free markets.* New York: Clarkson N. Potter.

———. 1965. *The guaranteed income.* New York: Doubleday.

Thompson, Gayle B. 1975. Blacks and social security benefits: Trends, 1960–73. *Social Security Bulletin* 38 (April): 30–40.

Tocqueville, Alexis de. 1966. *Democracy in America.* New York: Harper and Row.

Townsend, Joseph. 1786. *A dissertation on the Poor Law, by a well-wisher to mankind.* London: Printed for C. Dilly.

Trattner, Walter I. 1974. *From poor law to welfare state: A history of social welfare in America.* New York: Free Press.

Trow, Martin. 1966. Two problems in American public education. In *Social problems: A modern approach*, ed. Howard S. Becker. New York: John Wiley.

Tuckerman, Joseph. 1874. *On the elevation of the poor: A selection from his reports as minister at large in Boston.* Boston: Gray, Little and Wilkins.

Turner, Ralph. 1960. Sponsored and contest mobility and the school system. *American Sociological Review* 25 (December): 855–67.

Udry, Richard J. 1966. Marital instability by race, sex, education, and occupation using 1960 census data. *American Journal of Sociology* 72 (September): 203–9.

———. 1967. Marital instability by race and income based on 1960 census data. *American Journal of Sociology* 72 (May): 673–4.

United States Bureau of the Census. 1971. *Current population reports.* Series P-60, No. 81. Characteristics of the low income population, 1970. Washington, D.C.: U.S. Government Printing Office.

United States Bureau of the Census, 1972. *Census of population: 1970 general population characteristics. Final report PC (1)-B34. New York.* Washington, D.C.: U.S. Government Printing Office.

———. 1973. *Census of population: 1970. Detailed characteristics. Final report PC(1)-D1. U.S. summary.* Washington, D.C.: U.S. Government Printing Office.

———. 1974. *Statistical Abstracts of the U.S., 1974,* 95th ed. Washington, D.C.: U.S. Government Printing Office.

———. 1975. *Statistical abstracts of the United States, 1975,* 96th ed. Washington, D.C.: U.S. Government Printing Office.

———. 1976a. *Current population reports.* Series P-60, No. 101. Money income in 1974 of families and persons in the United States. Washington, D.C.: U.S. Government Printing Office.

———. 1976b. *Current population reports.* Series P-60, No. 102. Characteristics of the population below the poverty level: 1974. Washington, D.C.: U.S. Government Printing Office.

———. 1976c. *Current population reports.* Series P-60, No. 103. Money income and poverty status of families and persons in the United States 1975 and 1974 revisions. (advance report) Washington, D.C.: U.S. Government Printing Office.

———. 1977. *Current population reports.* Series P-60, No. 104. Household money income in 1975 and selected social and economic statistics of households. Washington, D.C.: U.S. Government Printing Office.

United States Bureau of Labor. 1910–13. *Report on the condition of woman and child wage earners in the United States,* 19 vols. Washington, D.C.: U.S. Government Printing Office.

United States Commissioner of Labor. 1886. *First annual report: Industrial depressions.* Washington, D.C.: U.S. Government Printing Office.

———. 1894. *Seventh special report: The slums of Baltimore, Chicago, New York and Philadelphia.* Washington, D.C.: U.S. Government Printing Office.

———. 1897. *Eleventh annual report: Work and wages of men,*

women and children. Washington, D.C.: U.S. Government Printing Office.

———. 1903. *Eighteenth annual report: The cost of living and retail prices of food.* Washington, D.C.: U.S. Government Printing Office.

United States Department of Health, Education, and Welfare. 1976a. *The measure of poverty: A report to Congress as mandated by the Education Amendments of 1974.* Washington, D.C.: U.S. Government Printing Office.

———. 1976b. *Social security programs throughout the world, 1975.* Research Report No. 48. Office of Research and Statistics. Washington, D.C.: U.S. Government Printing Office.

United States Department of Labor, Bureau of Labor Statistics. 1974. Marital family characteristics of the labor force, March 1974. Special Labor Force Report 173.

United States Social and Rehabilitation Service. 1977. Aid to families with dependent children: Standards for basic needs; state maximums, and other methods of limiting money payments; federal matching provisions under the Social Security Act, July 1976. NCSS Report D-2. 7/76. Washington, D.C. (mimeographed).

Vanecko, James. 1970. Resources, influence, and issue resolution in large urban political systems: The case of urban renewal. Ph.D. dissertation, University of Chicago. Chicago.

Wade, Richard C. 1958. Urban life in western America, 1790–1830. *American Historical Review* 64 (October): 14–30.

Ware, Caroline. 1965. *Greenwich Village.* New York: Harper and Row.

Warner, Amos G. 1894. *American charities.* New York: Thomas Y. Crowell.

Weber, Max. 1946. *From Max Weber: Essays in sociology,* ed. H. H. Gerth and C. Wright Mills. New York: Oxford University Press.

———. 1947. *The theory of social and economic organization,* ed. Talcott Parsons. New York: Oxford University Press.

Wiebe, Robert H. 1967. *The search for order 1877–1920.* New York: Hill and Wang.

Weir, Paula E. 1976. Urban family budgets updated to autumn 1975. *Monthly Labor Review* 99 (July): 40–44.

Wilensky, Harold L. 1965. The problems and prospects of the welfare state. Introduction to the paperbound edition of *Industrial society and social welfare,* by Wilensky and Charles N. Lebeaux. New York: Free Press.

———. 1966. Class, class consciousness, and American workers.

In *Labor in a changing America*, ed. William Haber, pp. 12–28. New York: Basic Books.

———. 1975. *The welfare state and equality: Structural and ideological roots of public expenditures.* Berkeley: University of California Press.

———. 1976. The "new corporatism," centralization, and the welfare state. *Sage Contemporary Political Sociology Series.* Series/Number 06–020. Vol. 2.

———. 1977. Comment on Zald's review of the welfare state and equality. *American Journal of Sociology* 82 (January): 862–65.

Wilensky, Harold L., and Lebeaux, Charles N. 1965. *Industrial society and social welfare.* New York: Free Press (paperback ed.).

Williamson, John B. 1973. Beliefs about the welfare poor. *Sociology and Social Research* 58 (October): 163–75.

———. 1974. Beliefs about the motivation of the poor and attitudes toward poverty policy. *Social Problems* 21 (June): 635–48.

Wilson, James Q. 1960. *Negro politics.* New York: Free Press of Glencoe.

Windham, Douglas M. 1970. *Education, equality, and income redistribution: A study of public higher education.* Lexington, Mass.: Heath.

Wrong, Dennis H. 1969. Social inequality without social stratification. In *Structured social inequality: A reader in comparative social stratification,* ed Celia S. Heller, pp. 513–20. London: Macmillan Co.

Yates, John V. N. 1823. *Report of the Secretary of State on the relief and settlement of the poor.* Reprinted in *Poverty, U.S.A., the almshouse experience.* New York: Arno Press, 1971.

Young, Michael. 1958. *The rise of the meritocracy.* London: Thames and Hudson.

Zald, Mayer N. 1977. Demographics, politics, and the future of the welfare state. *Social Service Review* 51 (March): 110–24.

Zald, Mayer N., and Denton, Patricia. 1963. From evangelism to general service: On the transformation of the YMCA. *Administrative Science Quarterly* 8 (June): 214–34.

Zelinsky, Wilbur. 1973. *The cultural geography of the United States.* Englewood Cliffs, N.J.: Prentice Hall.

Index